𝔗𝔥𝔢 𝔅𝔬𝔰𝔱𝔬𝔫 𝔊𝔩𝔬𝔟𝔢
COOKBOOK

The Boston Globe
COOKBOOK

Revised Edition

by Margaret Deeds Murphy

Edited and Introduced by Gail Perrin,
Food Editor, *The Boston Globe*

Photography by Georgiana Silk

The Globe Pequot Press

Chester, Connecticut 06412

Library of Congress Catalogue Number: 81-82608
ISBN: 0-87106-048-5

Printed in the United States of America
Revised Edition
Fourth Printing

Art direction, cover and book design by Barbara Marks

Illustrations on pages 195 and 223 by Lauren Brown
Typesetting by IceType of Greens Farms, Connecticut
Cover and color printing by Eastern Press, Inc. of New Haven, Connecticut
Text printing and binding by The Book Press of Brattleboro, Vermont

Line cut illustrations of household and kitchen items
used with permission from *Old American Kitchenwares*,
by Louise K. Lantz. Everybody's Press, publisher.

Foreword

Capturing the flavor of New England cooking is a little like trying to put the aroma of fresh-baked bread into a jar. It's definitely there but elusive all the same.

Yet somehow veteran cook Margaret Deeds Murphy has performed the magical feat, extracting and preserving the New England essence between these covers.

True, there are a number of "general" cookbooks on the market. But none of them is geared to the cook eager to turn out some area classics that reflect a maximum of taste with a minimum of effort.

The Boston Globe Cookbook is an outgrowth of *The Boston Globe Cook Book for Brides,* first published in 1948. The original version relied almost solely on recipes that had been submitted by various readers to Confidential Chat, a reader exchange dating back to 1884. "Chat" contributors, who use pen names such as "Suburban Secretary," have but one rule when it comes to recipes: all must be "tried and true," personal favorites that work every time.

Margaret Murphy has culled the best from the Chat barrel, updated other "tried and true" classics and introduced new ideas streamlined for the busy homemaker who wants to cook well without having to use every pot and pan in the kitchen—or every minute of the day.

She is informative without being pedantic and concentrates on the most important element of any cuisine—good taste. And she shows how good taste need not be expensive taste. While there are touches of the elegant, those touches do not rely on caviar, lobster or champagne. Also, while there are touches of convenience, she helps hamburger without resorting to a commercial mix.

Perhaps the most important thing, however, is that Margaret Murphy has embodied the spirit of the *Globe,* first put forth by founder Gen. Charles H. Taylor, whose words are on the *Globe* cornerstone today. Said Taylor:

"My aim has been to make the *Globe* a cheerful, attractive and useful newspaper that would enter the homes as a kindly, helpful friend of the family. . . . My ideal for the *Globe* has always been that it should help men, women and children to get some of the sunshine of life, to be better and happier because of the *Globe."*

Gail Perrin
Food Editor, *The Boston Globe*

Other cookbooks by Margaret Deeds Murphy

The Cook It and Freeze It Cookbook
Food Processor Cookery
Meat Makes the Meal
Fondue, Chafing Dish and Casserole Cookery
Freezer Cookery
The Farberware Turbo Oven Cookbook

Known to her friends as Maggie, **Margaret Deeds Murphy** shares here the expertise she has culled from a lifetime of professional cooking. She is the former head of General Foods Corporation's recipe test kitchen and has developed recipes for a number of well-known national food companies. She is a member of the American Home Economics Association, the Boston chapter of Home Economists in Business, and is a board director of the Cape Cod Seafood Council.

Gail Perrin is the food editor of *The Boston Globe* and the former editor of the Woman's Page. She has worked as the newspaper's assistant metropolitan editor and began her career in 1954 at the *Washington Daily News*.

Contents

Foreword
v

First Things
1

Appetizers and Beverages
11

Appetizers
12

Beverages
26

Breads
33

Pasta
69

Eggs, Cheese, and Dairy
85

Eggs
86

Cheese
92

Dairy
97

Soups
105

Sauces
121

Seafood
129

Shellfish
130

Finfish
138

Meats and Poultry
149

Dried Legumes and Cereals
177

Dried Legumes (Beans)
178

Cereals
187

Salads and Salad Dressings
193

Vegetables
211

Barbecues
231

Cakes and Cookies
241

Cakes
242

Cookies/Bars
251

Pies and Desserts
259

Pies
260

Desserts
269

Cooking For Two
281

Preserving and Pickling
297

Candy
309

Index
316

First Things

First Things

A cookbook generally reflects the taste of its author, as much as he or she may try to avoid it—and this one is no exception. As you read through this book, you will note a scanty representation of mixes and ready prepared foods. This is a cookbook, after all, and my feeling is that directions on the packages are quite adequate as a rule. It's also true that I use few mixes or prepared foods in my own cooking.

You will also find that over the years mixes are reformulated so that many recipes incorporating mixes will have to be revised: another good reason not to have them in great numbers in a cookbook which one hopes will be useful for many years.

Salt is one of the controversial items in our diet. And because it is easier to add salt than to remove it, I've written many of the recipes in the book to include less salt than you may be accustomed to. Try them the way they are written first, and then increase the salt next time if you feel the need.

Tips on Food Preparation

Here are some tips which may help you in your daily cooking:

• If you plan to peel many **small onions,** chill them well in the refrigerator; then peel under water to keep the odor and tears under control.

Peel all onions from the root end. For some reason the peel comes off more easily. If you prefer to use onion powder, ¼ teaspoon equals the flavoring power of one medium onion. Remember, though, that fresh chopped onions often are intended to provide bulk in a recipe.

Grating **onions?** Leave the stem end on to give yourself a handle when getting down to the end of the onion.

• When peeling **garlic,** put the garlic clove on a board or table and press with the flat of a knife until the garlic breaks. The skin will peel off readily then. If you are using garlic powder instead of fresh garlic, ⅛ teaspoon garlic powder equals 1 clove garlic.

If a whole clove of garlic is used for seasoning and is to be removed before food is served, stick garlic on a toothpick. It is easy to find and remove.

• In cleaning **leeks,** be sure to pull the leaves apart and rinse out all the sand. If you slice the bulb and leaves in half lengthwise they clean more easily.

• When you are dicing **celery, carrots,** or any long vegetable by hand, cut into strips, then cut strips into short lengths and pile together as many as can be cut conveniently at once, to save time and effort. Use a paring knife to cut into strips, a boning size knife to cut crosswise into cubes.

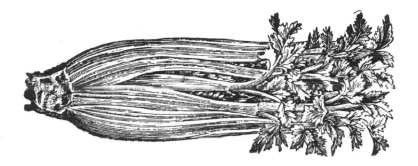

• It is easier to peel **apples** for pie if they are cut into quarters, peeled with a small sharp paring knife, and then cored. If you are peeling a lot of apples, drop the peeled ones into cold salt water (about 1 teaspoon per quart water) to keep them from turning brown.

• To cut **corn** from the cob, break ears in half and cut down through corn onto a paper plate.

To remove corn silk more easily, cut corn husks at stem end and pull back toward tip. Corn silk comes off with husk. Any that may be left can be removed with a small brush.

• Separate **yolks and whites of eggs** when cold. But let stand to reach room temperature before beating, for more volume. Cover while standing.

Egg yolks, stored in a small dish and covered with cold water, will keep fresh several days in the refrigerator.

Chop **hard cooked eggs** with a pastry blender.

• Use **pastry blender** to mix sugar, butter, and flour for cookie bars or other desserts.

• Grease cup before measuring **honey, molasses, or syrup,** and they will not cling to cup.

• Put **lemons** or **limes** on table, roll and press under hand to soften and get more juice from them. If you use a lot of limes, a lime juicer is a big aid in extracting juice.

• To help separate cold **bacon slices,** roll package either from side or from end.

• When measuring **shortening** from the container, dip spoon in hot water. The shortening comes off the spoon easily into the measuring cup. Another trick: To measure shortening, use a measuring cup larger than needed and put in water to make up difference. For instance, to get ½ cup shortening, put ½ cup water in a 1-cup measuring cup, add shortening to full measure, pour off water, and you have ½ cup shortening that's easily removed.

- To prevent **brown sugar** from hardening, empty contents of newly opened package into a jar. Add a piece of apple or a folded dampened paper towel. Cover and store in refrigerator. (A snugly fastened plastic bag works well too.)
- Devein cooked **shrimp** with a beer can opener. Run pointed end down back of shrimp. Rinse shrimp before using.
- Make your own **seasoned salt** with 3 tablespoons onion salt, 2 tablespoons each garlic and celery salt, and 1 tablespoon paprika. Mix well and store in a shaker with a lid. Makes about ½ cup.
- Have a special **pepper mill** in which you put equal parts of black pepper, white pepper, and whole allspice: a nice flavoring combination for meats, fish, or vegetables.
- Keep a jar of **buttered bread crumbs** in the refrigerator to be ready when needed.

Kitchen Equipment

A recent catalog from a company which specializes in small kitchen equipment and related items really was a collection for the person who has everything. My favorite item was a gurgling fish-shaped decanter for beverages. The question uppermost in my mind as I read through the many offerings was where on earth one would store even a tenth of the available objects.

Which is a sneaky way to get into the subject of kitchen equipment, and rule number one: Never buy a new item unless there is a place to store it where it is readily available to use. A brand new food processor stuck away on a top shelf of a cupboard isn't worth much—it's easier to keep on working with the old stuff than to get down the processor. That is the first thing one should remember when considering a purchase.

Everyone has favorite pieces of equipment: perhaps a **yogurt maker,** an **ice cream freezer** (electric, of course), a special **coffee maker,** a **pressure cooker** or a **slow cooker,** an **electric skillet** or **crepe maker,** a **fish poacher** or a **steamer.** It is generally a piece of equipment that fits one's life style. I won't attempt to present here a complete list of small equipment; whatever is your own favorite, enjoy it and the products it produces.

There are many really small pieces of equipment which I couldn't get along without. One is a **timer** separate from the one on the range. If it is necessary for me to leave the kitchen while some cooking which needs timing is going on, the timer goes with me. Or if the recipe says beat two minutes, the timer tells me when two minutes are up. It is a piece of equipment, small and inexpensive as it is, which enables me to do more than one job at a time.

Several **cutting boards** are essential to me, with one side of each marked near the handle with red fingernail polish to indicate that that is the onion side. Another essential is a Robo knife sharpener, not to mention my knives.

Good **measuring cups** are a must in cooking. I recommend sets of ¼, ⅓, ½, and 1-cup **dry measuring cups,** so called because whatever dry ingredient is being measured, the cup is filled to overflowing and then leveled off with a spatula. For liquid use **glass measuring cups** where the full measure is below the top lip of the cup. They come in 1-cup, 2-cup, and 1-quart sizes.

Several sizes of **whisks** and a good **small grater,** for lemon and orange peel and onions, are always in use. The best grater has a plastic rim, a stainless steel grating surface, and a handy "leg" so it can be used on a flat surface. I use two **mortars and pestles** in my kitchen. One is a wooden set which is used to crush dried herbs and seeds; the other, china, is used for garlic and anything liquid. The **garlic press** stays busy, too. There are plenty of **wooden spoons** and **rubber pan scrapers** and of course the **pepper mill.**

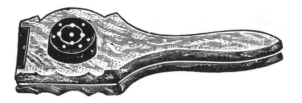

But let's assume you have your basic equipment and consider some of the more sophisticated kitchen tools, starting with the food processor.

• **Food Processor:** This is one of the biggest kitchen helpers that have come along recently. When using it learn to analyze the recipes and do the jobs that require the food container to be only rinsed or wiped out first. That means just one final washing. Read well all the information that comes with the processor. You will be surprised at the many operations it performs and the small number of things not recommended for the processor. Plan to use it to save time and energy. Grinders have almost become obsolete.

• **Microwave Oven:** The principle behind this oven is the use of a particular type of high-frequency radio energy called microwaves. They permeate the food and activate the molecules of the food to create the heat which cooks the food very rapidly both inside and out. Microwave cooking is primarily cooking by time. Whether you use this oven for a great deal of your food preparation or only as an adjunct to your regular range will probably depend on whether you are willing to take the time to learn a new way to cook.

Once you've invested in a microwave oven, read the instructions very carefully and follow them to the letter. Even in developing an oven from the basic premise of the microwave, different manufacturers have different approaches to its use. But do learn to use it for many things. If it is only used to thaw foods and heat coffee, you've wasted your money and are not realizing the energy savings the microwave oven is designed to make possible.

• **Convection Oven:** These are not an innovation, having been in use by bakeries for years; but the handy portable ovens designed for home use are relatively new. The principle behind the convection oven is heat that is propelled around the oven by a fan so that it hits the food from all sides at once. (A regular range oven has heat penetration primarily from the bottom after it has reached temperature. Regular ranges with the oven based on the convection principle are now also on the market.) Because of this

**Blueberry Cheese Cake
with Fresh Blueberry Topping
(recipes on page 250)**

bombardment of heat the convection oven bakes beautifully at a lower temperature and in less time. Again, read the directions. Some pans respond better to this kind of heating than others. You will be surprised to know, if you do not have a convection oven, that it broils and can be converted to a food dehydrator with a few shelves which are an extra equipment option. It can also be used as a proofing (rising) oven for bread, as a slow cooker, and to incubate milk for yogurt and cottage cheese. The convection oven also saves energy because of the lower heat and shorter time.

• **Blender:** Even though the food processor takes over many operations which were once done in the blender, the blender can still see plenty of use: mixing beverages, grinding coffee beans, making mayonnaise, chopping a few nuts or a small amount of crumbs, things of that nature. One objection to the blender has always been the chore of scraping the food out of that tall narrow container, but it certainly has fulfilled its purpose and will continue to be useful for a long time.

Everyone who likes to cook and does a lot of it has some one beloved gadget. An example: A number of years ago I acquired a three-pronged fork in Switzerland. The three prongs form a circle and are designed to hold hot potatoes boiled in their jackets so they can be more easily peeled. In Switzerland the potatoes are served with *raclette*, a melted cheese dish. I, however, use the fork to hold hot potatoes while I peel them for potato salad. It is an inexpensive little implement with a plain wooden handle, but has certainly given more value than its cost.

Metric Equivalents

There is still a question about how rapidly there will be a conversion from our present measuring standards to metric. It is a certainty that standard measuring recipes and equipment will be around for a long time. Many companies are putting both standard and metric weights on their packages and have been for a long time, and a few are using recipes with both measurements indicated. But they are the minority for the moment.

Perhaps it will help to remember that 1 kilogram is a little more than two pounds (2.205), 1 liter is a little more than a quart (33.8 ounces) or 1 gallon is 3.785 liters. About the only place where these liter measurements have made an impact is in the liquor and wine industry.

Metric Conversion Chart

Weight

Multiply ounces × 28.35 to get grams	gm	
Multiply pounds × 0.454 to get kilograms	kg	

Volume

Multiply teaspoons	× 5	to get milliliters	mL
Multiply tablespoons	× 15	to get milliliters	mL
Multiply ounces	× 30	to get milliliters	mL
Multiply cups	× 0.24	to get liters	L
Multiply pints	× 0.47	to get liters	L
Multiply quarts	× 0.95	to get liters	L
Multiply gallons	× 3.8	to get liters	L
Multiply inches	× 2.5	to get centimeters	cm

Temperature

To change from Fahrenheit to Celsius:

Subtract 32 from Fahrenheit, divide by 9 and multiply by 5. This will give you the Celsius. In Celsius, freezing is 0°—in Fahrenheit it is 32°.

To change from Celsius to Fahrenheit:

Multiply Celsius by 9 and divide by 5 and add 32.

Liquid and Dry Measure Equivalents

g = grams (dry measure)   kg = kilograms   dL = deciliters   L = liters
The metric amounts represented here are the nearest equivalents.

a pinch = slightly less than ¼ teaspoon
a dash = a few drops
3 teaspoons = 1 tablespoon
2 tablespoons = 1 ounce = ¼ dL (liquid), 30 g (dry)
4 tablespoons = ¼ cup = 2 ounces = ½ dL (liquid), 60 g (dry)
1 jigger = 3 tablespoons − 1½ ounces
8 tablespoons = ½ cup = 4 ounces = 1 dL
2 cups = 1 pint = ½ quart = 1 pound* = ½ L (liquid), 450g (dry)*
4 cups = 32 ounces = 2 pints = 1 quart = 1 L
4 quarts = 1 gallon = 3¾ L
8 quarts (dry) = 1 peck = 7¼ kg
4 pecks (dry) = 1 bushel

Dry ingredients measured in cups will vary in weight

Appetizers and Beverages

Numbers refer to pages where recipes appear in this book.

Both connote a party, and so this chapter is devoted mostly to party food.

Appetizers   12

Clams Casino   13

Cranberry Meatballs   13

Spinach Cheese Squares   14

Barbecue Spare Ribs   14

Hot Cheese   15

Scallops in Bacon   15

Stuffed Baked Mushrooms   15

Fiesta Surprise   16

Beer Cheese Dunk   16

Corned Beef and Cheese Spread   17

Mushroom "Liver" Canapes   17

Crabmeat Spread   17

Chopped Egg Dip   18

Cheese Crock   18

Clam Dip   18

California Dip   19

Apple Cottage Cheese Dip   19

Savory Vegetable Dip   19

Bean Dip   20

Party Chicken Wings   20

Lobster Ramona   21

Pickled Green Beans   21

Marinated Mushrooms   21

Maine Stuffed Eggs   22

Quick Pate   22

Nuts and Bolts   23

Wine Cheese Sticks   23

Vegetables for Parties   24

Beverages   26

Spiced Mocha Frosted   27

Fruit Milk Shakes   27

Chocolate Milk Shake   28

Chocolate Frosted   28

Chocolate Banana Milkshake   28

Chocolate Banana Frosted   28

Orange Nog   28

Egg Nog   29

Spiced Tea   29

Pink Punch   29

Wine Punch   30

Easy Fruit Punch   30

Party Punch   31

Apple Cranberry Punch   31

Hot Cocoa   31

Hot Spiced Wine   32

Hot Cranberry Juice Combo   32

Appetizers

A party should be fun for everyone, including the person or persons giving the party. One of the requisites for the party-giver's good time is organization. As many years as I've been connected with food, I seldom invite people for cocktails or dinner without having a written plan. With a plan as a checklist, you can stop worrying about whether you've done or not done even the minor things.

I like best to invite either a small group of six or eight for drinks and a sit-down dinner, or a large number for a buffet.

For a small group I seldom spend time on elaborate dips or hors d'oeuvres, preferring to spend it on the dinner food. Before dinner, instead of a first course at the table, I'll have a good cheese and crackers and a bowl of chilled shrimp with cocktail sauce or a bowl of crisp vegetables. Sometimes the vegetables come to the table instead of a salad.

For an informal buffet supper party I'll spend more time on appetizers, as they are actually part of the menu and blend into the buffet table when it is set up.

Some rules I try not to break.

• Keep a written record of guests, date, and food, particularly if you're new at cooking and have only a few specialties you prepare for guests.

• Plan to do things in advance as much as is possible. Many recipes, such as cheese dips, can be made as much as a week in advance with proper storage. Certainly silver can be polished, glasses washed, and pesky jobs of that nature accomplished early on.

• When deciding on the menu, particularly for large parties, avoid dips that are too thin and drippy—think of your carpet and people's clothes!

• Remember someone is always on a diet, so have plenty of crisp, fresh vegetables for nibblers, and low-calorie beverages. In fact today, with so many people choosing a light, dry wine as a predinner drink, it is wise to have chilled wine available. If there are guests who are not intimate friends, try to make discreet inquiries as to their preference in drinks, and have it available. Always have non-alcoholic beverages for people who want them.

• More and more people are having cooperative parties where the hostess furnishes the main dish and the other participants bring the remainder of the meal (by preparty plan, not helter skelter) and even their own predinner beverage. This method of entertaining, particularly if the same group gets together often, is practical and fun, as no one person shares all the cost or all the work.

• Another trend in parties is to make them thematic—built around a particular country or holiday or a special type of food. Here again, a plan would be worked out ahead of time and parts of the menu assigned to guests.

• Unless it is something especially simple, it is really wise to try out a new recipe on the family at least once before serving it for a party.

Any way you slice it, parties are extra work, but the work can be cut to a minimum by planning.

Clams Casino

Cherrystone clams are small quahogs. Many people steam open clams. I think steaming makes them tough so I use a knife (although sometimes with varying results). If you don't dig your own clams, perhaps the fish store people will show you how to open them some day when they are not busy.

2 dozen cherrystones or small quahogs
6 teaspoons lemon juice
¼ cup finely minced green pepper
¼ cup finely minced onion
2 or 3 slices bacon cut into ¾-inch squares (about 72 pieces)

Scrub clams well to remove dirt and sand. Open carefully to retain juice. Use a clam knife, if possible. (Illustrated instructions for shucking clams are on page 131.) Leave clam and juice in deepest half of shell and place on a baking dish. (A base of rock salt in which to set clams will keep them from tipping.) Sprinkle clams with lemon juice, green pepper, and onion, and put 2 or 3 small squares bacon on each clam. Bake at 450° F for 5 to 8 minutes or until bacon is crisp. Serve hot. Makes 24.

Cranberry Meat Balls

The combination of flavors and colors makes this a particularly pretty, as well as a very good, hot hors d'oeuvre.

½ cup uncooked oatmeal
1 egg
2 tablespoons water
1 tablespoon grated onion
1 teaspoon salt
1 teaspoon Worcestershire sauce
1 pound ground beef
2 tablespoons butter or margarine
¼ cup (about) flour
1 can (8 ounces) jellied cranberry sauce
1 can (8 ounces) tomato sauce
½ cup dry white wine

Mix oatmeal, egg, water, onion, salt, and Worcestershire sauce and let stand about 5 minutes. Mix lightly with beef and shape into 40 small meat balls.

Heat butter in large skillet. Roll meat balls in flour and brown quickly in butter, removing as browned. When all are browned, return to skillet. Mash cranberry sauce and blend with tomato sauce and wine. Pour over meat balls. Cover and simmer about 30 minutes. Serve in a chafing dish or keep hot over a candle warmer. These meat balls may be prepared in advance and reheated. Makes 40 meat balls.

Spinach Cheese Squares

4 eggs
¼ cup cooking oil
½ teaspoon salt
½ teaspoon freshly grated
    nutmeg
1 cup buttermilk biscuit mix
1 package (10 ounces) frozen
    chopped spinach, thawed
2 cups firmly packed grated
    Swiss cheese (about 8 ounces)

A close relative of a quiche, but easier to make and very tasty for a party. The squares are better warm and can be reheated in the oven or in a covered skillet over low heat.

Beat together eggs, oil, salt, nutmeg, and biscuit mix. Stir in spinach and cheese. Spoon into a well-greased and floured 9×9×2-inch pan and bake at 400° F for 30 to 35 minutes. Cut while still warm into 1½-inch or slightly smaller squares. Makes 36 squares if cut 1½ inches.

Barbecue Spare Ribs
(pictured between pages 230 and 231)

5 pounds pork spare riblets*
Salt and freshly ground pepper

Barbecue sauce

½ cup chopped Spanish onions
2 tablespoons butter or
    margarine
1 tablespoon Dijon mustard
1 chicken bouillon cube
½ cup water
½ cup dry white wine
2 tablespoons Worcestershire
    sauce
2 tablespoons lemon juice
1 teaspoon sugar

These tiny ribs make hearty cocktail fare, and are particularly popular for informal outdoor gatherings. Serve with plenty of napkins.

Cut the ribs into individual fingers. Arrange on rack in pan. Sprinkle with salt and pepper and bake at 425° F for 30 minutes.

Meanwhile combine ingredients for sauce, bring to boil, then simmer, covered, for 10 minutes.

Reduce oven temperature to 375° F and bake and baste ribs frequently with sauce for another 30 minutes. Serve hot or cold. Makes enough for about 15 people.

* *If riblets are not available, use regular spare ribs; have meat man cut rack in two crosswise and then cut between ribs.*

Hot Cheese

Sometimes simple recipes are too good to believe. This one, from a neighbor, is one of those. The cheese mixture could be prepared several days in advance and refrigerated until party time, then heated.

Grate cheese and mix with mayonnaise and onion and put into a small ovenproof dish which can be used for serving. Heat at 350° F for about 20 minutes or until mixture bubbles. Serve hot with crackers and crisp vegetables. Makes about 2 cups.

1 package (10 ounces) sharp white cheese
1 cup mayonnaise (not salad dressing)
1 tablespoon minced onion
Crackers and crisp vegetables

Scallops in Bacon

Let scallops marinate in lemon juice in refrigerator for about 4 hours or longer. Drain.

Cut bacon slices in thirds crosswise and wrap each scallop in a piece of bacon, securing with a toothpick. Put wrapped scallops on rack in shallow baking pan. Sprinkle with brown sugar. Bake at 425° F for 15 minutes or until bacon is browned. Serve hot. Makes about 50.

1 pint bay scallops
½ cup lemon juice
1 pound (about) bacon
Toothpicks
½ cup brown sugar

Stuffed Baked Mushrooms

For this recipe, brown or "natural" mushrooms should be lightly rinsed in cold water and patted dry with paper towels; white mushrooms need no washing. Never peel mushrooms.

Remove stems from mushrooms and reserve the caps. Chop the stems fine; saute them in oil until lightly browned, about 10 minutes. Mix lightly with bread crumbs, herbs, seasonings, melted butter, and lemon juice. Spoon mixture into mushroom caps and place in buttered flat pan. Bake at 350° F for 20 minutes. Serve hot. Makes 24.

24 medium (about 2-inch) mushrooms
¼ cup cooking oil
1 cup fresh bread crumbs
1 garlic clove, pressed
¼ cup chopped fresh parsley
½ teaspoon dried oregano or 1 teaspoon minced fresh oregano
½ teaspoon salt
Freshly ground pepper to taste
¼ cup melted butter
1 tablespoon lemon juice

Fiesta Surprise

1 can (6¾ ounces) deviled ham
3 tablespoons chopped stuffed
olives
1 tablespoon prepared mustard
1 teaspoon horseradish
1 package (8 ounces) cream
cheese
1 tablespoon milk
½ teaspoon onion salt
½ cup (about) chopped fresh
parsley
Crackers or potato chips

The combination of deviled ham and cream cheese will be a pleasant surprise to your guests, and nice for you, since it is a make-ahead.

Combine ham, olives, mustard, and horseradish, stirring to blend. Shape into a 3- to 4-inch round ball on a 6- or 8-inch serving plate. Cover with plastic wrap and chill for several hours or overnight.

Some time before ready to serve, soften cream cheese and beat in milk and onion salt. Frost chilled ham ball with cream cheese and cover with chopped fresh parsley. Serve with crisp crackers or potato chips. Makes enough for 12 or 15 people.

Beer Cheese Dunk

1 round loaf (about 8 inches) rye
or pumpernickel bread,
unsliced
1 jar (16 ounces) pasteurized
processed cheese spread
1 package (8 ounces) cream
cheese
½ cup beer

This spectacularly good idea came from the same neighbor who gave me ''Hot Cheese.''

Early in the day cut a slice off top of bread and hollow out inside of bread, leaving a ½-inch-thick shell. Cut bread removed from center of loaf into ½-inch cubes and let them air dry.

Warm cheese spread and cream cheese to room temperature and mix with beer to blend.

When ready to serve, pour cheese mixture into bread shell, place on a platter, and surround with bread cubes. Have toothpicks for dunking. Serves about 20.

Corned Beef and Cheese Spread

This is a pretty service for a party; choose a plate to show off the red rind of the cheese. Refrigerate unused half of cheese for future use.

Cut cheese in half crosswise. Carefully hollow out one half, leaving a shell about ⅛ inch thick. Grate cheese. (Makes 2½ cups.) Mince corned beef, and add to it the mayonnaise, relish, and horseradish. Mix well and fold in cheese. Spoon about ⅓ of mixture into shell and refill as needed. Serve surrounded with small rye or pumpernickel rounds. Makes about 3½ cups spread.

from Suburban Secretary
Confidential Chat Column

1 Edam cheese, about 2 pounds
1 can (12 ounces) corned beef
½ cup mayonnaise
¼ cup sweet pickle relish
2 teaspoons horseradish
Small rye or pumpernickel rounds

Mushroom "Liver" Canapes

Suburban Secretary says men particularly like this. The "liver" in the name probably alludes to the many well-loved pates that, unlike this one, are actually made from liver.

Saute mushrooms in butter until brown. Mix with cream cheese, mayonnaise, and seasonings. Chill well. Serve with assorted crackers. Makes about 1 cup.

from Suburban Secretary
Confidential Chat Column

¼ pound fresh mushrooms, finely minced
2 tablespoons butter
1 package (3 ounces) cream cheese, softened
⅓ cup mayonnaise
½ teaspoon salt
⅛ teaspoon garlic powder
⅛ teaspoon pepper
Assorted crackers

Crabmeat Spread

Mix all ingredients lightly together. Chill. Serve in a pretty bowl with round butter crackers. Makes 1 cup.

from Suburban Secretary
Confidential Chat Column

1 cup finely flaked crabmeat
2 tablespoons snipped fresh parsley
1 tablespoon finely minced onion
3 tablespoons mayonnaise
¼ teaspoon curry powder
1 teaspoon lemon juice
Round butter crackers

Chopped Egg Dip

2 hard cooked eggs, finely
   chopped
1 pint dairy sour cream
1 clove garlic, finely minced
1 teaspoon dry mustard
1 tablespoon horseradish
1 green pepper, finely chopped
1 tablespoon minced fresh
   parsley
2 tablespoons chili sauce
Radishes

Blend together all ingredients except radishes. Chill. Serve decorated with thin slices of radish. Good with potato or corn chips. Makes about 2 cups.

from Khadejah
Confidential Chat Column

Cheese Crock

¾ pound sharp cheddar cheese
¼ pound Danish blue cheese,
   crumbled
2 tablespoons butter or
   margarine, softened
1 teaspoon dry mustard
1 teaspoon Worcestershire
   sauce
Dash Tabasco sauce
Onion or garlic salt to taste
¾ cup (about) beer

This cheese crock is nice to have on hand to serve when unexpected guests arrive. It is also very popular at parties. Serve with a variety of crisp crackers.

Grate cheddar cheese and mix with blue cheese, butter, and seasonings. Gradually beat in beer until mixture is smooth and spreadable.

Store in refrigerator in covered crocks or jars. Keeps several weeks. Makes 2½ to 3 cups.

Clam Dip

1 package (8 ounces) cream
   cheese
1 can (6½ ounces) minced clams
1 teaspoon lemon juice
1 teaspoon Worcestershire
   sauce
Dash Tabasco sauce
Salt and pepper to taste
Crackers or chips

This is the traditional clam dip, which first came on the scene in the 1940s. It is still popular and disappears first.

Let cream cheese stand at room temperature to soften. Drain clams, saving liquid. Combine cream cheese with clams, lemon juice, and seasonings, stirring to blend. If necessary to get a dipping consistency, add a teaspoon or so of clam juice. Serve with potato or corn chips and crackers. Makes about 2 cups.

California Dip

Another classic party dip, easy to make and tasty.

Combine soup mix and sour cream, stirring to blend well. Chill in refrigerator several hours before serving. Garnish with chopped parsley. Serve with potato or corn chips. Makes about 2 cups.

Variation

Use 1 cup sour cream and 1 cup plain yogurt instead of all sour cream.

1 envelope (1.375 ounces) onion
   soup mix
1 pint dairy sour cream
Chopped fresh parsley
Potato or corn chips

Apple Cottage Cheese Dip

A simple mixture, particularly popular with people who want neither fish nor meat. Nice with sesame crackers.

Mix apples and lemon juice. (Leaving some red skin on part of the apples gives a little color.) Add all remaining ingredients and mix lightly. Serve with assorted crackers. Makes 1½ cups.

1 cup finely chopped apples,
   some with peel
1 tablespoon lemon juice
1 cup creamed cottage cheese
½ teaspoon celery salt
½ teaspoon onion salt
½ teaspoon curry powder
Assorted crackers

Savory Vegetable Dip

A good dip, keeps under refrigeration. If you have any left over, add a bit more yogurt and use as a salad dressing for a green salad.

Squeeze all liquid out of spinach. Combine spinach with all remaining ingredients. Chill at least 3 hours or overnight. Serve as a dip with crisp vegetables and/or crackers. Makes 3 cups.

1 package (10 ounces) frozen
   chopped spinach, thawed
½ cup sour cream
½ cup plain yogurt
1 cup mayonnaise
1 package (2 ounces) country
   vegetable soup mix
3 green onions, finely chopped
1 can (8 ounces) sliced water
   chestnuts, drained and
   chopped

Bean Dip

¾ cup dried pinto beans
2½ cups water
½ teaspoon salt
2 tablespoons lemon juice
1 tablespoon mayonnaise
1 teaspoon Worcestershire
   sauce
1 clove garlic, mashed
¼ teaspoon Tabasco sauce
2 green onions, chopped
1 additional green onion, thinly
   sliced

Serve bean dip at room temperature. It may be made in advance and refrigerated, but get it out in time to warm up before the party. Crisp vegetables and crackers should be served with bean dip.

Wash beans and soak overnight in water. Add salt and cook, covered, until tender: about 2 hours. Drain. Combine with lemon juice, mayonnaise, Worcestershire, garlic, Tabasco, and 2 green onions in a blender or food processor and blend until smooth.

When ready to serve, spoon the dip into a serving bowl. Garnish with additional onions. Serve with crisp vegetables or corn chips. Makes 1½ cups dip.

Party Chicken Wings

2½ pounds chicken wings
2 cups dry bread crumbs
1 envelope (1¼ ounces) taco
   seasoning mix
1 jar (16 ounces) taco sauce

A flavor of Mexico is imparted to these chicken wings by the taco seasoning and sauce. They are always a favorite at parties.

Cut off wing tips (save for chicken broth). Separate wings at joint with a sharp knife. Mix bread crumbs and taco seasoning until well blended. Dip each piece of wing into taco sauce and then roll in bread crumb mixture, being sure to coat thoroughly. Place on a lightly greased baking sheet and bake at 375° F for 30 to 35 minutes. Serve hot or cold. Makes about 40 pieces, depending on size of wings.

Lobster Ramona

When I feel rich enough to serve lobster, my favorite way is to cut the cooked lobster in bite-size pieces, keep it hot in lemon butter sauce over a candle warmer, and provide toothpicks for spearing the pieces. This recipe for Lobster Ramona is excellent, too.

Mince lobster, celery, and green onion very fine. Mix lightly with sour cream, catsup, mustard, and salt and pepper. Serve in a pretty bowl surrounded with rye bread rounds and/or round butter crackers. Makes about 1½ cups.

1 cup cooked lobster
1 stalk celery
1 green onion
¼ cup dairy sour cream
6 tablespoons catsup
½ teaspoon Dijon mustard
Salt and freshly ground pepper to taste
Rye bread rounds or round butter crackers

Pickled Green Beans

Serve pickled green beans, drained, as a finger food.

Choose fresh young beans and snip off stem end. Steam or cook in a small amount of water for about 8 to 10 minutes or until tender-crisp. Cool and pack into a large jar.
Combine all remaining ingredients in a saucepan and bring to a boil. Pour hot over beans in jar. Cover and let stand in refrigerator for several days before using. Makes about 1 quart.

1½ pounds green beans
1½ cups cider vinegar
¼ cup firmly packed brown sugar
¼ teaspoon salt
1 garlic clove, cut in half
1 tablespoon pickling spice

Marinated Mushrooms

These tasty mushrooms are better if made ahead of time.

Cut a slice off stem end of mushrooms and rinse under running water. Combine with all remaining ingredients. Simmer 15 minutes. Marinate, covered, in the refrigerator. Will keep several weeks. To serve, drain and serve with toothpicks. Makes 2 cups.

2 cups small whole mushrooms (about ¾ pound)
1 cup water
½ cup cooking oil
2 tablespoons lemon juice
1 stalk celery
1 clove garlic
¼ teaspoon dried rosemary
¼ teaspoon dried thyme
½ bay leaf
½ teaspoon chili powder
½ teaspoon salt
6 peppercorns

Maine Stuffed Eggs

12 eggs, hard cooked
1 can (3¾ ounces) sardines,
   drained
4 teaspoons lemon juice
2 teaspoons horseradish
½ teaspoon salt
Freshly ground pepper to taste
6 tablespoons mayonnaise
8 to 10 stuffed olives, sliced

If 24 halves of eggs is more than you want, halve the recipe. In that case the leftover sardines can be doused liberally with lemon juice and served on oblong pieces of buttered toast.

Remove shells from hard cooked eggs and cut in half lengthwise. Carefully remove yolks and put into a bowl with drained sardines. Mash together with a fork or spoon until well blended. Add lemon juice, horseradish, salt, pepper, and mayonnaise and mix well. Pile lightly into egg whites. The sardines add enough bulk so that the filling in each half egg will be generous. Decorate each egg with a slice of stuffed olive. Keep chilled in refrigerator until ready to use. Makes 24 halves.

Quick Pate

1 tablespoon butter or
   margarine
½ teaspoon chopped garlic
2 tablespoons chopped onion
1 tablespoon cognac
2 tablespoons sherry
1 pound liverwurst
Softened butter
Crackers or melba toast

A lot of the flavor of this pate will depend on the flavor of the liverwurst. Buy a good, spicy one to be enhanced with the seasonings in the recipe.

Heat butter in a small saucepan and cook garlic and onion over low heat until transparent. Stir in cognac and sherry. Remove from heat. Peel rind from liverwurst, cut into pieces and blend well with garlic and onion. Spread softened butter on inside of a 2-cup mold and pack pate into mold. Chill for several hours. To serve, unmold on plate and serve with crackers or melba toast. Makes 2 cups.

Nuts and Bolts

This recipe can be halved; but if you have freezer capacity, it is a good snack to make in quantity and keep on hand.

In a large roasting pan (at least 5-quart capacity) mix cereals and nuts. Combine butter with seasonings. Pour over cereal mixture. Stir well. Bake at 200° F for 2 hours, stirring every half hour. Cool. Store in airtight jars in freezer. Makes about 4½ quarts. To serve, thaw to room temperature.

3 cups thin pretzel sticks
3 cups Rice Chex cereal
3 cups Wheat Chex cereal
3 cups Cheerios cereal
1 pound mixed nuts
1 pound butter or margarine, melted
3 tablespoons Worcestershire sauce
4 teaspoons garlic salt
4 teaspoons celery salt

Wine Cheese Sticks

You will find wine cheese sticks very popular. They can be made well in advance of a party, another asset.

In a bowl, mix flour, paprika, and rosemary. (If using dried leaf rosemary, crush to powder in a mortar and pestle.) Blend in butter and half the cheese. Add wine and mix with a fork until the pastry can be shaped into a ball. If necessary, add a few more drops of wine. Chill for 1 or 2 hours.

Roll pastry on a well-floured pastry cloth into a 12×16-inch rectangle. Sprinkle with half the remaining cheese. Fold half the pastry over cheese and roll again to 12×16 inches. Sprinkle with remaining cheese and repeat. Divide pastry in quarters and roll each quarter into a 6×3-inch rectangle. With a pastry cutter or a sharp knife cut each rectangle into strips 3 inches long and ½ inch wide. Transfer strips to baking sheet and bake at 350° F for 12 to 15 minutes. Repeat until all sticks are baked. Store in airtight container. Makes about 8 dozen.

1 cup all-purpose flour
½ teaspoon paprika
¼ teaspoon dried rosemary
6 tablespoons butter or margarine, softened
4 ounces sharp cheddar cheese, grated (1 cup)
1½ tablespoons chilled dry white wine

Vegetables for Parties

The French call them *crudités*, we call them crisp fresh vegetables, but by any name they have become part of the appetizer scene whether eaten as is or served with a spread or dip. The choice of vegetables is endless. I'll list them alphabetically, with suggestions for preparation.

ANISE can be cut in sticks and eaten with salt or used to dunk.

ARTICHOKES appear at parties mostly as artichoke hearts, though the leaves of cooked artichokes can be dunked. Never used raw.

ASPARAGUS: Raw asparagus is delightful when dipped in a cold mixture. Choose thin asparagus for serving raw and cut tip end about 3 inches long.

BEANS: Crisp, young green beans are excellent raw. Cut off both ends. Pieces should be about 2 inches long.

BROCCOLI: Trim heads from stalk and cut heads in 2 or 3 pieces lengthwise, depending on size. Pretty and good raw.

BRUSSELS SPROUTS: Cut fresh Brussels sprouts in 2 or 3 pieces (depending on size) and use as a dipper.

CARROTS can be peeled and julienned or made into carrot curls. For julienne strips, cut tiny sticks about 3 inches long and very thin. For curls, use larger carrots and cut length of carrot with potato peeler to make thin strips; curl, fasten with toothpick, and store in ice water for several hours. Remove toothpick to serve.

CAULIFLOWER: Use raw flowerets as is or cut in pieces, depending on size.

CELERY: Use from second layer of stalks into center to make julienne strips. Hearts can be quartered lengthwise with leaves left on.

CUCUMBERS: If waxed, peel; otherwise use with peel on. Cut into slices crosswise, or in lengthwise strips about 2 to 3 inches long.

ENDIVE, Belgian: Endive leaves are excellent as a dipper, larger ones can be cut in half lengthwise.

GREEN ONIONS add variety to vegetables. Cut green tops off so only an inch or so remains and choose small onions.

JERUSALEM ARTICHOKES are a tuber—no relation to either Jerusalem or artichokes, but the root of a variety of the sunflower plant. Peeled and thin sliced, they make a good addition to the dunkers.

JICAMA is a root tuber which, when peeled and thin-sliced, makes a very good crisp, water chestnut-like vegetable to use for dipping. Choose smaller size, as the larger may be woody.

MUSHROOMS: There are so many other uses for mushrooms as appetizers that I seldom use them for dunking. But there is no reason why one cannot. Use small mushrooms whole, cut larger ones in quarters.

PEAS: Snow peas or young tender undeveloped pea pods can add interest to the crisp vegetables.

PEPPERS: Green or red peppers can be seeded and cut into strips. They are flavorful and add color.

RADISHES are always welcome. If you buy (or grow) radishes with leaves, strip off all but the tiniest leaves. Radish "roses" may be made by slicing into the red peel with a small, sharp knife, top to bottom, leaving bottom of cut attached to radish. Soak in ice water.

RUTABAGAS, peeled and sliced thin, add a nice flair.

SUMMER SQUASH (zucchini or yellow) need not be peeled. Scrub well and cut in medium thin slices.

TOMATOES: Cherry tomatoes are a popular item.

All of these vegetables, except mushrooms, can be prepared ready to serve the day before the party. Store in plastic bags with ice cubes and securely fastened with tie or rubber band. Refrigerate each separately, then when ready to serve, arrange vegetables to look like bouquets in bowls with cracked ice.

Beverages

Beverages are an essential part of our daily diet, as we should drink at least eight glasses of liquid a day in the form of water, milk, fruit juice, and similar beverages.

This short section on beverages will not attempt to give directions for making tea or coffee as there are many fine methods for both, each of which has its advocate.

Instead, I have chosen a few party recipes together with some family ideas to induce both children and adults to drink more milk. Cutting down on calories? Remember to buy nonfat milk either in dry form to be reconstituted or in liquid form. Ice milk and sherbets can be substituted for the richer ice creams. You will also be getting less of the saturated fats.

Fruit Milk Shakes

These good beverages can be varied to suit tastes and seasons. They are perfect for the blender, but can be whipped up with a fork and a whisk.

To 1 cup nonfat or regular milk, add one of the ingredient combinations.

Blend in blender until smooth, or mash fruit with fork and beat in milk and seasonings until blended. These amounts make 1 serving. They can be varied by adding a small scoop of ice cream.

1 banana, peeled and cut up
2 tablespoons honey

or

1 ripe pear, peeled and core removed
2 tablespoons sugar
¼ teaspoon cinnamon

or

½ cup crushed strawberries
3 tablespoons sugar

or

½ cup applesauce
¼ teaspoon nutmeg

Spiced Mocha Frosted

A pleasant drink for a refreshment, served with cookies or sandwiches.

Mix chocolate, coffee, and cinnamon and add about 1 cup of the milk. Cook and stir until chocolate is melted and mixture blended. Slowly add remaining milk and sugar to taste, stirring. Divide between 6 tall glasses and add a scoop of ice milk to each. Makes 6 servings.

2 squares unsweetened chocolate, grated
2 tablespoons instant coffee
½ teaspoon cinnamon
1 quart nonfat milk
½ cup (about) sugar
1 pint vanilla ice milk or ice cream

Chocolate Milk Shake

2 tablespoons cocoa syrup
    (recipe below)
1 cup cold nonfat or regular
    milk

cocoa syrup

1 cup cocoa
1½ cups sugar
⅛ teaspoon salt
1¼ cups hot water
1 teaspoon vanilla extract

A chocolate milk shake is popular with all ages. If you prepare your own cocoa syrup, it is less expensive than commercial chocolate syrup.

Blend well and serve. Makes 1 serving.

Cocoa Syrup: Combine cocoa, sugar, salt, and hot water. Cook and stir over moderate heat for 5 minutes. Cool and add vanilla extract. Store, covered, in the refrigerator. Makes 2¼ cups.

Variations

Chocolate Frosted: Add one scoop chocolate ice cream.

Chocolate Banana Milk Shake: Add one-half sliced banana and blend in blender.

Chocolate Banana Frosted: Add one-half sliced banana and one scoop chocolate ice cream and blend in blender.

Orange Nog

1 egg
¼ cup frozen orange juice
    concentrate
1 cup milk
2 teaspoons honey
Crushed ice

Orange nog can substitute for breakfast when one is in a rush. In any event it's a nourishing beverage and flavorful.

Combine egg, juice concentrate, milk, and honey in blender and blend on high for about 10 seconds. Serve over crushed ice. Makes 1 serving.

Variation

Add one-half banana, sliced.

Egg Nog

An egg nog was a treat we always looked forward to as children when we were ill. It's a good way to get milk into the diet.

2 eggs
2 tablespoons honey or sugar
2 cups nonfat or regular milk
½ teaspoon vanilla extract

Combine all ingredients and blend in blender, or in a bowl with rotary beater or whisk. Makes 2 servings.

Variation

For adults: Add ½ cup heavy cream, whipped, and ½ cup brandy. Makes 4 servings.

Spiced Tea

The tea can be prepared in advance and poured over the crushed ice when ready to serve. An especially pleasant beverage for a hot summer day.

2½ cups water
1 stick cinnamon (about 2 inches)
6 whole cloves
6 individual tea bags
½ cup sugar
½ cup orange juice
¼ cup lemon juice
¼ cup cranberry juice
Crushed ice

Heat water with cinnamon and cloves until boiling. Remove tags from the tea bags and add to boiling water. Remove from heat, cover, and steep 5 minutes. Strain and add sugar and fruit juices. Chill. Serve over crushed ice. Makes 4 servings.

Pink Punch

A refreshing combination of juices which would go well with both sandwiches and cookies.

1½ quarts cranberry juice cocktail
¼ cup lime juice
1 quart apple juice
2 cans (6 ounces each) frozen limeade concentrate
4½ cups water
Fresh mint

Combine juices and water and chill well. Serve over ice and garnish with fresh mint. Makes 4 quarts or about 26 5-ounce servings.

Easy Fruit Punch

2 cups sugar
2 cups water
¾ cup lemon juice
1 can (46 ounces) pineapple
    juice
1 quart bottled sparkling water,
    chilled
Orange ice ring (recipe below)

Orange Ice Ring

Orange juice
Fruit in season

A pretty punch and a good combination of fruit flavors. An ice ring can be made of any fruit juice with a flavor compatible with the punch in which it is to be used, or of plain water.

Combine sugar and water and boil 5 minutes. Cool and mix with lemon and pineapple juices. Chill well. When ready to serve, pour into a 6- to 8-quart punch bowl; add sparkling water and ice ring. Makes about 20 5-ounce servings.

Orange Ice Ring: To make an ice ring, start a day in advance. Use a 6-inch or 8-inch ring mold (depending on the size of the punch bowl). A 6-inch ring mold takes 3 cups of juice; an 8-inch mold, 5 cups. Pour juice into mold and allow to freeze partially. This takes several hours (cover the juice with a piece of aluminum foil so it will not frost the freezer). When partially frozen, take off the foil and with a sharp knife or skewer, poke fruit in season into the partially frozen juice. Use fresh strawberries, or quarters of thin orange slices with the peel left on, or pineapple chunks. The mold should be frozen overnight.

Wine Punch

⅔ cup sugar
2 cups orange juice
4 bottles (25.4 ounces each)
    sauterne, chilled
1 bottle (25.4 ounces) burgundy,
    chilled
Ice block to fit bowl
1 bottle (25.4 ounces) dry
    champagne, chilled
Thin orange slices
Fresh mint sprigs

An easy punch to prepare and special to serve for a special occasion. If you don't want to prepare the whole recipe at once, buy two splits of champagne and make half at a time.

Combine sugar and orange juice and stir until sugar is dissolved. Chill. In an 8-quart punch bowl mix sauterne and burgundy wines with orange juice. Add ice block. When ready to serve, pour in champagne. Garnish with thin orange slices and fresh mint sprigs. Makes about 35 5-ounce servings.

Party Punch

Small cookies would go nicely with this party punch. As Precious Gifts says, the recipe can be doubled with no problems.

Combine orange and cranberry juices in a 4-quart punch bowl. Add ginger ale and ice cream divided into 8 pieces. Stir. Makes about 20 5-ounce servings.

1 quart chilled orange juice
1 quart chilled cranberry juice
1 quart chilled ginger ale
1 pint vanilla ice cream

from Precious Gifts
Confidential Chat Column

Apple Cranberry Punch

Festive to look at with its rosy cranberry blush and just the right tart flavor for a good punch.

Combine juices and pineapple tidbits (including juice) and chill well. When ready to serve, pour into punch bowl and add ice cubes and ginger ale. Makes about 20 5-ounce servings.

1 quart cranberry juice cocktail
3 cups apple juice
½ cup fresh lemon juice (2 to 3 lemons depending on size)
1 can (8½ ounces) pineapple tidbits
1 tray ice cubes
1 quart ginger ale

Hot Cocoa

Hot cocoa and cookies will always be a favorite snack. If there is any left over, chill it and serve as "chocolate milk."

Mix cocoa and sugar with water and bring to a boil; cook, stirring, 3 minutes. Add milk and heat just to the boiling point (but do not boil). Beat with a rotary beater or whisk until frothy. Add vanilla. If desired, top each serving with a few marshmallows. Makes 5 5-ounce servings.

5 tablespoons cocoa
4 tablespoons sugar
½ cup water
1 quart nonfat milk
½ teaspoon vanilla extract
Tiny marshmallows (optional)

Hot Spiced Wine

2 bottles (25.4 ounces each) dry
   red wine
¾ cup sugar
1 stick cinnamon (about 2
   inches)
4 whole cloves
3 or 4 lemon slices
10 thin orange slices

*A very easily made hot wine that hits the spot on a cold
day.*

Combine wine and sugar and heat slowly, stirring to dissolve sugar. Add cinnamon; stick cloves
into lemon slices and add them to wine also. Heat
below boiling point for 10 minutes. Strain and
serve hot in cups with an orange slice in each
serving. Makes 10 5-ounce servings.

Hot Cranberry Juice Combo

1 quart cranberry juice cocktail
1 can (18 ounces) pineapple
   juice
1 teaspoon whole cloves
1 stick cinnamon (about 3
   inches)

*Serve up with plenty of doughnuts for a refreshment for
a cold evening.*

Combine all ingredients and bring slowly to a
boil. Cover and simmer 15 minutes. Strain to remove spices. Serve hot. Makes about 10 5-ounce
servings.

Breads

Numbers refer to pages where recipes appear in this book.

Ingredients 34
Techniques 36
White Bread 41
Oaten Wheat Bread 41
Honey Wheat Bread 42
French Bread 43
Down East Health Bread 44
Herbed Batter Bread 44
Rye Bread with Orange and
    Caraway 45
Anadama Bread 46
Bubble Coffee Cake 47
Parker House Rolls 48
(Rich Yeast Dough)
Hamburger Rolls 48
Crescent Rolls 48
Cloverleaf Rolls 49
Hot Cross Buns 49
Refrigerator Rolls 50
Potato Refrigerator Rolls 51
Pecan Rolls 52
Cranberry Bread 53
Cranberry Orange Bread 54
Cranberry Nut Bread 54
Banana Bread 55
Banana Nut Bread 55
Banana Fruit Cake 55
Banana Apricot Bread 55
Banana Date Bread 55
Banana Carrot Bread 56
Apple Bread 56
Blueberry Fruit Nut Bread 57
Pumpkin Orange Bread 57
Wheat Date Nut Bread 58

Zucchini Bread 58
Boston Brown Bread 59
Sour Cream Coffee Cake 60
Fried Bread 60
Fried Yeast Bread 60
Cornbread 61
Cornsticks 61
Buttermilk Cornbread 61
Irish Soda Bread 61
Raisin Soda Bread 61
Brown Soda Bread 61
Basic Muffins 62
Cheese Muffins 62
Bacon Muffins 62
Raisin Muffins 62
Blueberry Muffins 62
Bran Muffins 63
Raisin Bran Muffins 63
Honey Bran Muffins 63
Refrigerator Buttermilk Bran
    Muffins 63
Yeast Raised Muffins 64
Buttermilk Biscuits 64
Baking Powder Biscuits 65
Sweet Biscuit Shortcake 65
Cheese Biscuits 65
Herb Biscuits 65
Drop Biscuits 65
Wheat Germ Biscuits 65
Jonnycake 66
(West of Narragansett Bay)
Jonnycake 66
(East of Narragansett Bay)
Whole Wheat Popovers 67

Breads
Yeast and Baking Powder

Bread making is such a joy. It can never be a bore because even the most routine recipes can be varied to produce new and interesting results. The care and baking of bread, whether it is a yeast or a baking powder product, is a labor of love.

In order to make that labor of love as easy and perfect as possible, here is a short course in baking.

Ingredients

Flour

Wheat flour is the ingredient used in the largest quantity in bread recipes. Its purpose is to provide gluten, which gives bread its texture and, of course, bulk. White flour has the highest content of gluten forming properties. For this reason it is usually used as at least part of the flour in recipes where other flours are incorporated. Without white flour, the bread has a heavy texture.

All-purpose white can be purchased as a bleached or unbleached flour. Either is satisfactory for baking, though unbleached is preferred by some because it has gone through less milling.

Bread flour is also available. It has a higher gluten content which is good for baking bread. While all-purpose flour can be used for other products (such as pastry, baking powder breads, or cakes) where gluten is not a factor, bread flour should be saved for yeast breads.

Whole wheat flour is wheat flour which has bran left in the flour. Do not sift whole wheat flour.

Other specialty flours such as soy, rye, buckwheat, corn, millet, and oat are available, some only in specialty stores. As a rule they are used in small quantities to enhance the flavor. Cake flour can be purchased also. It is very low in gluten and designed to give lightness of texture to cake products.

Yeast

Yeast is used in recipes to make the products rise. It is temperamental in that it requires moderate temperature, 105°–115° F, to become active and create a good result. Liquids too cold or too hot are enemies of yeast. In some specialized recipes temperatures of 120°–130° F are suggested. With these recipes the higher temperature is satisfactory as it is still in the high warm range.

Yeast can be purchased in individual airtight packages as active dry yeast. This same dry yeast also comes in bulk, in jars. One scant tablespoon is equivalent to one package. After bulk yeast is opened, store tightly covered in the refrigerator. Yeast packages are dated and should be used before that date or fairly close to its expiration. Also available are moist yeast cakes; a 0.6-ounce cake is interchangeable with one package or one tablespoon of active dry yeast. It is not wise to purchase bulk yeast unless one does a great deal of baking, as it deteriorates faster than the hermetically sealed packages.

Other Leavening Agents

Baking powder, baking soda, and cream of tartar are the leavening agents for quick breads, so named because they do not require the long rising period of those made with yeast. Modern recipes and those in this book can be used with any brand of baking powder. It is usually mixed with flour and/or other dry ingredients. Cream of tartar is occasionally found in recipes.

In preparing quick breads, do not overbeat. Plan to bake immediately after mixing, as once the baking powder, soda, or cream of tartar is mixed with liquid, it begins to act.

Sweetening

In yeast products, something sweet such as sugar, honey, or molasses is needed to cause the yeast to form gas and the bread to rise. Sweetening is also used to give flavor and improve texture, the latter particularly in quick breads.

Liquids

Liquids used in baking vary from water to wine and run the gamut in between. Liquid is necessary to dissolve the yeast or baking powder, bind the ingredients, and give flavor and consistency to the product. Liquids used in yeast breads should be warmed. Those in quick breads are used cold.

Other Ingredients

Shortening and eggs improve texture and add flavor. The shortening can vary from solid white shortening to butter, margarine, or cooking oil. Use shortening specified in recipe. Sometimes spices, nuts, or fruits are used for flavor and texture.

Techniques

Making yeast products teaches one patience, if nothing else. They should not be hurried, although they can be slowed down to a degree. Once you get your hand into bread making, mixing, kneading, watching for the proper rising, all become second nature.

Mixing

Use a bowl that is large enough so that the ingredients can be easily handled. An electric mixer or vigorous hand beating at the first stage can begin the formation of the gluten. After enough flour has been worked into the liquid so that the dough may be handled, it is then kneaded.

Kneading

Use a clean flat surface sprinkled with a little flour. Flour your hands and take the dough from the mixing bowl. Shape it into a ball and begin to knead.

Fold the dough toward you and, with the heel of palms, push the dough ball away from you; then turn it one-quarter of the way around; repeat the folding, pushing, and turning motions. Knead the dough until it is smooth and elastic, about 10 minutes. Add more flour to board and hands as needed, but try not to add more than necessary. Toward the end of the kneading time, beginners will be surprised at the very small amount of flour needed.

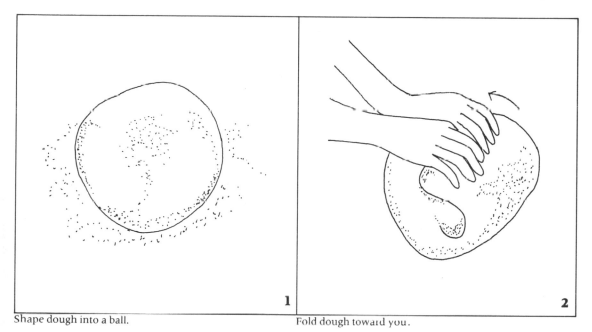

1 Shape dough into a ball.

2 Fold dough toward you.

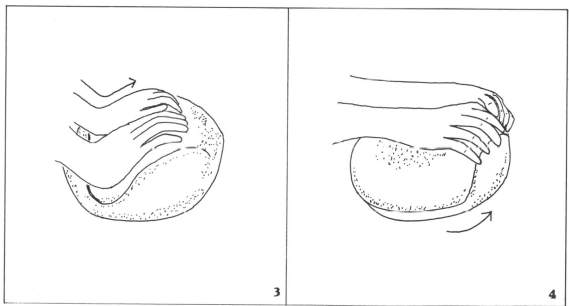

3 Push away with the heel of your palms.

4 Turn it one-quarter of the way around.

Rising

A place that is free from drafts and with a temperature of about 85° F, makes the best nest in which to raise the bread. This can be achieved in several ways. In the unlit oven place a large bowl of boiling water and set the bread in another bowl beside it or over it. If your oven has a pilot light or an electric bulb, that alone may be sufficient heat. Cover the bread with plastic wrap and a clean towel during this period. Check after one hour. The dough when sufficiently risen should double in size. If you press the tips of two fingers lightly into the dough and the dent stays, the dough is doubled. Since many factors can govern the temperature surrounding the dough, check rising whenever you make bread; do not count on time only.

If recipe calls for two risings (this helps make a finer textured bread), punch bread down in center, turn dough over in bowl. Re-cover and let rise again until doubled in bulk, about 30 minutes.

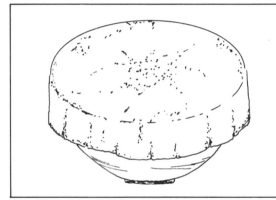

1

Cover bowl with plastic wrap and a clean towel.

2

Check after one hour.

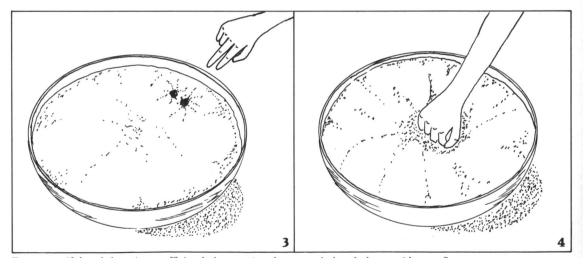

3

Test to see if dough has risen sufficiently by pressing the tips of two fingers into the dough. If the dents stay, the dough has doubled.

4

Punch dough down with your fist.

**Anadama Bread (recipe on page 46)
and Blueberry Muffins (recipe on page 62)**

Shaping

For making bread into loaves, cut the dough into the number of pieces the recipe says (two pieces for two loaves, three for three, etc.). Directions vary for shaping. Here are two methods; I suggest you try both, and follow the one which gives you the most satisfactory loaf.

One suggestion: Roll each piece into a rectangle, using a rolling pin, gently but firmly, to remove gas bubbles. Then begin with upper short side and roll toward you. Seal with thumbs. Seal ends also and fold ends under. Carefully transfer to a greased bread pan putting sealed side on bottom.

Another suggestion: Cut bread mass into required size pieces. Knead each piece two or three minutes and with hands shape into loaf. Put into greased bread pan.

Bread then must be allowed to rise again in the pan. Place in the 85° F space, cover, and let rise until double in bulk, one to two hours. Use the two finger test, pushing gently into one end of the loaf. If dent stays, bread is ready to bake.

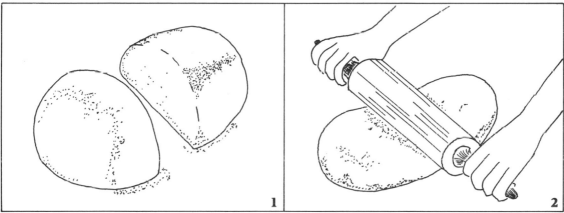

For two loaves, cut the dough into two pieces.   Roll one piece of dough into a rectangle.

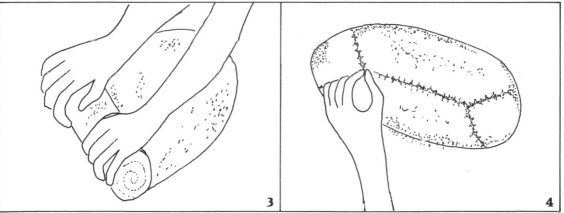

Begin with short side and roll toward you.   Fold ends under and seal ends and edge by pinching seams together.

Baking

Follow temperature given and put bread in a preheated oven. Place bread so heat can go around the pans. At end of time suggested, remove a loaf from pan and tap on bottom or side. If bread sounds hollow and is nicely browned, it is done.

Remove loaves from pans and cool on a rack. I like to rub tops of the hot bread with butter or margarine and save the wrappers from the quarters for this purpose. This makes a soft crust. If you like a crisp crust, do not butter the top.

Storing Bread

Cooled bread can be frozen. Wrap in freezer wrap, seal, label, and date. You can freeze for two to three months.

Bread left unfrozen for immediate use should be kept in a cool place (not the refrigerator) in a plastic bag kept closed with a closure.

Final Note

If you are going to bake a lot of loaf bread, get a good bread knife for cutting. That is a necessity for nice, neat slices.

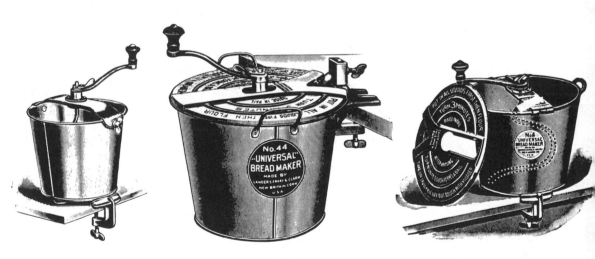

Old-fashioned bread makers

White Bread

This white bread is delicious when served warm. It freezes very well and is always a treat.

Combine sugar, salt, butter, evaporated milk, and boiling water in a very large bowl. Add 4 cups flour and yeast and beat 2 minutes with an electric mixer or by hand. Gradually add remaining flour until mixture is thick enough to knead.

Turn out on a lightly floured surface and knead for 10 minutes or until dough is smooth and elastic. Put into a greased bowl and turn to grease dough. Cover and let rise until double in bulk.

Punch down, turn dough in bowl and let rise again until double in bulk. Punch down.

Cut dough into 4 pieces and let rest 10 minutes, covered.

Shape into loaves and put into 4 greased 9×5×3-inch loaf pans. Let rise, covered, until double in bulk. Bake at 400° F for 30 to 35 minutes. Makes 4 loaves.

¼ cup sugar
1½ tablespoons salt
6 tablespoons butter or margarine
1 can (13 ounces) evaporated milk
1⅔ cups boiling water
12 cups (about) unbleached all-purpose flour
2 packages active dry yeast

Oaten Wheat Bread

A slightly heavier textured bread, but very flavorful.

Mix oatmeal, whole wheat, dry milk, brown sugar, and butter in large bowl. Add boiling water and stir to blend. Cool to room temperature. Soften yeast in warm water and stir into oatmeal mixture. Stir in all-purpose flour until mixture is stiff enough to knead. Turn out onto a lightly floured surface and knead for ten minutes until smooth and elastic. Put into a greased bowl and turn to grease dough. Cover and let rise until double in bulk. Punch down.

Cut dough into 2 pieces. Shape into loaves and put into greased 9×5×3-inch loaf pans. Let rise, covered, until double in bulk. Bake at 375° F for 35 minutes. Makes 2 loaves.

1 cup uncooked quick oatmeal
1 cup whole wheat flour
⅔ cup nonfat dry milk powder or granules
½ cup firmly packed brown sugar
2 tablespoons butter or margarine
2 cups boiling water
1 envelope active dry yeast
½ cup warm water
6 to 7 cups all-purpose flour

Honey Wheat Bread

1 quart milk
½ cup butter or margarine
6 tablespoons honey
2 tablespoons salt
8 cups whole wheat flour
2 packages active dry yeast
4 cups (about) all-purpose flour

A few years back I bought some aluminum 1-pound meat loaf pans. They measure 7¾×3⅝×2¼ inches. Very often instead of 3 loaves of bread in 9×5×3-inch pans, I make 4 in the smaller size. Bake at the same temperature for 10 minutes less time.

Heat together milk, butter, honey, and salt just until bubbles begin to form around edge of milk. Butter does not need to be completely melted. Remove from heat and beat in 4 cups whole wheat flour and yeast. Beat until well blended.

Stir in remaining whole wheat flour and add enough white flour to make dough stiff enough to knead.

Turn out on a lightly floured surface and knead 10 minutes or until dough is smooth and elastic. Put into a greased bowl and turn to grease dough. Cover and let rise until double in bulk.

Punch down, turn dough in bowl and let rise again until double in bulk. Punch down.

Cut dough into 3 pieces and let rest 10 minutes, covered. Shape into loaves and put into greased 9×5×3-inch loaf pans. Let rise, covered, until double in bulk. Bake at 375° F for 35 to 40 minutes. Makes 3 loaves.

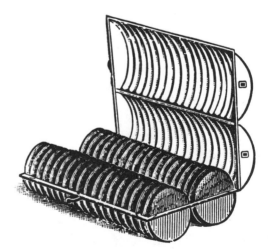

French Bread

Commercial French bread is baked in an oven into which steam is introduced. This accounts for the crisp crust. It is difficult to achieve the commercial effect in a home oven, but this home-baked French bread is mighty good anyway.

2 packages active dry yeast
2 tablespoons sugar
2 teaspoons salt
7 to 8 cups unbleached all-purpose flour
2 cups very warm tap water
2 tablespoons butter or margarine, softened
3 tablespoons cornmeal
2 to 3 tablespoons water for brushing

Combine yeast, sugar, salt, and 2 cups flour in a large bowl. Mix well and stir in the 2 cups warm water and the butter. Beat 2 minutes. Then gradually stir in remaining flour until dough is stiff enough to knead. Knead on a lightly floured surface until dough is smooth and elastic. Place in a greased bowl and turn to grease dough. Cover and let rise until double in bulk.

Cut dough into 2 pieces and knead each piece 2 to 3 minutes. Shape into a 15-inch roll and place on a baking sheet which has been sprinkled liberally with cornmeal. Cut 4 to 5 gashes across the top of each loaf with scissors and brush with water. Cover and let rise until double in bulk. Brush again with water and bake at 400° F for 20 minutes or until browned. Cool on rack. Makes 2 loaves.

Note: Some authorities suggest placing a pan of boiling water in the bottom of the oven while the French bread is baking. The steam supposedly makes a more crusty loaf of bread. It has never seemed to make much difference in my oven, so the judgment is yours.

Variation

Whole Wheat French Bread: Substitute 4 cups whole wheat flour for 4 cups of the all-purpose flour. Directions for mixing remain the same.

Down East Health Bread

½ cup enriched cornmeal
½ cup nonfat dry milk powder
   or granules
2 cups boiling water
⅓ cup molasses
1 tablespoon salt
¼ cup margarine
2 packages active dry yeast
1½ cups whole wheat flour
4 cups (about) all-purpose flour

A well-flavored bread with a lot of good ingredients. Good fresh and makes excellent toast.

Combine cornmeal and dry milk. Stir gradually into boiling water. Add molasses, salt, and margarine. When cool to touch, stir in yeast and whole wheat flour and beat for 2 minutes.

Stir in white flour until mixture is stiff enough to knead. Knead on a lightly floured surface until smooth and elastic, about 10 minutes, adding flour as needed.

Place dough in a greased bowl, turn to grease dough. Cover and let rise until double in bulk (about 2 hours). Punch dough down. Divide in half and knead, each piece 3 minutes. Shape into loaves and place in greased 9×5×3-inch pans. Cover and let rise again until double in bulk. Bake at 375° F about 45 minutes. Makes 2 loaves.

Herbed Batter Bread

½ cup warm water (105°–115° F)
1 package active dry yeast
½ cup warm dairy sour cream
3 tablespoons butter or
   margarine, softened
3 tablespoons sugar
1 teaspoon salt
1 teaspoon Italian herb
   seasoning
1 egg
2 to 2½ cups all-purpose flour

A loaf of herbed bread would accompany a salad meal well; or plan to bake it at the same time as a casserole dish for supper.

Measure water into large bowl. Add yeast and stir until softened. Add cream, margarine, sugar, salt, herbs, and egg. Beat in 2 cups flour until well blended, about 1 minute. Stir in enough additional flour to make a soft dough (one which will hold its shape when a spoon is pulled out of it). Cover and let rise until double in bulk, about 40 minutes. Stir down. Spoon dough into a greased 1-quart casserole. Cover and let rise until double in bulk, 40 to 50 minutes. Bake at 375° F for 35 minutes or until brown. Remove from casserole and cool on rack. Makes 1 loaf.

Rye Bread with Orange and Caraway

In some circles this is called "Swedish Rye Bread." Whether that claim to national origin stands up or not, it is still a very good recipe.

Combine sugar, water, and yeast in a small bowl and let stand 5 minutes.

Heat milk with salt, molasses, and shortening until lukewarm. Add yeast and 1½ cups of the rye flour and beat for 2 minutes. Stir in remaining rye flour, orange rind, and caraway seed. Gradually stir in white flour until dough is stiff enough to knead. Knead on a lightly floured surface until smooth and elastic. Put dough in a greased bowl and turn to grease dough. Cover and let rise until double in bulk, about 2 hours. Punch down and divide into 2 pieces. Cover and let rest 10 minutes. Shape into loaves and put into greased 8×4×2¼-inch loaf pans. Cover and let rise until double in bulk, about 1½ hours. Bake at 375° F for 25 to 30 minutes or until nicely browned. Remove from pan and cool on rack. Cool before cutting. Makes 2 loaves.

1 tablespoon sugar
½ cup lukewarm water
1 package active dry yeast
1½ cups milk
1 tablespoon salt
¼ cup molasses
2 tablespoons shortening
3 cups rye flour
1 tablespoon grated orange rind
2 teaspoons caraway seed
3 cups (about) all-purpose flour

Anadama Bread
(pictured between pages 38 and 39)

½ cup yellow cornmeal
3 tablespoons cooking oil
¼ cup molasses
2 teaspoons salt
¾ cup boiling water
1 package active dry yeast
¼ cup warm water
1 egg
2¾ cups all-purpose flour
Extra cornmeal

Supposedly a New England fisherman became angry with his wife because all she gave him to eat, day after day, was cornmeal and molasses. One night he tossed flour and yeast into the cornmeal and molasses, put it all into the oven and baked it. He sat down to eat a loaf of bread for a change, mumbling "Anna, damn her!"—shortened to Anadama.

Stir together in a large mixing bowl the cornmeal, oil, molasses, and salt. Add the boiling water and mix well. Cool to lukewarm.

Dissolve yeast in the warm water. Add yeast, egg, and half the flour to the lukewarm cornmeal mixture. Beat 2 minutes on medium speed of mixer or by hand. Scrape sides and bottom of bowl frequently.

Add rest of flour and mix with a spoon until flour is thoroughly blended into batter. Spread batter evenly into greased loaf pan, 8½ × 4½ × 2¾-inch or 9 × 5 × 3-inch. Batter will be sticky. Smooth out top of loaf by flouring hand and patting into shape.

Let rise in warm place until batter reaches top of 8½-inch pan or 1 inch from top of 9-inch pan. Sprinkle top with a little cornmeal. Bake at 375° F for 50 to 55 minutes. Crust will be dark brown. Immediately remove from pan and cool on rack. Makes 1 loaf.

from The Royal Family
Confidential Chat Column

Bubble Coffee Cake

Bubble Coffee Cake is a good recipe for a morning coffee. Instead of cutting, break it apart with 2 forks. It can be served with or without butter.

Combine milk, ¼ cup sugar, 4 tablespoons butter, and salt and cool to lukewarm. Meanwhile, soften yeast in warm water. Mix yeast and milk mixtures in a large bowl. Beat in egg and 2 cups flour and continue beating 2 minutes. Stir in additional flour until a fairly stiff dough is formed. Place dough in a greased bowl. Cover and let rise until double in bulk. Punch down and allow to rest 10 minutes.

Grease an 8-inch bundt cake pan and sprinkle half the pecans on bottom.

Mix ½ cup sugar with cinnamon.

Pinch off small pieces of dough and form into round 1½-inch balls. Dip first in melted butter, then in sugar and cinnamon. Place in bundt pan. Continue until all dough is used and then sprinkle remaining cinnamon-sugar and pecans on top. Cover and let rise until double in bulk. Bake at 350° F for 30 to 35 minutes. Invert at once on serving plate. Makes 1 cake.

½ cup scalded milk
¼ cup sugar
4 tablespoons butter or margarine
½ teaspoon salt
1 package active dry yeast
¼ cup warm water
1 egg
4 to 5 cups all-purpose flour
¼ cup chopped pecans
½ cup sugar
1 teaspoon cinnamon
3 tablespoons melted butter

Parker House Rolls
or Rich Yeast Dough—with variations

5 cups (about) all-purpose flour
½ cup sugar
1½ teaspoons salt
2 packages active dry yeast
1 cup milk
¼ cup butter or margarine
2 eggs
½ cup melted butter or
    margarine for brushing

Parker House rolls are named after Boston's Parker House hotel, established 1855. They are more of a shape than a recipe since any rich yeast dough recipe can be formed into Parker House rolls. These rolls freeze well.

In a large bowl, mix 2 cups flour with sugar, salt, and yeast. Heat together milk and butter until bubbles appear around the edge of the milk. Pour at once into flour mixture and beat 2 minutes. Add eggs and beat until well blended. Gradually add remaining flour until mixture is stiff enough to knead. Knead on a lightly floured surface until smooth and elastic. Place in a greased bowl, turn to grease dough. Cover and let rise until double in bulk, about 2 hours.

Turn dough out onto a lightly floured board and with a floured rolling pin, roll dough ¼ to ½ inch thick. Cut with a floured 3-inch round cutter. Brush lightly with melted butter and make a crease across the center of the cut dough with the dull edge of a knife. Fold one half over the other half. Place fairly close together on a greased pan or cookie sheet. Brush with melted butter. Cover lightly and let rise again until double in bulk, about 1 hour.

Bake at 375° F for 15 to 20 minutes or until lightly browned. Brush hot rolls with butter. Makes about 3½ dozen rolls.

Other shapes into which rich yeast dough may be formed:

Hamburger Rolls: Roll raised dough ½ inch thick. Cut with a 4-inch biscuit cutter. Brush with butter and place on a greased cookie sheet. Cover and let rise until double in bulk. Bake at 375° F for 15 to 20 minutes or until lightly browned.

Crescent Rolls: Roll raised dough in 9-inch circles about ¼ inch thick. Brush with melted butter. Cut into 8 wedges. Roll from large side. Shape into crescents and place on a greased cookie sheet.

Cover and let rise until double in bulk. Bake at 375° F for 15 to 20 minutes or until nicely browned.

Cloverleaf Rolls: Shape raised dough into tiny balls. Dip in melted butter and place 3 in each section of a greased muffin tin. Let rise until double in bulk and bake at 375° F for 15 to 20 minutes or until nicely browned.

Hot Cross Buns: Make ½ recipe rich yeast dough, adding 1 teaspoon cinnamon to dry ingredients. Knead ½ cup currants or raisins into risen dough. Form into 1½-inch balls and place in a greased 8×8×2-inch pan. Brush with egg yolk diluted with 2 teaspoons water. Cover. Let rise until double in bulk, about 1 hour. Bake at 375° F for 30 minutes or until lightly browned. Remove from pan and cool on rack. When cooled, form cross on top with frosting made by mixing ¾ cup confectioners sugar with a few drops of hot water.

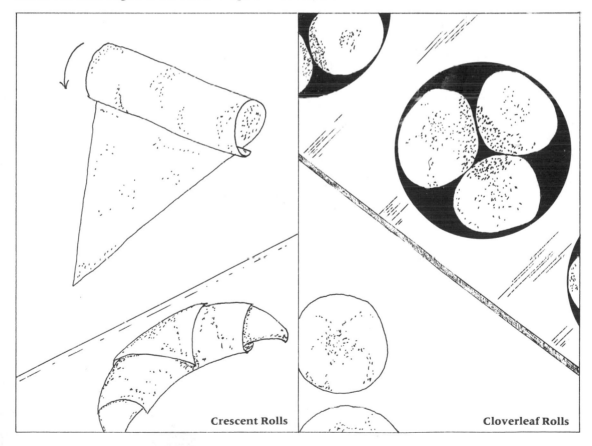

Crescent Rolls

Cloverleaf Rolls

Refrigerator Rolls

2 packages active dry yeast
¼ cup lukewarm water
¾ cup milk
½ cup butter or margarine
¼ cup sugar
½ teaspoon salt
2 eggs, well beaten
4 cups all-purpose flour
5 tablespoons melted butter or
   margarine

This recipe for rolls came to me many years ago from a dear family friend. They are marvelously easy to make and to eat. They show up at all my holiday meals. Some of our most circumspect friends will eat four or five at one sitting.

Combine yeast and water and let stand to soften yeast. Combine milk, butter, sugar, and salt in a 6-cup saucepan and heat just until butter is melted. Cool to lukewarm. Add yeast and eggs and stir in flour gradually until a soft dough is formed. Spoon into a 2-quart bowl and store, covered, in the refrigerator 24 hours.

To bake: Divide dough into fourths. On a floured surface, roll each fourth into a circle ¼ inch thick. Cut each circle into 8 wedge-shaped pieces. Starting at wide end roll each wedge into a crescent. (See illustration on page 49.) Dip in melted butter and place on baking pan. A 15×10-inch jelly roll pan is best since it has a rim so that the butter on the rolls won't spill into the oven during baking. Cover and let rise at room temperature until doubled in bulk. This takes about 1½ to 2 hours depending on the temperature of the room. Bake at 425° F for 10 to 12 minutes. This makes 32 rolls. If there are any left over, they freeze well; or, you may note, the recipe can be divided.

Potato Refrigerator Rolls

A rich roll with an extra flavor from the potatoes. You can use instant potatoes to make the mashed potatoes if you wish.

1 cup mashed potatoes
¾ cup butter or margarine, softened
½ cup sugar
2 teaspoons salt
2 eggs
2 packages active dry yeast
½ cup lukewarm water
1 cup milk, scalded and cooled
7 cups (about) all-purpose flour
Melted butter for brushing

Mix potatoes with butter, sugar, salt, and eggs in a large bowl. Soften yeast in water and mix with cooled milk and potato mixture. Beat for 2 minutes. Gradually stir in flour until stiff enough to knead. Knead on a lightly floured surface until smooth and elastic. Put into a greased bowl and turn to grease bread. Cover and let rise until double in bulk. Punch down. Place in a greased 2-quart casserole. Butter top of bread and cover with casserole lid. Place in refrigerator until ready to bake, at least 24 hours. About 1 hour before baking, remove desired amount of dough and shape into rolls. Place on greased baking sheet, spread rolls with melted butter. Cover and let rise until double in bulk, about 1 hour. Bake at 400° F for 15 to 20 minutes. The whole recipe makes 5 dozen medium sized rolls. Dough will keep under refrigeration up to 1 week.

Pecan Rolls

Dough

2 packages active dry yeast
½ cup sugar
2 teaspoons salt
5 cups all-purpose flour
1 cup milk
½ cup butter or margarine
2 eggs

Pecan Filling

1 cup (about) butter or
    margarine, melted
2⅓ cups firmly packed brown
    sugar
1½ cups chopped pecans
¾ cup whole pecans

Luscious homemade pecan rolls are welcomed by family and friends and also make a lovely gift at Christmas. An easy way to cut up pecan rolls is to take a short length of clean string, put under roll where you want to cut, bring up ends, and cross.

Dough: Combine yeast, sugar, salt, and 2 cups flour in a bowl. Heat milk and butter in saucepan just until bubbles begin to form around edge of milk. Butter does not need to be completely melted. Remove from heat and add to yeast mixture. Beat 2 minutes with an electric mixer or by hand. Add eggs and beat until blended. Slowly stir in remaining flour until a dough is formed which will not stick to the hands. Turn out on a lightly floured surface and knead until smooth and elastic, about 10 minutes. Put into a greased bowl and turn to grease dough. Cover and let rise until double in bulk, about 2 hours.

When dough has risen to double, cut into 3 pieces. Roll each into a rectangle, about ¼ inch thick, 8 inches wide, and 12 inches long.

For filling, spread each rectangle with about 2 tablespoons melted butter, sprinkle with about ⅓ cup brown sugar and ½ cup chopped pecans. Roll tightly from long side and seal edge. Cut each into 12 slices.

Divide remaining butter (melt more if there is not enough to cover bottom of pans) among three 8-inch round cake pans. Sprinkle with remaining sugar and place ¼ cup whole pecans in each pan. Place 12 slices, cut side down, in each pan. Cover and let rise until double in bulk about 1 hour. Bake at 375° F for about 25 minutes or until nicely browned.

Place rack over large baking pan and turn out rolls from pans at once on rack over pan. If any syrup or nuts go onto pan, they can be retrieved and put back on rolls. Serve hot or cool, or wrap in freezer wrap and freeze. Makes 3 dozen pecan rolls.

Cranberry Bread

A basic cranberry bread which makes marvelous sandwiches when combined with softened cream cheese.

Mix flour, sugar, baking powder, and salt together in a bowl. Beat egg with milk and cooking oil. Stir into dry ingredients just to blend. Fold in cranberries and nuts. Spoon into a greased 9×5×3-inch baking pan. Bake at 350° F for 60 to 70 minutes or until a cake tester inserted in center comes out clean. Cool bread in pan 10 to 15 minutes. Remove carefully from pan and cool on rack. To store, wrap in plastic wrap or aluminum foil. During hot weather, store bread in refrigerator.

Wrap in freezer wrap, seal, label, and date to freeze up to 3 months. Makes 1 loaf.

3 cups all-purpose flour
1 cup sugar
4 teaspoons baking powder
1 teaspoon salt
1 egg
1½ cups milk
2 tablespoons oil
1 cup fresh cranberries, coarsely
  chopped
½ cup chopped nuts

Cranberry Orange Bread

2 cups all-purpose flour
1 cup sugar
1½ teaspoons baking powder
½ teaspoon baking soda
½ teaspoon salt
¼ cup shortening
1 teaspoon grated orange rind
¾ cup orange juice
1 egg
1 cup fresh cranberries, coarsely
    chopped

Cranberries have a unique place in New England history. They were first cultivated in Dennis on Cape Cod and from that small beginning have grown to one of our prime fruit crops. If you have a food processor, chop the cranberries and nuts in it.

Mix flour, sugar, baking powder, soda, and salt in a bowl. Cut in shortening with 2 knives or a pastry blender. Beat together orange rind, juice, and egg. Mix into dry ingredients just to blend. Stir in cranberries. Spoon into a greased 9×5×3-inch loaf pan. Bake at 350° F for 60 to 70 minutes or until a cake tester inserted in center comes out clean. Cool bread in pan 10 to 15 minutes. Remove carefully from pan and cool on rack. To store, wrap in plastic wrap or aluminum foil. During hot weather, store bread in refrigerator.

Wrap in freezer wrap, seal, label, and date to freeze up to 3 months. Makes 1 loaf.

Variation

Cranberry Nut Bread: Add ½ cup chopped nuts with cranberries.

Banana Bread

Because bananas were brought here first by a New England sea captain, they have always been a unique part of our culinary heritage. This is a good banana bread with several variations.

½ cup shortening
1 cup sugar
3 eggs
1⅓ cups mashed ripe bananas
　(about 3 large bananas)
2⅓ cups all-purpose flour
3 teaspoons baking powder
½ teaspoon baking soda
½ teaspoon salt

Cream shortening and sugar until light and fluffy. Add eggs and bananas and beat for 2 minutes or until blended. Mix flour with baking powder, soda, and salt. Stir into banana mixture just to blend. Spoon into a greased 9×5×3-inch loaf pan. Bake at 350° F for 60 to 70 minutes or until cake tester inserted in center comes out clean. Cool bread in pan 10 to 15 minutes. Remove carefully from pan and cool on rack. To store, wrap in plastic wrap or aluminum foil. During hot weather, store bread in refrigerator.

Wrap in freezer wrap, seal, label, and date to freeze up to 3 months. Makes 1 loaf.

Variations

Banana Nut Bread: Add ½ cup chopped nuts with flour mixture.

Banana Fruit Cake: Add ½ cup each chopped nuts and chopped candied fruits with flour mixture.

Banana Apricot Bread: Add ½ cup finely chopped dried apricots with flour mixture.

Banana Date Bread. Add ½ cup chopped sugared dates with flour mixture.

Banana Carrot Bread

1 cup mashed bananas (about 2
   large bananas)
1 cup sugar
¾ cup oil
2 eggs
2 cups all-purpose flour
1 teaspoon baking soda
½ teaspoon salt
½ teaspoon cinnamon
¼ teaspoon nutmeg
1 cup finely grated raw carrot
   (about 3 medium carrots)

All quick bread loaves are better if allowed to cool and stored overnight before cutting. This is true of banana carrot bread, too.

Combine banana with sugar, oil, and eggs in a large bowl. Beat for 2 minutes at medium speed. Mix together dry ingredients and fold into banana mixture. Add carrots. Spoon into a well-greased and floured 9×5×3-inch loaf pan. Bake at 350° F for 1 hour or until cake tester inserted in center comes out clean. Cool in pan on rack 10 minutes. Remove loaf from pan and cool on rack. To store, wrap in aluminum foil or plastic wrap.

Wrap in freezer wrap, seal, label, and date to freeze up to 3 months. Makes 1 loaf.

Apple Bread

1 cup all-purpose flour
2 teaspoons baking powder
½ teaspoon baking soda
1 teaspoon salt
1¾ cups whole wheat flour
½ cup raw unprocessed bran
5 tablespoons brown sugar
2 eggs
¼ cup oil
1 teaspoon vanilla extract
1 cup peeled, cored, quartered
   apples (1 large apple)
1 cup plain yogurt
½ cup walnut meats

The flavor of this bread combines very well with cheese for a healthy sandwich.

Mix all-purpose flour with baking powder, soda, salt, whole wheat flour, and wheat bran.

Beat together sugar, eggs, oil, and vanilla. Chop apples very fine and mix into sugar mixture. Add yogurt alternately with dry ingredients, stirring just to blend after each addition. Fold in nuts. Spoon into a greased 9×5×3-inch loaf pan. Bake at 350° F for 1 hour or until a cake tester inserted in center of loaf comes out clean. Cool in pan on rack 10 minutes. Carefully remove loaf from pan and cool on rack. To store, wrap in aluminum foil or plastic wrap. Store unused portion of bread in refrigerator.

Wrap in freezer wrap, seal, label, and date to freeze up to 3 months. Makes 1 loaf.

Blueberry Fruit Nut Bread

A moist loaf, makes a nice tea bread. One loaf to eat, one to freeze for future use.

In a bowl mix together flours, sugar, baking powder, soda, salt, and nutmeg. Beat eggs and mix with applesauce and oil. Stir into dry ingredients just enough to blend. Fold in blueberries and nuts. Spoon into 2 greased and floured 8×4×2¼-inch loaf pans. Bake at 350° F for 50 minutes or until a cake tester inserted in center of loaves comes out clean. Cool in pans on rack for 10 minutes. Remove from pans and cool on rack. When cooled, wrap in aluminum foil or plastic wrap to store. Store unused portion in refrigerator. Wrap in freezer wrap, seal, label, and date to freeze up to 3 months. Makes 2 loaves.

* *If dry pack frozen blueberries are used, rinse and drain.*

1 cup whole wheat flour
2 cups all-purpose flour
1 cup granulated sugar
1 tablespoon baking powder
½ teaspoon baking soda
½ teaspoon salt
½ teaspoon nutmeg
2 eggs
1 cup commercial applesauce
¼ cup oil
2 cups fresh or dry pack frozen blueberries*
½ cup chopped nuts

Pumpkin Orange Bread

Cream shortening and sugars until light and fluffy. Beat in eggs. Stir in pumpkin and water. Mix flour with baking powder, soda, salt, and spices and fold into pumpkin mixture.

Remove seeds from orange, cut into pieces and grind, rind and all, in a blender, grinder, or food processor. Stir into batter. Fold in nuts and raisins. Spoon batter into 2 well-greased 9×5×3-inch loaf pans. Bake at 350° F for 1 hour or until cake tester inserted in center comes out clean. Cool in pan on rack for 10 minutes. Remove loaves carefully from pans and cool on rack. To store, wrap in aluminum foil or plastic wrap.

Wrap in freezer wrap, seal, label, and date to freeze up to 3 months. Makes 2 loaves.

⅔ cup shortening
2 cups granulated sugar
⅔ cup firmly packed brown sugar
4 eggs
1 can (16 ounces) pumpkin
⅔ cup water
3⅓ cups all-purpose flour
½ teaspoon baking powder
½ teaspoon baking soda
1 teaspoon salt
1 teaspoon cinnamon
½ teaspoon cloves
½ teaspoon nutmeg
1 orange
⅔ cup chopped nuts
⅔ cup chopped raisins or dates

Wheat Date Nut Bread

¼ cup butter or margarine,
  softened
½ cup firmly packed brown
  sugar
2 eggs
1 cup small curd cottage cheese
⅔ cup chopped dates
2 cups whole wheat flour
4 teaspoons baking powder
¼ teaspoon baking soda
¼ teaspoon salt
½ teaspoon cinnamon
½ cup milk

Wheat date nut bread is baked in a round pan for a change. It is full of healthful ingredients.

In a large mixing bowl, beat together butter and sugar. Add eggs, cottage cheese, and dates and beat to blend.

Mix flour with dry ingredients and add alternately with milk to creamed mixture, beating just to blend. Spoon batter into a greased 8-inch round cake pan. Bake at 350° F for 60 minutes or until a cake tester inserted in center comes out clean. Cool in pan on rack for 5 minutes. Then cut in wedges or slices.

The bread can be baked in disposable aluminum pans for gifting.

from The Fiddler's Wife
Confidential Chat Column

Zucchini Bread

4 eggs
2 cups granulated sugar
1 cup cooking oil
1 teaspoon vanilla extract
3½ cups all-purpose flour
¾ teaspoon baking powder
1½ teaspoons baking soda
1 teaspoon cinnamon
1 teaspoon salt
2 cups grated, unpared zucchini
  (about 3 medium)
1 cup raisins

Zucchini squash grows so well around here that bread made with it is very popular. Since this recipe makes 2 loaves, freeze one. If you've not tasted it, you'll be surprised at its cake-like flavor.

Beat eggs until light; then gradually beat in sugar, then oil and vanilla. Mix flour with remaining dry ingredients and add alternately with zucchini to egg mixture stirring until all dry ingredients are just moistened. Fold in raisins. Spoon into 2 greased and floured 9×5×3-inch loaf pans. Bake at 350° F for 55 minutes or until a cake tester inserted in center comes out clean. Cool in pans on rack for 10 minutes. Remove from pans and cool on rack. To store, wrap in plastic wrap or aluminum foil. Refrigerate unused portion.

Wrap in freezer wrap, seal, label, and date to freeze up to 3 months. Makes 2 loaves.

Boston Brown Bread

Very good commercial Boston brown bread can be bought, but no New England cook book would be complete without a recipe so you can make your own. Traditionally, brown bread is served with Boston baked beans.

2 cups buttermilk
¾ cup molasses
1 cup Kellogg's All-Bran cereal
1 cup whole wheat flour
1 cup cornmeal
2 teaspoons baking soda
2 tablespoons sugar
1 teaspoon salt
½ cup raisins

Mix buttermilk, molasses, and bran cereal. Let stand 10 minutes or until all liquid is absorbed by bran.

Mix flour, cornmeal, soda, sugar, salt, and raisins. Fold into bran mixture, stirring just to blend. Fill into greased molds, ⅔ full; this recipe will make three 1-quart molds or two 1½-quart molds.

Cover molds tightly, with either a greased lid or greased aluminum foil. Put molds upright into a large kettle, add water halfway to top of molds. Bring to a boil, cover, then keep water simmering to steam breads for 3 hours. Uncover molds and bake in oven at 250° F for 20 to 30 minutes or until tops are dry. Remove bread from molds and serve hot. To store, cool bread and wrap in aluminum foil. Reheat in foil in top of double boiler.

To cook in a pressure cooker: Set molds on rack in pressure cooker. Add water to depth of 2 inches. Steam 15 minutes with valve open. Close and steam 60 minutes longer for large mold, 40 minutes for small. Reduce heat at once. If you wish a little drier bread, bake as directed in steaming directions above.

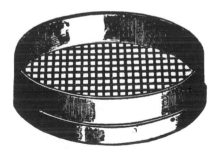

Sour Cream Coffee Cake

½ cup butter or margarine,
  softened
1 cup granulated sugar
2 eggs
1 teaspoon vanilla extract
1 cup dairy sour cream
1 teaspoon baking soda
2 cups all-purpose flour
¼ teaspoon salt
1½ teaspoons baking powder
¼ cup chopped nuts
¼ cup brown sugar
1 teaspoon cinnamon

A few years back sour cream coffee cake hit the coffee klatch circuit. It became popular at once and is good enough to deserve a place in our baking section.

Beat butter, granulated sugar, eggs, and vanilla together until light and fluffy. Stir in sour cream and soda, mixing well. Mix flour, salt, and baking powder and fold into sour cream mixture. Do not beat.

Spoon half of batter into a well-greased 9-inch angel cake pan. Mix nuts, brown sugar, and cinnamon and spoon half on batter in pan. Spoon in remaining batter and sprinkle with rest of nut mixture. Bake at 350° F for 45 minutes or until cake tester inserted in cake comes out clean. Let stand 5 minutes and then invert pan on a plate and remove cake. Serve warm. Makes 1 cake.

Fried Bread

2 cups all-purpose flour
2 teaspoons baking powder
2 tablespoons sugar
½ teaspoon salt
2 tablespoons shortening
¾ cup (about) milk
Fat or oil for frying
Maple syrup

This is a typically New England dish. It can either be made of white bread dough or this recipe. Serve with maple syrup.

Mix dry ingredients and blend in shortening with a fork. Stir in milk with a fork until a soft dough is formed. On a lightly floured surface, knead bread for 2 or 3 strokes. Pat smooth to ½ inch thickness. Cut into 3-inch squares with a floured knife. Fry in 375° F fat or cooking oil until lightly browned, 3 to 4 minutes. Drain on paper towels. Serve hot with maple syrup. Makes 6 servings.

Fried Yeast Bread: After first rising of white bread dough (recipe page 41), roll amount of dough needed on a lightly floured surface to ¼-inch thickness. (One fourth of dough will make about 16 pieces.) Cut into strips 2½ inches wide and then into diamonds or squares. Fry in fat or oil heated to 375° F until lightly browned, 3 to 4 minutes. Drain on paper towels and serve hot with maple syrup. Makes 16 pieces.

Cornbread

In this area, stone ground cornmeal is not hard to find and many prefer it to other kinds. Cornbread is an easy hot bread to make for dinner.

1 cup all-purpose
3½ teaspoons bal
½ teaspoon salt
2 tablespoons sugar
1 cup yellow cornmeal
1 egg
1 cup milk
¼ cup oil or melted bacon fat

Mix all dry ingredients in a bowl. Combine egg, milk, and oil or bacon fat. Stir into dry ingredients just to blend. Spoon into a well-greased 8×8×2-inch pan. Bake at 425° F for 40 minutes or until nicely browned. Cut into squares and serve hot. Makes 16 squares.

Variations

Cornsticks: Bake cornbread batter in greased cornstick pans at 425° F for 15 minutes or until nicely browned. Makes 12.

Buttermilk Cornbread: Decrease baking powder to 1½ teaspoons and add ½ teaspoon soda. Substitute 1 cup buttermilk for 1 cup milk.

Irish Soda Bread

In Connemara we visited a farm where we had butter-milk with flecks of butter in it. There are innumerable recipes for Irish soda bread. To our own, we added the butter to make up for our anemic buttermilk.

3½ cups all-purpose flour
2 teaspoons salt
1 tablespoon sugar
2 teaspoons baking soda
2 tablespoons butter or
  margarine
1¾ cup buttermilk

Mix flour, salt, sugar, and soda in bowl. Blend butter into flour mixture with fork. Add butter-milk and stir with fork until all flour is dampened. Flour hands and shape dough to fit into a well-greased 8-inch round cake pan. Cut across top from side to side to make an X. Bake at 400° F for 35 minutes or until nicely browned. Remove from pan and cool on rack. Do not cut Irish Soda Bread until well cooled. Then cut into thin slices and serve with butter. Makes 1 loaf.

Variations

Raisin Soda Bread: Stir ½ to 1 cup raisins into batter with buttermilk.

Brown Soda Bread: Decrease all-purpose flour to 1 cup. Add 2¾ cups whole wheat flour.

Basic Muffins

2 cups all-purpose flour
1 tablespoon baking powder
½ teaspoon salt
2 tablespoons sugar
1 egg
1 cup milk
3 tablespoons oil or melted
  butter or margarine

A basic muffin recipe can have many variations. If you get the basic recipe down pat, you can add a lot of favorite flavors to it. Remember that muffin batter should never be beaten—just stirred to barely blend dry and liquid ingredients.

Mix dry ingredients in a bowl. In another bowl, beat together egg, milk, and oil or melted butter. Add to dry mixture and stir just to blend. Fill 3-inch (top measure) muffin tins that have been greased (or lined with paper liners) about ⅔ full and bake at 400° F for 20 to 25 minutes. Makes 12 to 15 medium muffins.

Variations

Cheese Muffins: Mix ½ cup grated American cheese with dry ingredients.

Bacon Muffins: Add ½ cup crumbled crisp fried bacon to dry ingredients.

Raisin Muffins: Add ½ cup raisins to dry ingredients.

Blueberry Muffins
(pictured between pages 38 and 39)

2 cups all-purpose flour
1 tablespoon baking powder
½ teaspoon salt
¼ cup sugar
½ teaspoon cinnamon
1 cup fresh blueberries*
1 egg
1 cup milk
3 tablespoons oil

Muffins go together in a hurry and bake quickly. They add a personal touch to a meal. During blueberry season make them often, spiked with this popular New England berry.

Mix flour with dry ingredients in a bowl. Stir in blueberries. In another bowl beat together egg, milk, and oil. Add to flour mixture and stir just to blend.

Fill 3-inch (top measure) muffin tins that have been greased (or lined with paper liners) about ⅔ full and bake at 400° F for 20 to 25 minutes. Makes 12 to 15 medium size muffins.

* Frozen blueberries can be used; thaw before using.

Bran Muffins

Nothing tastes as good as warm bran muffins at breakfast, lunch, or dinner.

Combine milk and bran and let stand. Mix flour with dry ingredients. Add egg and shortening to bran and beat well. Stir in dry ingredients just to blend. Fill 3-inch (top measure) muffin tins that have been greased (or lined with paper liners) ⅔ full. Bake at 400 ° F for 25 minutes. Makes 12 muffins.

Variations

Raisin Bran Muffins: Add ½ cup raisins to batter.

Honey Bran Muffins: Substitute ¼ cup honey for sugar in recipe. Add honey to bran and milk. Directions for mixing remain the same.

1¼ cups milk
1½ cups Kellogg's All-Bran cereal
1½ cups all-purpose flour
3½ teaspoons baking powder
½ teaspoon salt
⅓ cup sugar
1 egg
5 tablespoons soft shortening or oil

Refrigerator Buttermilk Bran Muffins

A handy way to have hot muffins when you want them.

Crush cereal to make 3 cups. Measure 1 cup and combine with boiling water. Set aside to cool.

Cream butter and sugar until light. Add eggs and beat well. Mix flour, soda, salt, and buttermilk powder. Add to creamed mixture alternately with water, stirring just to blend. Stir in moistened cereal, remaining 2 cups cereal, and raisins. Put batter into a container which can be tightly covered and store in the refrigerator. Will keep up to 5 weeks.

To bake: Fill greased or paper-lined 3-inch (top measure) muffin tins ⅔ full. Bake at 375° F for 20 to 25 minutes. Makes 28 muffins.

4 cups Ralston Bran Chex cereal
1 cup boiling water
½ cup butter or margarine, softened
1 cup sugar
2 eggs
2½ cups all-purpose flour
2½ teaspoons baking soda
½ teaspoon salt
½ cup buttermilk powder*
2 cups water
1 cup raisins

* *2 cups fresh buttermilk can be used. Omit buttermilk powder and 2 cups water.*

Yeast Raised Muffins

3 cups all-purpose flour
1 package active dry yeast
¾ cup nonfat dry milk powder
  or granules
2 tablespoons brown sugar
2 teaspoons salt
½ cup butter or margarine,
  softened
2 cups hot tap water
1½ cups whole wheat flour
½ cup raw unprocessed bran

These yeast muffins do not need any kneading. Serve them piping hot.

Mix well all-purpose flour, yeast, dry milk, sugar, and salt in a bowl. Cut softened butter into pieces over flour mixture. Gradually add hot water to flour mixture and beat 2 minutes. Stir in whole wheat flour and bran. Mixture should be thick enough so that when the spoon is lifted from batter, it will hold its shape. Cover with plastic wrap and a towel and let rise about 1 hour or until doubled in bulk. Stir down.

Grease well 2½ dozen 3-inch (top measure) muffin tins. Half fill with batter. Let rise about 45 minutes or until doubled in bulk. (Do not cover.) Bake at 425° F for 15 to 20 minutes or until nicely browned. Let stand about 3 minutes before removing from pan. If 2½ dozen is too many at one time, the muffins freeze well.

Buttermilk Biscuits

2 cups all-purpose flour
1 teaspoon baking powder
½ teaspoon baking soda
½ teaspoon salt
4 tablespoons buttermilk
  powder*
5 tablespoons shortening
⅔ cup (about) water

Mix together flour, baking powder, soda, salt, and buttermilk powder in a bowl. Cut in shortening with a pastry blender or 2 knives until texture of dry crumbs. With a fork, stir in water to form a soft dough. Turn out on a lightly floured surface and knead 2 or 3 times. Pat into a ½-inch-thick rectangle. Cut with a floured 2-inch biscuit cutter or use a knife and cut square biscuits. Place on a greased baking sheet and bake at 425° F for 12 to 15 minutes or until nicely browned. Makes about 14.

* *⅔ cup fresh buttermilk can be used. Omit buttermilk powder and water.*

Baking Powder Biscuits

It is possible to make very good biscuits from a commercial mix, but sometimes there is no mix on hand and biscuits are easy to whip up from scratch. For a tender biscuit, use a light hand.

2 cups all-purpose flour
1 tablespoon baking powder
1 teaspoon salt
4 tablespoons shortening
¾ cup (about) milk

Mix together flour, baking powder, and salt in a bowl. Cut in shortening with a pastry blender or 2 knives until texture of dry crumbs. With a fork, stir in milk to form a soft dough. Turn out on lightly floured surface and knead 2 or 3 times. Pat into a ½-inch-thick rectangle. Cut with a floured 2-inch biscuit cutter or use a knife and cut square biscuits. Place on a greased baking sheet. For crusty biscuits, place 2 inches apart; for softer biscuits, place close together. Bake at 425° F for 12 to 15 minutes or until nicely browned. Makes about 14.

Variations

Sweet Biscuit Shortcake: Increase shortening to 6 tablespoons, add 3 tablespoons sugar to dry ingredients, and decrease milk to ⅔ cup. Roll or pat dough to ¼ inch thick. Spread with softened butter. Cut with 3-inch round cutter and place one biscuit on top of other on baking sheet to bake until nicely browned. To serve, separate biscuits, cover bottom half with fruit, place top on fruit, and add more fruit to top. Serve with plain or whipped cream. Makes 5 to 6 shortcakes.

Cheese Biscuits: Add ⅔ cup grated cheese to flour mixture with shortening.

Herb Biscuits: Add 4 tablespoons finely chopped fresh parsley and 2 tablespoons of your favorite herb, chopped, such as rosemary or tarragon or thyme, with the milk. Or mix 1 teaspoon powdered sage or poultry seasoning with the dry ingredients.

Drop Biscuits: Increase milk in biscuit recipe to 1 cup. Drop biscuit dough by tablespoonfuls onto a greased baking sheet. Bake as directed.

Wheat Germ Biscuits: Substitute 1 cup of whole wheat flour for 1 cup all-purpose flour and add ¼ cup wheat germ to dry ingredients.

Jonnycake

Neither yeast nor baking powder leavened, Jonnycake from Rhode Island is something else again. These recipes are courtesy of the Society for the Propagation of the Jonnycake Tradition in Rhode Island.

The Jonnycake should be made only from white stone ground meal ground in Rhode Island from flint corn. If you can't get flint cornmeal, use stone ground white cornmeal and don't tell anyone. Store unused cornmeal in the refrigerator to keep its fresh flavor.

The name Jonny with no "h" probably evolved from the original "journey cake," as the first cakes were called.

Jonnycake
West of Narragansett Bay

1 cup white cornmeal
½ teaspoon salt
1 cup bubbly boiling water
3 or 4 tablespoons milk or cream
1 teaspoon sugar or molasses
   (optional)

Mix all ingredients to mashed potato consistency, adding more liquid if necessary. Drop by spoonfuls onto hot greased griddle to make cakes ½ inch thick and 2½ inches across. Fry 6 to 8 minutes on each side until there is a brown crunchy crust and inside is done. Makes 12 Jonnycakes.

Jonnycake
East of Narragansett Bay

1 cup white cornmeal
½ teaspoon salt
1⅞ cups cold milk

Mix all ingredients into thin, soupy consistency. Ease large spoonfuls to hot greased griddle to make cakes about ⅛ inch thick and 5 inches across. Fry 2 to 3 minutes on each side or until brown. Makes 8 Jonnycakes.

Whole Wheat Popovers

Popovers do not fall into either a yeast or baking powder category, but they are a bread, so we include them in this chapter. If I am baking something else at the 425° F temperature which does not need to have the oven opened, I bake the popovers at the same time.

½ cup whole wheat flour
½ cup all-purpose flour
½ teaspoon salt
2 eggs
1 cup milk
1 tablespoon oil

Combine all ingredients in a bowl and beat with rotary beater until batter is smooth, 1½ to 2 minutes. Spray 3-inch (top measure) aluminum muffin tins with Pam and grease lightly with oil. Fill about half full of batter. Bake at 425° F for 45 minutes. Do not open oven. Remove from pans at once and serve hot. Makes 9.

Popovers may be made with 1 cup all-purpose flour, leaving out the whole wheat called for in the recipe. The recipe may be divided in half if 9 is too many. Popovers can be baked in tin muffin pans but are more satisfactorily baked in aluminum. If you have iron popover pans, use them (and then you will not need the Pam).

Pasta

Numbers refer to pages where recipes appear in this book.

Egg Noodles   71
Spinach Noodles   72
Macaroni with Cream   73
Macaroni and Cheese with Vegetables   73
Saucy Macaroni Casserole   74
Cottage Cheese Casserole   74
Sausage Macaroni Bake   75
Rigatoni with Carbonara Sauce   75
Macaroni Casserole for Eight   76
Lasagna   76
Noodles with Pesto   77
Noodles Romanoff   77
Chicken and Noodles   78
Egg Noodles Alfredo   79
Sea Scallops with Spaghetti   79
Linguine with White Clam Sauce   80
Spaghetti with Meat Balls   80
Vegetable Sauce for Spaghetti   81
Squash Tomato Sauce   81
Spaghetti Sauce   82
Italian Spaghetti with Pork   82
Potato Gnocchi   83

Pasta

This chapter gives just a sampling of a food product, possibly developed in Naples, Italy, that goes back many centuries. Tradition has it that in 1789, Thomas Jefferson sent a trusted courier to Naples to learn how to make "maccaroni" and to find a suitable mold in which to make it. The mission was successful and that same year Mr. Jefferson served what we now call spaghetti, fragrant with cheese and butter, at a formal dinner.

The Italian word *pasta* covers the field of macaronis, spaghettis, and noodles—all basically made from flour and eggs. About as wide a variant as you'll find is a special pasta such as spinach noodles or potato gnocchi, though various flours are used also.

All members of the pasta family are good with countless sauces and go into many a casserole, the macaronis and noodles more likely candidates than spaghetti.

But increasingly today there is a tendency to make more lightly sauced pasta dishes, in which fresh garden vegetables are combined with fresh herbs to sauce the pasta.

If you follow the trend, you will be using more pasta; you will sauce it with lighter combinations of vegetables and meat, fish, or cheese; and your spaghetti is more likely to be cooked al dente. You may even be making your own pasta.

In cooking with pasta, use fresh herbs whenever possible. The general rule is to use three times more fresh herbs than dried. Freshly grated Parmesan cheese is superior, and it is a breeze to make, especially if you have a food processor.

For many years I have been cooking all pastas in far less water than the directions indicate. This uses less energy (to heat the water), besides saving water. The pasta may be a bit more al dente when cooked in less water, but there is no loss of quality.

Here are some of the old pasta favorites, as well as new recipes to give you a base for doing your own thing.

Egg Noodles (recipe on page 71)
with Sauce (recipe on page 74)

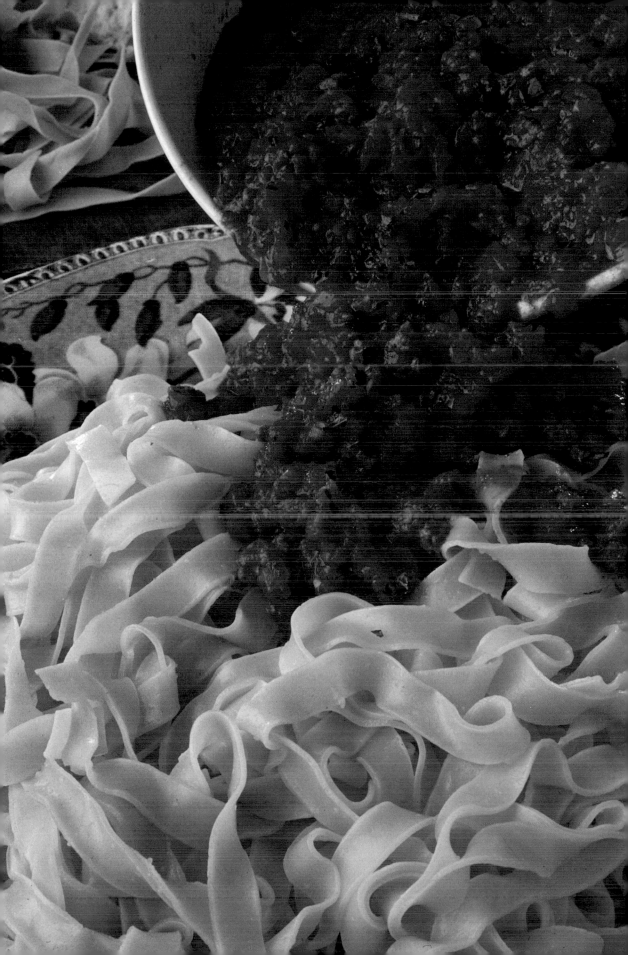

Egg Noodles
(pictured between pages 70 and 71)

If you have a food processor, noodles can be made in it; the food processor recipe book will tell you how.

Mix flour and salt in a bowl or on a board. Make an indentation in center and add egg yolk mixed with water. Work flour into egg yolk with fingers until the mixture is blended. If too dry, add a few drops more water. Put some additional flour on the board and knead the dough about 5 minutes, or until smooth and elastic. Cover with plastic wrap and let rest 20 minutes.

Divide dough into 3 parts and roll each part until very thin. Dust top of rolled noodle dough lightly with flour. Fold dough over on itself and cut into ¼- to ½-inch wide strips. Separate and let dry.

Noodles can be used at once or dried and stored in a covered container. This recipe makes about 8 ounces.

To cook, boil 2 quarts water with 2 teaspoons salt. Add noodles and boil 5 to 15 minutes, depending on dryness of noodles. Serve buttered or use in a recipe.

1 cup all-purpose flour
¼ teaspoon salt
1 egg yolk, lightly beaten
2 tablespoons water
Additional flour
2 quarts boiling water
2 teaspoons salt

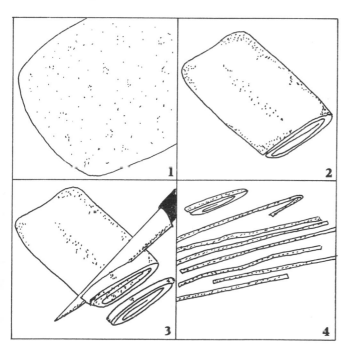

Spinach Noodles

1 package (10 ounces) frozen
   chopped spinach, thawed
½ cup water
¼ teaspoon salt
1½ cups (about) all-purpose
   flour
2 eggs
2 quarts boiling water
1 teaspoon salt
¼ cup butter

These pretty noodles can be served with a sauce or buttered as suggested.

Cook spinach with ½ cup water and salt, covered, in a 1-quart saucepan for about 5 minutes. Drain. Allow to cool and squeeze out all possible liquid. Chop fine.

Put flour on a board or other suitable work surface and make an indentation in center. Put in eggs and spinach and work flour into eggs and spinach with fingers to make a dough. It should not be sticky, so add a little additional flour if necessary. Bring dough together in a ball and let rest a few minutes. Clean off work surface and knead dough until smooth and elastic.

Cut dough into 2 or 3 pieces and roll each piece on a lightly floured surface until thin but not too thin. Lift dough with floured rolling pin and place each rolled piece on a clean cloth to dry on surface so that it will not stick to itself when folded to cut. This takes several hours, depending on humidity.

When dough is dry enough to cut, fold dough in half from long side. Cut into ½- to ¼-inch strips, toss lightly with fingers to separate and unroll. Set aside to dry.

To cook, heat about 2 quarts water to boiling in saucepan and add 1 teaspoon salt. Add noodles and boil about 5 to 10 minutes, or until desired texture is reached. Drain and toss with ¼ cup butter. Makes 4 servings.

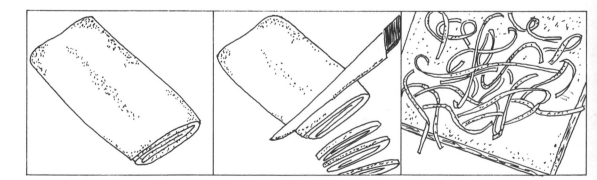

Macaroni with Cream

Serve macaroni with cream as an accompaniment to almost any meat or fish dish. After you've made it once, perhaps you'll wish to add some chopped fresh herbs to your own taste.

Cook macaroni in boiling water with 2 teaspoons salt about 8 minutes. Drain and put macaroni back in pan. Shake and stir over low heat until all liquid is evaporated. Add half-and-half, nutmeg, and salt to taste, and cook and stir over low heat until cream is absorbed, about 10 to 12 minutes. Cut butter into small pieces. Remove macaroni from heat and stir in butter. Sprinkle with chopped parsley. Makes 4 servings.

½ pound macaroni
2 quarts boiling water
2 teaspoons salt
1 cup half-and-half
½ teaspoon grated nutmeg
Dash salt
4 tablespoons butter
4 tablespoons chopped fresh parsley

Macaroni and Cheese with Vegetables

The vegetables give a nice texture and flavor to the macaroni and cheese. Fill out the menu with green beans, cole slaw, and apples baked at the same time as the casserole.

Cook macaroni in a quart of water until al dente, about 9 minutes. Drain.

Clean and dice celery. Chop onion. Heat butter in a saucepan and cook celery and onion until tender, but not browned. Stir in flour and let bubble. Slowly add milk, stirring until mixture comes to a boil and is thickened. Add cheese, salt, and pepper and stir until cheese is melted. Mix with macaroni. Spoon into buttered 1½-quart casserole. Sprinkle with bread crumbs and bake at 350° F for 30 minutes or until bubbling. Makes 4 servings.

½ pound elbow macaroni
1 quart boiling water
2 stalks celery
1 medium onion
¼ cup butter or margarine
3 tablespoons flour
2 cups milk
½ pound American process cheese, diced
1 teaspoon salt
Freshly ground pepper to taste
½ cup buttered dry bread crumbs

Variation

Omit celery and onions for a regular macaroni and cheese casserole.

Saucy Macaroni Casserole

(sauce pictured between pages 70 and 71)

Sauce

3 tablespoons bacon fat or oil
2 medium onions, chopped
1 clove garlic, chopped
½ pound ground beef
1 can (28 ounces) peeled,
  crushed tomatoes
1 teaspoon salt
Freshly ground pepper to taste
1 cup water
1½ teaspoons chili powder

½ pound uncooked macaroni
1 cup grated cheddar cheese

Prepare the sauce early in the day, refrigerate, but reheat before combining the casserole.

Heat fat in skillet and cook onion and garlic until soft. Add beef and cook 3 to 5 minutes longer. Add tomatoes, salt, and pepper, and simmer, covered, about 30 minutes. Stir in water and chili powder.

When ready to cook, layer the sauce with the uncooked macaroni and cheese, starting with macaroni and ending with sauce and cheese, in a buttered 2-quart casserole. Bake covered 35 minutes. Uncover and bake 15 minutes longer. Makes 4 to 6 servings.

Quick version

Substitute 5 cups of your favorite commercial spaghetti sauce for this sauce.

Cottage Cheese Casserole

½ pound ziti macaroni
3 quarts boiling water
2 teaspoons salt
¼ cup chopped onion
2 tablespoons olive or other
  cooking oil
¼ cup chopped fresh parsley
Dash Tabasco sauce
½ teaspoon salt
1½ tablespoons Worcestershire
  sauce
2 cups small curd cottage cheese
2 cups dairy sour cream
½ cup buttered dry bread
  crumbs

Ziti is another form of macaroni (or pasta). When combined in this casserole with cottage cheese and sour cream, it makes a tasty dish. Add buttered steamed zucchini, a small green salad, and hot bread and you have a good dinner.

Cook ziti in boiling water with 2 teaspoons salt for about 8 minutes, stirring once or twice. Drain.

Saute onion in oil until tender. Mix with cooked ziti. Combine parsley, seasonings, cottage cheese, and sour cream, and stir into ziti and onions. Spoon into a buttered 2-quart casserole and sprinkle crumbs on top. Bake at 350° F for 30 to 35 minutes or until bubbly. Makes 4 servings.

Sausage Macaroni Bake

Black Jack's macaroni casserole can be put together, and even refrigerated over night.

Heat oil in skillet and saute garlic for about 2 to 3 minutes. Remove and discard garlic. Add onion to oil and saute until translucent. Remove onion to a large casserole. Saute sausage pieces. Remove, drain well.

Cook macaroni in boiling water with salt 6 to 8 minutes. Drain and cool it with cold water. Combine with the sausages, tomatoes, oregano, and 2 cups of the cheese cubes, stirring well. Spoon into the large casserole and put 1 cup cheese cubes on top. Bake at 325° F until cheese is melted and brown and casserole is bubbly, 20 minutes. If the casserole has been prepared in advance and refrigerated, allow 40 minutes. Makes 6 servings.

from Black Jack
Confidential Chat Column

1 tablespoon oil
1 garlic clove(peeled, whole)
1 large onion, chopped
¾ pound sweet Italian sausages, cut in pieces
1 pound macaroni
2 quarts boiling water
1 teaspoon salt
1 large can (1 pound, 13 ounces) whole tomatoes
1 tablespoon dried oregano
3 cups ½-inch cheddar cheese cubes

Rigatoni with Carbonara Sauce

If you don't often use the less common pastas, you'll like the change offered by this recipe. Tomato and lettuce salad, crisp rolls, and fruit for dessert can make the meal.

Cook rigatoni in boiling water with salt, stirring once or twice, for about 10 minutes. Drain and keep hot in a saucepan.

Meanwhile fry bacon in oil until crisp. Add wine and cook until wine has evaporated. Add bacon, eggs, and cheeses to hot cooked rigatoni and stir to coat. If the rigatoni is not hot enough to cook eggs, place saucepan over low heat for 1 minute, stirring. To serve, sprinkle with parsley and serve with additional Parmesan cheese. Makes 4 servings.

1 pound rigatoni macaroni
3 quarts boiling water
2 teaspoons salt
6 slices bacon, diced
2 tablespoons olive or other cooking oil
½ cup dry white wine
3 eggs, lightly beaten
¼ cup grated Romano cheese
¼ cup grated Parmesan cheese
¼ cup chopped fresh parsley
Additional Parmesan cheese

Macaroni Casserole for Eight

⅓ pound elbow macaroni
2 quarts boiling water
2 teaspoons salt
½ cup grated Parmesan cheese
½ cup milk
1 egg, lightly beaten
¼ cup margarine
½ cup chopped onions
1½ pounds frankfurters, sliced
   1 inch thick
1 can (8 ounces) tomato sauce
¾ cup shredded mozzarella
   cheese
½ cup sliced pitted black olives
½ teaspoon salt
¼ teaspoon nutmeg
¼ teaspoon cinnamon
⅛ teaspoon pepper

Cook macaroni in boiling water with 2 teaspoons salt 8 to 10 minutes. Drain. Add Parmesan cheese, milk, egg, and 3 tablespoons of the margarine. Mix well.

Saute chopped onion in remaining 1 tablespoon margarine until tender. Add with frankfurters, tomato sauce, cheese, olives, and seasonings to macaroni mixture. Mix well.

Turn into a buttered 2-quart casserole. Bake, uncovered, at 350° F about 20 minutes or until bubbly. Makes 8 servings.

from Field Of Wheat
Confidential Chat Column

Lasagna

¾ cup chopped onion
1 garlic clove, chopped
3 tablespoons olive oil
¾ pound ground beef
1 can (8 ounces) tomato sauce
1 can (6 ounces) tomato paste
1 cup water
½ teaspoon dried oregano or 1½
   teaspoons chopped fresh
   oregano
½ teaspoon dried basil or 1½
   teaspoons chopped fresh
   basil
1 whole clove, crushed
8 ounces lasagna noodles
3 quarts boiling water
2 teaspoons salt
2 cups ricotta or small curd
   cottage cheese
½ cup grated Parmesan cheese
8 ounces sliced mozzarella
   cheese

Lasagna can be prepared in advance, refrigerated, and heated when ready to serve. Meatless lasagna can be made by omitting the ground beef. With or without meat, this is a hearty dish and usually a green salad, hot bread, and fruit suffice for a complete menu.

Saute onion and garlic in olive oil until tender. Add meat and brown. Add tomato sauce, tomato paste, 1 cup water, herbs, and clove. Cover and simmer about 30 minutes.

Meanwhile cook lasagna in boiling water with salt about 10 minutes or until al dente. Drain.

Place half of lasagna in the bottom of a buttered 13×9-inch casserole. Spread half of the ricotta, Parmesan, and mozzarella cheeses over lasagna. Add half the meat sauce. Repeat layers. If you would like to save a few slices of mozzarella to put on top of the second layer of meat sauce, do so. Bake in 350° F oven 45 minutes. Makes 6 servings.

Noodles with Pesto

Fedora Bontempi says that if you do not have fresh basil, you can soften ½ cup dry basil leaves in a little luke-warm water. I have always used fresh.

The sauce called *pesto* is traditionally made in a mortar and pestle (hence the name), but this tradition was established before blenders. If you wish to use a mortar and pestle, use one with about a 2-cup capacity. Put garlic, basil, and dash of salt in mortar and mash with pestle until well blended. Add cheese and olive oil alternately a little at a time, pounding and mixing to blend after each addition. Add pine nuts, if desired, pounding and mixing until they are blended.

If you choose to use a blender (a food processor is a little too large for this operation), put in garlic (it need not be minced), basil leaves, a dash of salt, and a bit of the cheese and olive oil. Blend, then add remaining cheese and dribble in the remaining olive oil and optional pine nuts, blending until smooth. To serve, cook pasta (egg noodles, spaghetti, or linguine) in 2 quarts boiling water with 2 teaspoons salt until al dente: 6 minutes for noodles, 8 minutes for spaghetti or linguine. Drain and mix with pesto. Makes 4 servings.

4 cloves garic, minced
12 leaves fresh basil
Dash salt
⅔ cup grated Parmesan cheese
½ cup olive oil
2 tablespoons pine nuts (optional)
1 pound egg noodles or 8 ounces spaghetti or linguine
2 quarts boiling water
2 teaspoons salt

Noodles Romanoff

January's Carnation says this dish is easy and elegant. It would make part of a buffet menu.

Cook noodles in boiling water with 1 teaspoon salt until tender, 10 to 12 minutes. Drain well.

In a large bowl mix sour cream and cream cheese, blending well. Add onions, Worcestershire sauce, ½ teaspoon salt, and pepper. Transfer to a greased 1½-quart casserole or baking dish. Sprinkle top with Parmesan cheese and paprika. Bake at 350° F for 30 minutes. Makes 6 servings.

from January's Carnation
Confidential Chat Column

½ pound egg noodles
2 quarts boiling water
1 teaspoon salt
2 cups dairy sour cream
1 package (8 ounces) cream cheese, softened
¼ cup finely chopped onions
1 teaspoon Worcestershire sauce
½ teaspoon salt
Dash pepper
¼ cup grated Parmesan cheese
Paprika

Chicken and Noodles

1 stewing hen, about 4 pounds
Water to cover
1 stalk celery
1 peeled carrot
1 medium onion
6 to 8 peppercorns
Bouquet garni (sprig parsley,
   sprig fresh thyme, bay leaf)
1 teaspoon salt
1 recipe egg noodles
3 tablespoons butter or
   margarine
3 tablespoons flour

Make the bouquet garni by tying the herbs in a piece of cheesecloth. This dish is wonderful in winter. The chicken can be cooked the day ahead.

Cut stewing hen into serving pieces and wash well. If there is an excess of fat, remove it and save for other cooking. Put pieces of chicken in a pot, add water to cover and celery, carrot, onion, peppercorns, bouquet garni, and salt. Bring to a boil, reduce heat and simmer until chicken is tender, about 2½ hours. Remove chicken to platter and carve.

Strain broth and put back in pot. Bring to boil, add noodles and boil 5 to 15 minutes depending on how dry the noodles are. Remove noodles from broth with a slotted spoon into a serving dish.

Melt butter in a saucepan. Add flour and let simmer 1 minute. Measure 2½ cups chicken broth and add to flour-butter. Cook and stir until mixture boils and is thickened.

Serve chicken and noodles with gravy. This recipe will serve 4, with chicken left over for salad or other recipes. The leftover chicken could also be removed from the bone and frozen in a carton with some of the chicken broth or gravy. It will keep 3 to 4 months at 0° F.

Egg Noodles Alfredo

This famous dish from Alfredo's restaurant in Rome is a grand way to use your chafing dish. But if you have no chafing dish, an electric skillet or a large heavy skillet or saucepan will do as well.

1 pound egg noodles, ⅛ or ¼ inch wide
2 quarts boiling water
2 teaspoons salt
¼ pound sweet butter, softened
⅔ cup heavy cream
1 cup grated Parmesan cheese
Additional grated Parmesan cheese

Cook noodles in boiling water with salt until al dente, about 6 minutes. Drain.

Melt half the butter in a chafing dish or electric skillet set at low heat. Stir in the cream and ⅓ cup of cheese. Add hot noodles and with a fork and spoon toss noodles gently in a folding process, adding remaining cheese and butter. Mix and blend until noodles are well coated and creamy. Serve very hot with additional cheese sprinkled on the noodles. Makes 4 servings.

Sea Scallops with Spaghetti

A tasty change with spaghetti. Serve with a romaine, sliced radish, and black olive salad with Italian dressing; crusty rolls; and for dessert, Neapolitan ice cream.

1 pound sea scallops, fresh or frozen
2 strips bacon
1 small green pepper, seeded and diced
¼ pound sweet Italian sausage meat
1 medium red onion, sliced
1 can (10¼ ounces) meatless spaghetti sauce
½ cup tomato sauce
½ pound thin spaghetti
2 quarts boiling water
2 teaspoons salt

If frozen, thaw scallops and cut into thirds or quarters. Cook bacon until crisp and reserve. In bacon fat, saute green pepper, sausage meat, and onions until lightly browned. Remove from pan and saute scallops until golden brown. Return pepper, sausage, and onion to skillet with scallops. Crumble bacon and add with spaghetti sauce and tomato sauce, mixing well. Simmer 5 minutes.

Cook spaghetti in boiling water with salt 8 to 10 minutes. Drain. Serve with scallop sauce. Makes 4 servings.

Linguine with White Clam Sauce

½ pound linguine
2 quarts boiling water
2 teaspoons salt
¼ cup olive or other cooking oil
1 large clove garlic, chopped
2 tablespoons flour
2 cans (7 ounces each) clams, or
    1½ cups minced raw clams
    with juice
¼ cup chopped fresh parsley
1½ teaspoons dried basil or 1½
    tablespoons chopped fresh
    basil
Salt and freshly ground pepper
    to taste

This is one recipe where canned clams are really excellent, and this from a clammer. Served with a salad and hot crisp bread, it is a good quick dinner.

Cook linguine in boiling water with salt for about 10 minutes, stirring once or twice. Drain.

Heat oil and cook garlic about 1 minute. Add flour and juice from clams. Bring to a boil, stirring. Add clams, parsley, and basil and simmer 5 minutes, stirring. Taste and add salt and pepper. Serve over hot cooked linguine. Makes 4 servings.

Spaghetti with Meat Balls

1 pound ground beef
1 clove garlic, chopped
2 tablespoons chopped fresh
    parsley
½ teaspoon salt
Freshly ground pepper to taste
2 slices white bread, crumbled
2 eggs
3 tablespoons chopped onion
¼ cup olive oil
1 can (1 pound, 12 ounces)
    tomatoes in puree
1 can (6 ounces) tomato paste
1½ teaspoons dried basil or 1½
    tablespoons chopped fresh
    basil
Freshly ground pepper to taste
½ pound thin spaghetti, cooked
Grated Parmesan cheese

Spaghetti and meat balls always seem to call for a good green salad, Italian bread, red wine, and fruit and cheese for dessert.

Mix ground beef with garlic, parsley, salt, pepper, bread, eggs, and onion until blended. Shape into 12 to 16 meat balls. Put on a cookie sheet and chill in freezer about 30 minutes.

Heat oil in a large skillet and brown chilled meat balls on all sides. When browned, add tomatoes, tomato paste, basil, and pepper. Cover and cook over low heat for 1 to 1½ hours, stirring occasionally.

Cook spaghetti as directed. Serve meat balls with hot spaghetti and Parmesan cheese. Makes 4 servings.

Vegetable Sauce for Spaghetti

A quickly prepared sauce for a spaghetti dish. Green bean and onion salad and hard rolls are suggested to partner it.

Chop pepper, onions, and carrots. Saute in butter or oil until tender. Add tomato soup and water and heat to boiling. Stir in cheese.

Cook spaghetti in boiling water with salt for 8 to 10 minutes. Drain. Mix with vegetable sauce. Taste and add salt and pepper as needed. Makes 4 servings.

from Cosmas
Confidential Chat Column

1 large green pepper, seeded
2 onions
2 large carrots, peeled
¼ cup butter or olive oil
1 can (10¾ ounces) condensed
    tomato soup
½ soup can water
½ pound diced American
    process cheese
½ pound spaghetti
2 quarts boiling water
2 teaspoons salt
Salt and freshly ground pepper
    to taste

Squash Tomato Sauce

Take advantage of summer vegetables to make this lovely light vegetable sauce for spaghetti. Adding whole wheat bread and a lettuce and bean sprout salad will make a nourishing meal. If you prefer, use all zucchini.

Heat oil in skillet and saute onion and garlic until tender, not browned. Add squash, tomatoes, and seasonings. Bring to a boil, reduce heat, and simmer, covered, about 20 minutes. Uncover and simmer 5 minutes longer.

Cook spaghetti in boiling water with salt for 8 to 10 minutes while sauce is simmering. Drain. Serve with sauce and Parmesan cheese. Makes 4 servings.

* *In the winter, use 2 cups of canned tomatoes.*

¼ cup oil
1 large onion, chopped
1 clove garlic, chopped
3 cups diced yellow summer
    squash (2 to 3 medium)
3 cups diced zucchini (2 to 3
    medium)
4 medium size ripe tomatoes,
    peeled and diced*
Freshly ground pepper to taste
½ teaspoon each dried basil,
    oregano, and thyme; or 2
    teaspoons Italian seasoning
½ pound spaghetti or linguine
2 quarts boiling water
2 teaspoons salt
Grated Parmesan cheese

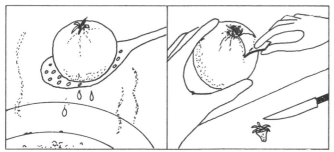

Put tomato into boiling water for thirty seconds, then drain. Cut around core with a knife, and discard. Peel away the skin with a knife or your fingers.

Spaghetti Sauce

1 tablespoon butter
2 tablespoons olive oil
2 tablespoons bacon fat
1 large onion, finely chopped
1 carrot, finely chopped
1 stalk celery, finely chopped
¾ pound ground beef
¼ pound Italian sausage meat
⅔ cup dry white wine
4 teaspoons tomato paste
1¼ cups beef broth
1 tablespoon pound cake
  crumbs
Salt and freshly ground pepper
  to taste
1 pound spaghetti, cooked as
  directed

This spaghetti sauce is excellent—and no, the spices have not been forgotten. The spoonful of cake crumbs, which smooths out the flavor, was a trick I learned from an Italian-American friend years ago. Use hot or sweet Italian sausage. Your choice.

Combine butter, oil, and bacon fat in a large skillet. Add vegetables and saute over moderate heat until lightly browned. Add beef and sausage and crumble and cook until lightly browned. Add wine, tomato paste, beef broth, and cake crumbs. Cover and simmer over low heat for 2 to 3 hours, stirring occasionally. Before serving, taste and add additional salt and pepper, if necessary. Serve over hot cooked spaghetti. Makes 4 to 6 servings.

Italian Spaghetti with Pork

2 teaspoons olive oil
2 large onions, chopped
1 green pepper, seeded and
  chopped
2 cloves garlic, chopped
1 pound lean pork chops cut in
  very small pieces
1 can (6 ounces) tomato paste
1 tomato paste can cold water
½ pound mushrooms, sliced, or
  1 can (4 ounces) sliced
  mushrooms
2 bay leaves
½ teaspoon dried thyme
1 pound spaghetti
3 quarts boiling water
2 teaspoons salt
¼ cup butter
1 or more cups grated Parmesan
  cheese

Eliza sent Yrrej's recipe to Chat when a reader asked for a repeat of the recipe. Her comment, "It's scrumptious."

Heat oil. Add onion and green pepper. When onion is golden brown, add garlic. Cook on low heat for five minutes. Add meat. When brown, add tomato paste and cold water. Stir. Add mushrooms, bay leaves, and thyme. Cook slowly, covered, until meat is tender, adding additional water, if necessary.

Cook spaghetti in boiling water with salt for 8 to 10 minutes. Drain. Stir in butter and sauce. Add cheese. Makes 6 servings.

from Yrrej
Confidential Chat Column

Potato Gnocchi

Potato gnocchi, or dumplings, can be served with the same sauce as spaghetti. To my taste, though, they are better with melted butter and Parmesan and a meat dish.

2 pounds potatoes (about 6 medium)
Water to cover
2 cups (about) flour
2 egg yolks, lightly beaten
½ teaspoon salt
2 quarts boiling water
Melted butter
Grated Parmesan cheese

Scrub potatoes and boil in water to cover until tender but firm, about 25 minutes.

Drain and peel immediately and rub through a ricer. Place potatoes on a well-floured surface and mix with flour. The mixture should be about ⅔ potatoes and ⅓ flour. Make an indentation in mixture and add egg yolks and salt. Mix and knead into a soft dough which is easily handled. Cut off small chunks of dough and roll quickly on a well-floured surface into finger size rolls. Cut into 1-inch pieces. Press center of each piece with a finger. As they are made, put gnocchi on a floured board and sprinkle with flour to keep them from sticking together.

Boil a few gnocchi at a time in boiling water. Stir, and when gnocchi come to top, remove with a slotted spoon. Put into a serving dish and pour on some melted butter. Continue until all gnocchi are cooked. Sprinkle finished gnocchi with Parmesan cheese. Makes 4 to 6 servings.

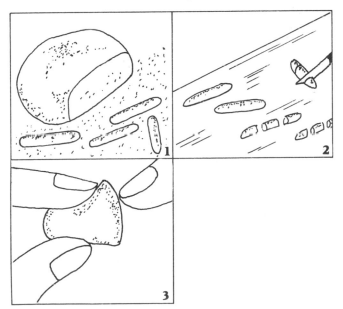

Eggs, Cheese, and Dairy

Numbers refer to pages where recipes appear in this book.

Cooking Eggs   87
French Omelets   88
Western Omelet   89
Cheese Souffle   89
Mushroom Sauce   89
Swiss Cheese Pie   90
Quiche Lorraine   90
Brunch Eggs   90
Eggs Benedict   91
Cheese   92
Ricotta Croquettes   93
Cheese, Bacon, and Tomato   94
Saturday Cheese Sandwich Special   94
Swiss Cheese Fondue   95
Presto Pizza   96
Dairy   97
Yogurt   99
Pancakes   100
Blueberry Pancakes   100
Corn Pancakes   100
Clam Pancakes   100
Men's Favorite Griddle Cakes   101
Oatmeal Pancakes   101
Chicken Crepes   102
Creme Fraiche   103

Eggs, Cheese, and Dairy

Almost every chapter in this book contains recipes using eggs, cheese, and other dairy products. They are a universal part of our cooking and when one must go on an eggless, milkless diet, a great void occurs.

In this chapter, devoted specifically to eggs, cheese, and dairy foods, we will try to give you a potpourri of recipes featuring them predominantly.

Eggs
A Few Words About Eggs

Grades found mostly at the grocers are AA and A. A yolk in a grade AA egg is higher and the white will spread less when the egg is broken. Also the appearance of the shell can knock an egg from AA to A. For most uses, however, Grade A is as good as AA; and, in fact, after a week in the refrigerator, an AA egg will become an A egg.

Egg size is average weight of a dozen. One dozen extra large must weigh at least 27 ounces; one dozen large, 24 ounces; and one dozen medium, 21 ounces.

Brown eggs are popular in New England, but nutritionists repeat over and over again that there is no difference nutritionally between a white and a brown. If white eggs are less expensive, buy them.

The old rule of thumb that if there is less than seven cents' difference between egg prices, the larger size is the best buy, still holds.

Remember that eggs are a perishable food and should be kept under refrigeration and will stay fresher longer if refrigerated.

Cooking Eggs

Because the protein of eggs can become toughened with high heat, medium heat is recommended for all egg cooking.

Hard Cooked Eggs: Use a teflon-coated, stainless steel, or enamel pan. Cover eggs with cold water. As the water starts to boil, stir eggs with a wooden spoon to keep the yolks suspended in the middle as much as possible. Reduce heat so that eggs cook below the boiling point and cook at that temperature 15 minutes.

Eggs in the Shell: Put eggs into cold water and let come to a boil. Reduce heat and simmer for as long as you like your eggs—2 minutes for rare; 3 minutes, medium; and 5 minutes, well done. A pinch of salt added to water will help keep eggs from cracking. Crack eggs in half with a sharp knife and remove cooked eggs with a spoon (stainless steel, if possible, since eggs tarnish silver) into a small dish. If you have egg cups, cut off the sharp end of egg and place rounded end in the egg cup. The egg is then eaten with a spoon from the shell.

Poached Eggs: If you have an egg poacher, use it as directed. Otherwise, poach eggs in a skillet of lightly salted water. Let water come to a boil, drop in egg, reduce heat, and let egg poach 3 to 5 minutes. If you oil the skillet lightly before putting in the water, the egg will not stick to the bottom and the skillet will be easier to clean. The white coagulates closer to the yolk if you stir the water round and round before adding the egg (eggs). Some like to add a small amount of vinegar to the water to help coagulate the whites.

Fried Eggs: A teflon-lined skillet is good; and if you are not on a diet, even in a teflon skillet add a little fat for flavor. Saved bacon fat, butter or margarine are best. Heat over medium heat until fat is hot. Add eggs and fry to doneness desired. If you like the white over the yolk cooked, put a lid on the skillet for a few minutes.

Scrambled Eggs: For each egg, add 1 tablespoon water or milk and season to taste with salt and pepper. Mix with a fork until white and yolk are completely blended. One egg, scrambled, looks like such a small portion, that most people figure 1½ to 2 eggs per person. Cook in bacon or sausage fat, butter, or margarine stirring egg in from edges until doneness desired is reached.

French Omelets

1 tablespoon butter or
   margarine
2 eggs
2 tablespoons water
Dash salt
Dash freshly ground pepper

Fillings for 2 eggs—any one of
   the following:

¼ to ⅓ cup shredded cheese
1 to 2 slices cooked crumbled
   bacon
¼ cup canned sliced
   mushrooms, drained
2 tablespoons chopped green
   pepper
2 tablespoons chopped cooked
   shrimp
¼ cup yogurt or cottage cheese

Use an 8-inch skillet with sloping sides. An omelet party is fun and they are so easily and quickly made that the guests can make their own while the hostess looks after toasted English muffins, coffee, etc. Put the various fillings in pretty bowls for omeleteers to mix and match.

The amount of fillings and eggs can easily be multiplied for a crowd. The fillings listed below are only suggestions. Bowls of bean sprouts, chopped fresh tomatoes, or green onions are a few more.

Put butter in skillet over medium high heat. Quickly mix eggs with water, salt, and pepper using a fork or whisk. Pour eggs into skillet and with a spatula, start drawing eggs in from outer edge to center. Tilt skillet so uncooked eggs will run to outer edges. Put filling (or fillings) you choose on one half of cooked omelet. Fold over other half and slide omelet onto plate. This cooking process should take only 1 to 2 minutes. Makes 1 omelet.

Note: Omelets should not be overcooked as they then break when you try to fold them.

Western Omelet

In 1 tablespoon of the butter, saute onion and green pepper until tender. Combine with ham.

Beat eggs and milk enough to blend whites and yolks well. Season with salt and pepper. Heat remaining butter in a 10-inch skillet. Pour in eggs, sprinkle ham mixture over eggs. Pull cooked edges into center until all eggs are cooked to suit. Fold and slide onto platter. Makes 4 servings.

4 tablespoons butter or
   margarine
½ cup chopped onion
¾ cup chopped green pepper
¾ cup chopped smoked ham
6 eggs
3 tablespoons milk
½ teaspoon salt
Freshly ground pepper to taste

Cheese Souffle

If you've been putting off making a souffle, don't. They aren't that complicated and once you've taken the plunge, you'll be sorry you didn't do it sooner. Just have the diners at the table before the souffle comes out of the oven. A green salad with lots of tomatoes and hot bread go well with this dish.

Heat butter in saucepan. Add flour, salt, and pepper and cook 1 or 2 minutes. Stir in milk and cook, stirring, until mixture comes to a boil and is thickened. Remove from heat and add cheeses and Tabasco. Stir until cheese melts.

Beat egg whites until very stiff. Beat egg yolks until thick and lemon colored. Fold yolks into cheese sauce, then fold in whites. Pour into a 1½-quart souffle dish. Bake at 425° F for 25 minutes. Serve immediately. Makes 4 servings. If you like, serve souffle with mushroom sauce (recipe below).

6 tablespoons butter or
   margarine
½ cup all-purpose flour
½ teaspoon salt
Freshly ground pepper to taste
2 cups milk
¼ pound natural sharp cheddar
   cheese, shredded
3 tablespoons grated Parmesan
   cheese
Dash Tabasco sauce
4 eggs, separated

Mushroom Sauce

Heat butter in saucepan and saute mushrooms until they are tender and any liquid has evaporated. Stir in flour and seasoning and cook 1 to 2 minutes. Stir in milk and cook, stirring, until mixture boils and is thickened. Serve hot. Makes 1½ cups.

4 tablespoons butter or
   margarine
¾ cup sliced fresh mushrooms
2 tablespoons flour
Dash salt
Freshly ground pepper to taste
1¼ cups milk

Swiss Cheese Pie

¾ cup chopped green onions
2 tablespoons butter or
    margarine
1 unbaked 9-inch pie shell
2 cups light cream
3 eggs, well beaten
1 cup shredded Swiss cheese
½ teaspoon salt
Freshly ground pepper to taste

This is a dish that could go into either the egg or cheese category. It is the beloved of the cocktail circuit, but was originally served with a light salad as a luncheon main dish.

Saute onions in butter until tender and spread on bottom of pie shell. Mix cream, eggs, cheese, and seasonings and pour over onions in pie shell. Bake at 425° F for about 40 minutes or until custard is firm in center.

Variation
Quiche Lorraine: Add 3 slices bacon, crisply cooked and crumbled, to onions.

Brunch Eggs

6 slices bacon
¾ cup chopped green pepper
½ cup chopped onion
2 packages (16 ounces each)
    frozen hash brown potatoes,
    thawed
½ teaspoon salt
Freshly ground pepper to taste
¼ cup milk or light cream
6 eggs
½ cup shredded cheddar cheese

Serve hot whole wheat toast with orange marmalade, lots of coffee, and as a starter, a fresh fruit cup to make this a pleasant brunch.

Cook bacon in a 10-inch skillet until crisp. Remove from skillet and set aside. Pour off all but about 3 tablespoons bacon fat. Mix pepper, onion, and potatoes and add to skillet. Cover and cook over moderately low heat 10 minutes. Uncover and turn potatoes to cook other side for about 5 minutes. Stir in seasonings and milk or cream.

Make 6 indentations in top of potatoes and break an egg in each indentation. Cover and cook over low heat until eggs are almost set, about 3 minutes. Sprinkle eggs with cheese and bacon which has been crumbled. Cover and cook until eggs are set, 3 to 5 minutes longer. Makes 6 servings.

Eggs Benedict

Chilled orange sections and hot tea add to eggs Benedict. Serves 2 or 4 people depending on appetites.

Grill ham and keep hot. Split English muffins, toast, and butter. Put on serving plates and top each with a ham slice, a poached egg, and hollandaise sauce. Makes 2 or 4 servings.

4 slices ham, cut to fit English muffins
2 English muffins
2 tablespoon butter or margarine
4 poached eggs (page 87)
1 recipe hollandaise sauce (page 123)

Cheese

There are so many fine American and imported cheeses, it is hard to know where to start.

The colonists brought their own methods of making their favorite cheeses when they settled. In 1851, the first cheddar cheese factory was established near Rome, New York. Today a great many of the cheeses which originated in Europe are made in this country. A recent ad by the cheese department of a large store claimed to have 180 varieties of cheese, so if I've left out any of your favorites, forgive me.

Cheeses are natural or processed. Natural cheese is made by the age-old method of separating curd from the whey of milk and continuing from there for various varieties. Pasteurized "process" cheese is made by blending fresh and aged natural cheeses which have been shredded, mixed, and heated (pasteurized) after which no further ripening occurs. Process cheese when melted is not stringy, and it melts easily. It is generally a mild flavor.

Natural cheeses obtain their flavors (called ripening) from the kind of milk used (French Roquefort is made from sheep's milk, Norwegian Gjetost from goat's milk), bacterial culture, and molds.

Soft unripened cheeses such as cottage cheese do not undergo any ripening process and should be used fresh.

Firm unripened cheeses such as mozzarella ripen from the outside or rind of the cheese, toward the center. The bacteria or mold on the outside helps to fix the flavor of the cheese.

Soft ripened cheeses ripen from the interior as well as the exterior. Brie, Camembert, and Liederkranz are examples.

Firm ripened cheese ripens through the entire cheese, and ripening continues as long as the temperature is favorable. Vermont cheddar, Colby, Edam, Gouda, provolone, and Swiss (Emmentaler) are examples.

Very hard cheeses are Parmesan, Romano, and sapsago. They ripen slowly because of their low moisture content.

Other cheeses such as blue (or "bleu"), Gorgonzola, Roquefort, and Stilton are ripened by veins of blue mold.

All natural cheese should be kept refrigerated. Cottage cheese, ricotta, and other soft unripened cheeses should be used within a few days after purchase.

Ripened or cured cheeses keep well in the refrigerator for several weeks if protected from mold contamination and drying out. Leave on the original wrapper and protect cut surfaces with foil or plastic wrap.

Ends and pieces that have dried out may be grated, kept refrigerated in a covered jar, and used in cooking.

Smelly cheeses such as Limburger or Liederkranz should be stored in a tightly covered container.

Small pieces of cheese, 1 pound or less, can be frozen up to 6 months. Varieties which freeze well are brick cheeses, cheddar, Edam, Gouda, Muenster, Swiss, provolone, and mozzarella. Wrap cheese in freezer paper and label, seal and date.

Except for cottage and cream cheese, all cheeses should be served at room temperature to bring out their distinctive flavor and texture. About 1½ hours should bring cheese to proper temperature depending on size of piece.

Neufchatel, Brie, Camembert, Limburger, Liederkranz, Bel Paese, Port du Salut, cheddar, Edam, Gouda, Swiss, Roquefort, blue, Stilton, Gorgonzola, fontina, Pont l'Eveque, and Muenster are among those that are good served with crackers and fruit for dessert.

Cooking cheeses include many of the above—such as Swiss, Edam, Gouda, Roquefort, blue, fontina, and cheddar—as well as processed cheeses, cottage cheese, cream cheese, ricotta, mozzarella, brick cheeses, Colby, provolone, Parmesan, and Romano.

Ricotta Croquettes

These little hot cheese croquettes make a nice hot hors d'oeuvre; or make them larger in size and serve as a main dish for luncheon or dinner.

Mix ricotta with onion, flour, egg, and salt. Shape into bite-size croquettes and dip in bread crumbs. Let air dry on wax paper for 10 minutes.

Heat 2 inches fat or oil in heavy skillet or electric skillet to 365° F and fry croquettes until nicely browned. Serve with dairy sour cream. Makes about 30.

1 pound ricotta cheese
2 tablespoons grated onion
¼ cup flour
1 egg
¼ teaspoon salt
1 cup seasoned bread crumbs
Fat or oil for frying
1 cup dairy sour cream

Cheese, Bacon, and Tomato

8 slices bacon, cut in half
8 slices whole wheat bread
4 tablespoons mayonnaise
16 thin tomato slices
8 slices sharp cheddar cheese

A favorite combination which makes a wonderful supper sandwich.

Pan fry bacon until done, but not crisp. Toast bread under broiler on one side. Spread untoasted side with mayonnaise and arrange two slices tomato on each. Put two halves of bacon on top of tomatoes, and a slice of cheese. Run under the broiler long enough to melt cheese, 2 to 3 minutes. Makes 4 servings.

Saturday Cheese Sandwich Special

2 tablespoons chopped onion
3 tablespoons chopped green
  pepper
1 fresh or canned chili pepper,
  seeded and chopped
2 tablespoons butter or
  margarine
1 small tomato, peeled and
  chopped (about ½ cup)
1½ cups grated American
  process cheese
¼ teaspoon salt
2 tablespoons mayonnaise

This tasty sandwich spread can double as an hors d'oeuvre spread in case of emergency.

Saute onion, green pepper, and chili pepper in butter until tender, not browned. Add tomato and cook a few minutes longer. Cool and mix with cheese, salt, and mayonnaise to blend well. Makes about 2 cups. Use as a cold sandwich spread or broil on bread for a hot sandwich. It will store for several weeks, covered, in the refrigerator.

Swiss Cheese Fondue

A fondue party is loads of fun—it is informal, and since the hostess is an active participant, guests don't feel as though they are causing work. One fondue pot is enough for each 4 persons, so if you plan to have more, borrow unless you already have more than one.

If you can buy long loaves of crusty bread, do so. Cut crosswise into 1½-inch slices and then cut each slice into pieces so that each piece has crust on one side. Allow bread to air-dry for about an hour and then cover with a clean cloth or plastic. For service arrange cubes in a bread basket lined with a bright napkin.

To make fondue:

Rub fondue pot on inside with cut garlic and discard garlic. Pour in wine. Set over heating unit of pot and heat to the boiling point. Add lemon juice. Sprinkle cheese with flour, mixing together, and add by spoonfuls to hot wine, stirring constantly with a wooden fork or spoon. Keep stirring until cheese is melted. Add kirsch or cognac and nutmeg or pepper and stir to blend.

Keep hot over heating unit. Each person in turn spears a piece of bread on a fork and twirls it in the fondue. Makes 4 servings.

Notes on Fondue

A crust forms in the bottom of the pan. Remove with a spatula and divide among the diners. Some think it is the best part of the fondue.

Serve a bowl of crisp vegetables with the fondue—and a hearty dessert, such as an apple pie with ice cream. A Chablis or Riesling is a good accompaniment to the fondue.

* Half Swiss and half Gruyere cheese can be used also.

2 loaves crusty Italian or French bread
1 clove unpeeled garlic, cut in half
2 cups dry white wine
1 tablespoon lemon juice
1 pound natural Swiss cheese, shredded or cut in fine cubes*
3 tablespoons flour
3 tablespoons kirsch or cognac
Freshly ground nutmeg or pepper to taste

Presto Pizza

Crust

2¼ cups sifted all-purpose flour
1 tablespoon baking powder
1 teaspoon salt
⅓ cup shortening
¾ cup milk
2 tablespoons margarine,
  melted

Filling

⅓ cup chopped green pepper
2 tablespoons chopped onion
1 cup tomato sauce
½ cup tomato juice
½ teaspoon dried oregano
1 pinch garlic powder
⅔ cup grated mozzarella cheese
8 slices salami, cut up
½ cup grated Parmesan cheese

The Islander sent this recipe in answer to a request from Lady Glencora, and the baking powder crust makes it "presto."

Mix flour, baking powder, and salt. Cut in shortening. Add milk and mix just enough to wet the dry ingredients. Place dough on lightly floured surface and knead gently 30 seconds.

Divide pizza dough in half. Press and pat each half into a 12-inch ungreased pizza pan. Brush with melted margarine.

In a mixing bowl, mix chopped pepper with onion, tomato sauce and juice, oregano, and garlic powder. Pour half over pizzas; reserve remaining half. Cover each pizza with grated mozzarella and pieces of salami. Pour remaining tomato sauce mixture over cheese. Sprinkle each pizza with ¼ cup grated Parmesan. Bake at 400° F for 15 minutes. Reduce heat to 300° F and bake 10 minutes more.

from The Islander
Confidential Chat Column

Dairy

Milk, like eggs, is a perishable commodity and should be treated with respect. Depending on your family size and consumption of milk, the largest container you can use efficiently will be the least expensive per ounce. Buy milk from a store that keeps it well refrigerated and get it into your refrigerator as soon as possible. Also, always buy pasteurized milk unless, under doctor's orders, you are using raw milk from a certified source. Watch the use date on the container and buy the milk with the latest date.

Milk is sold in many forms, and the following kinds are widely available:

Homogenized whole milk has been subjected to enough pressure so that the milk fat remains evenly distributed throughout the milk. Most homogenized milk has vitamin D added. It can be used for drinking or cooking.

Skim milk has had its butterfat removed. This removal of fat is the only difference between skim and whole milk. Skim milk can be used for drinking or cooking.

Low-fat milk is whole milk with all but 2% of the fat removed. It is a little richer to the taste than skim milk, but lower in calories than homogenized whole milk. Can be used for drinking or cooking.

Other kinds of milk in the dairy department are **buttermilk** and **chocolate milk.**

In the grocery department you can find other milk products, such as the following:

Condensed milk is a mixture of whole cow's milk and sugar, with about 60% of the water removed. It is canned under pressure, has excellent keeping qualities, and can be used for sweetening coffee and for making ice cream and desserts. Refrigerate after opening.

Evaporated milk is whole milk with about half the water removed and with vitamin D added. The milk is homogenized to distribute the fat evenly, pasteurized before it is put into the can, and sterilized after the can is sealed. It comes in 13-ounce and 6-ounce cans, sometimes referred to as tall and small cans. In the can, evaporated milk will keep for up to a year if stored in a cool place.

Evaporated milk also comes in a low-fat variation with both vitamins A and D added. This product contains only ¼ of 1 percent fat.

Evaporated milk can be used straight from the can; and in fact if regular evaporated milk is partially frozen it whips very well. It can also be diluted with water, or with other liquids to add flavor. After opening, refrigerate any left in the can at once.

Nonfat dry milk is skim milk with the water removed. It is fortified with vitamins A and D. It comes in powder or granular form and should be reconstituted with water according to directions on the package. Keep opened package in a cool, dry place.

Reconstituted, it can be used in any recipe where regular milk is called for. Some recipes call for dry milk mixed with the dry ingredients without reliquifying.

Cultured buttermilk powder is available for use in recipes calling for buttermilk. It does not reconstitute as a beverage, so directions on the carton should be followed. Refrigerator storage after opening is required.

Cream comes in several degrees of richness. Heavy or whipping cream is used mainly for whipped cream, and has not less than 30% butterfat. "All-purpose" cream can also be whipped. Light cream, for coffee or cooking, is not less than 18% butterfat.

Half-and-half is a mixture of half milk and half cream and contains 10 to 12% butterfat.

Dairy sour cream is light cream soured by culture or starter. It has a thick texture and a characteristic tartish flavor.

Yogurts take up a big space in the dairy department. There are so many varieties and flavors that it would be impractical to discuss them. Plain yogurt with no flavorings added (other than the bacilli that make yogurt) is used most in cooking. Yogurt can be made of regular, skim, or low-fat milk and will generally indicate on the carton which milk is used. A culture is introduced into the milk which, on standing, produces the texture and flavor of yogurt.

Yogurt

If you make your own yogurt, it costs about half what you pay for it; and it is so simple to make. These are the directions for making 1 quart of yogurt from 1 quart whole milk. It will be necessary to buy a small container of plain yogurt to have a starter.

1 quart whole milk
¼ cup plain yogurt

Bring milk to a full, rolling boil. Let it come to the top of the pan, but be careful it doesn't boil over. Cool the milk to 110° F. Stir occasionally so a skin does not form on top of the milk. When it has reached 110° F, take 1 cup of the warm milk and blend into the plain yogurt. Return this to the remaining milk and gently stir until mixed well. Pour into 2 pint containers or a china or glass bowl; cover.

The yogurt must now be kept in a warm place, 110 to 120° F, to incubate. One way is to turn the oven to lowest temperature (150° F) for 2 or 3 minutes, turn oven off, and place yogurt in oven. If there is a light in the oven, turn it on. Or if your oven has a pilot light, this will keep the oven warm enough. Or set a bowl of boiling water in the oven beside or below the yogurt. It will take 6 to 8 hours for the yogurt to set. If you think the oven is getting too cool, replace the boiling water.

Makes 1 quart yogurt. Store, covered, in refrigerator, where it will keep about 2 weeks. Save ¼ cup yogurt to start the next batch.

This yogurt may be used any way commercial yogurt can be used. Serve it with fruit, honey, or maple syrup, or use in recipes calling for yogurt.

Variation

For a less rich yogurt, use 2 cups whole milk and 2 cups liquid nonfat milk.

Pancakes

Pancakes, since they use milk, seem an ideal set of recipes for this dairy section.

We have always had a love affair with pancakes, or hotcakes as they are also called, and a breakfast or supper of hotcakes and sausage with butter and real maple syrup is tops.

There are plenty of good pancake mixes on the market, but if you don't make them that often and don't want an open box hanging around your cupboard—or if you prefer the made-from-scratch flavor—they are easy to make.

Pancakes

1½ cups all-purpose flour
3½ teaspoons baking powder
½ teaspoon salt
3 tablespoons sugar
1 egg, well beaten
3 tablespoons oil or melted
   shortening
1 cup (about) milk

Pancakes, since they use milk, seem an ideal set of recipes for this dairy section.

Mix flour with baking powder, salt, and sugar in a bowl. In another bowl, combine egg, oil, and milk. Add to flour and stir just enough to moisten the dry ingredients. Do not beat.

Heat griddle so that drops of water bounce off it, or to 400° F. Swipe some oil across griddle, and use a ¼-cup measure full of pancake batter to make each pancake. Cook until tops begin to rise and bubbles dot surface; turn and brown on other side, about 3 minutes altogether. Makes about 12 4-inch pancakes.

Variations

Blueberry Pancakes: Add 2 tablespoons more sugar to dry ingredients. Add 1 cup berries sweetened with 1 or 2 tablespoons sugar to the batter.

Corn Pancakes: Add to the batter 1 cup canned whole kernel corn, drained, or 1 cup fresh corn or frozen corn cut off the cob, thawed.

Clam Pancakes: Omit sugar from recipe; add 1 cup drained, chopped raw clams and 1 teaspoon grated onion to batter.

Men's Favorite Griddle Cakes

White Moonflower's griddle cakes are quick and easy to make and Canadian bacon goes well with them. The amount of baking powder is correct.

Select the best whole wheat flour, one which has excellent flavor and is ground fine. Sift the flour, but also add the bran which does not go through the sifter. Beat the egg, add the salt and sugar, then the sifted flour, baking powder, milk, and finally the butter. Beat well and drop by large spoonfuls on hot griddle. When light and fluffy, turn the griddle cakes to bake and brown the other side. Makes 15 to 16.

from White Moonflower
Confidential Chat Column

2 cups whole wheat flour
1 egg
½ teaspoon salt
1 tablespoon sugar
2 tablespoons baking powder
1½ cups milk
2 tablespoons butter, melted

Oatmeal Pancakes

Oatmeal pancakes make a fine supper dish with butter, syrup, and bacon. Serve fruit salad for dessert.

Combine oatmeal, flour, baking powder, and salt in a medium sized bowl. Stir until well mixed. Beat together milk, egg, and oil and stir into dry ingredients until just moistened. Heat griddle to 400° F and lightly grease. Fill a ¼-cup measure with batter and pour on hot griddle. Turn pancakes when tops begin to rise and edges look cooked. Makes about 10 4-inch cakes.

1 cup uncooked quick or old-fashioned oatmeal
¾ cup all-purpose flour
1 tablespoon baking powder
½ teaspoon salt
1 cup milk
1 egg
2 tablespoons oil

Chicken Crepes

Crepes

½ cup all-purpose flour
1 egg
1 egg yolk
⅛ teaspoon salt
1 teaspoon sugar
1 cup milk
2 tablespoons butter, melted

Chicken Filling

⅓ cup butter
½ cup flour
1½ cups half-and-half
1 cup well-seasoned chicken
    broth
Salt and freshly ground pepper
    to taste
2 cups finely chopped cooked
    chicken or turkey
½ cup chopped fresh mush-
    rooms
2 tablespoons dry sherry
½ cup dairy sour cream

Crepes are always spectacular to serve, but not that difficult to make. The crepes can be made way in advance and frozen, or the day ahead and refrigerated.

Crepes: Put flour in a bowl. Add all remaining ingredients and beat with whisk until very smooth. Chill for two hours. Grease a 6- or 7-inch crepe skillet and heat over moderate heat. Pour in about 2 tablespoons batter and tilt skillet so a thin layer is formed. Brown on one side only and remove to a wire rack to cool. Makes 16 crepes. When cooled, separate with pieces of plastic or wax paper, overwrap, and store overnight or freeze.

Chicken Filling: Heat butter and flour together in a saucepan for 2 minutes. Stir in half-and-half and broth and cook and stir until mixture boils and is thickened. Season to taste.

Divide sauce into 2 equal parts. In one half stir chicken, mushrooms, and sherry. Cool. Put a spoonful of this filling on the uncooked side of each crepe and roll crepe around filling. Place seam side down in one or two buttered flat casseroles or baking dishes the right size to hold crepes in one layer.

Into the remaining sauce stir the sour cream. Pour over the filled crepes. Bake at 400° F for 25 minutes or until bubbly. Makes 4 to 6 servings.

**Broiled Scallops and Bacon
(recipe on page 134)**

Creme Fraiche

Creme fraiche is usually made with heavy cream, but my own version, using light cream, is lower in calories and makes a delicious topping for fruit or other desserts. To me, the buttermilk version has a little more tangy flavor, but the same thickened cream results from either buttermilk or yogurt.

Mix cream well with buttermilk or yogurt. Pour into a jar and cover. Let stand in a warm place 8 to 12 hours or until cream thickens. Then refrigerate until well chilled. Serve as a topping for fruit or other desserts. Makes 2 cups. Will keep for 10 days to 2 weeks.

* *If you prefer a richer product, use heavy cream.*

2 cups light cream*
3 tablespoons buttermilk or plain yogurt

Soups

Numbers refer to pages where recipes appear in this book.

Garnishes for Soup   106
Quick Ideas For Enhancing Soup   107
Soup Stock   107
Clam Chowder   108
Vegetable Soup   108
New England Fish Chowder   109
Fish Chowder   109
Oyster Stew   110
Corn Chowder   110
Lamb Barley Soup   111
Tuna Chowder   111
Split Pea Soup   112
Bean Soup   112
Black Bean Soup   113
Lentil Soup   113
Onion Soup   114
Quick Supper Soup   114
Celery Soup   115
Herbed Beef Soup   115
Baked Bean Soup   116
Chilled Zucchini Soup   116
Gazpacho   117
Vichyssoise   117
Quick Soup Pick-Ups   118
Calico Chowder   118
Tomato Soup De Luxe   118
Cold Weather Soup   118
Beef Potage   119

Soups

Soup is one of my favorite foods, particularly if it is homemade. I try always to keep something on hand to make soup, however simple. If you want to get into soup making, there are ways to make it a fairly effortless project.

When the soup base is meat or chicken stock, always make it the day before you need the soup so that it can be chilled overnight for easy removal of the fat.

Chill meat used in stock separately. It will be easier to cut up to incorporate into the soup.

Save liquid from vegetables to use in soup stock. A clean coffee can with a plastic cover is a good container. Keep it in the freezer and add liquid as it accumulates. Don't save strong flavored cooking water such as that from cabbage, broccoli, and related vegetables unless you are particularly fond of it as a flavor; then save it separately from the more mild vegetables.

Everything is a candidate for the soup pot in my kitchen—leftover gravy, vegetables, bones from boning a steak or chicken. When I go shopping, I canvass the meat and poultry department for chicken necks, pork or beef bones, lamb breasts or bones. All make a good stock base for soup. And in fact if you mix up the kinds of meat and chicken in making the stock, it seems to me to have a better flavor. When you find these soup making items you can freeze them for future use.

Leftover vegetables also go into the soup. When preparing asparagus, snap off the tender tips and peel the tougher ends (not the very tough bottoms, but the part in between the tough bottom and the top you cook) and make cream of asparagus soup.

If you have a food processor, it is a great help in preparing soup. Vegetables can be processed to soup size in a jiffy or pureed for cream soups in a hurry.

Herbs and other seasonings can be added to canned soups to give them a little more personal flavor. There are some suggestions under the quick soup section below.

Garnishes for Soup

- Crisp ready-to-eat cereal (not sweetened)
- Snipped chives or parsley
- Croutons bought or homemade (toast buttered bread slices in a 300° F oven until lightly browned, trim, and cut into small squares; season, if you like, with garlic or savory salt)
- Popcorn
- Crisp bacon bits
- Slices of frankfurter
- Thin lemon slices
- Sour cream or yogurt
- Cheese crackers

Quick Ideas For Enhancing Soup

• Combine 1 can (10¾ ounces) condensed cream of chicken soup and 1 packet (2 ounces) dried vegetable soup mix with 2 soup cans water. Simmer about 5 minutes. Top with chopped parsley. Makes 3 servings.

• To 1 can (10½ ounces) condensed cream of mushroom soup, add ½ soup can water, ½ soup can dry white wine. Heat and sprinkle with crushed dried rosemary. Makes 2 servings.

• Combine 1 can (10½ ounces) condensed cream of mushroom and 1 can (10½ ounces) condensed cream of chicken with 1 soup can water and ½ soup can light cream. Blend and heat. Serve sprinkled with grated fresh nutmeg. Or chill heated soup and serve icy cold with snipped chives. Makes 4 servings.

• Dilute 1 can (10¾ ounces) condensed beef noodle soup with 1 soup can tomato juice. Add a dash of crushed dried oregano leaves and heat. Makes 2 servings.

• Combine 1 can (10¾ ounces) condensed cream of asparagus soup and 1 can (11¼ ounces) green pea soup. Add 1 teaspoon curry powder, 1 teaspoon instant minced onion, and 2 soup cans milk. Heat and serve topped with whipped cream; or heat, then chill and serve icy cold.

Soup Stock

After the stock has been cooked and strained, taste it to see if it has a good strong flavor. If it seems a little weaker than you'd like, add some beef or chicken bouillon cubes or boil the stock to concentrate it a bit more. (With power costs what they are, it is actually less expensive to add bouillon cubes.) But remember that you are going to add vegetables and other things to the stock which will help bring up the flavor.

Beef, pork, or chicken bones
  (about 2 to 3 pounds)
2 quarts water
1 onion, peeled
1 carrot, peeled
1 stalk celery
1 bay leaf
6 peppercorns
½ teaspoon salt

Cover bones with water, add remaining ingredients, and bring to a boil. If there is much scum which appears on the liquid after it begins to boil, skim it off and discard. Reduce heat, cover, and simmer. Beef or pork bones take about 3 hours or longer. Chicken and lamb bone flavor will be extracted with 1½ to 2 hours of simmering. Cool stock enough to handle and strain out bones and vegetables. Chill stock and bones separately overnight. (If bones have little or no meat on them, they can be discarded.) Remove fat from chilled soup and discard. This should make about 1½ quarts stock.

Clam Chowder

4 slices bacon, cut up, or 4 tablespoons diced salt pork*
1 medium onion, chopped
1 to 2 tablespoons flour
2 cups strained clam juice
1 medium potato, peeled and
 diced
Pinch of dried or powdered
 thyme (optional)
1 cup milk
1 cup chopped clams
Salt and freshly ground pepper
 to taste
Pilot crackers

Massachusetts clam chowder is famous world-wide. In its original form it was always made with diced salt pork, and most commercially prepared clam chowder has salt pork. At home, today, some homemakers use bacon instead. It is more likely to be on hand since it has many other uses. Another question is whether to add a whiff of thyme or not, and that is a matter of taste.

If you open and clean your own clams, strain the juice through cheesecloth to remove sand and possibly bits of shells. Wash the clams well and chop in a blender or food processor. Be certain to taste the clam chowder before adding salt; clams are inclined to be salty, so additional salt may not be needed.

Slowly cook bacon or salt pork in a 1½-quart saucepan until pieces are crisp. Add onion and cook, stirring, until tender but not browned. Stir in flour, then clam juice. Add potato (and thyme if desired), bring to a boil, cover, and simmer 15 minutes or until potatoes are tender. Stir in milk and reheat (but do not boil). Add clams and again reheat, but do not boil. Taste, and if needed, add salt and pepper. Clam chowder is sometimes served with a bit of butter floating on top; but in any event, serve with pilot crackers. Makes about 1 quart.

* If you use salt pork, remove the pieces from saucepan after frying and reserve. Sprinkle on top of clam chowder in bowls.

Vegetable Soup

1 medium onion, chopped
1 stalk celery, chopped
2 carrots, peeled and diced
2 tablespoons butter or
 margarine
2 tablespoons uncooked rice
1 cup canned tomatoes,
 chopped
1 quart beef stock
Salt to taste

If there is cooked meat left from making the stock, chop it finely and add to the soup.

Saute onion, celery, and carrots in butter for 5 minutes, stirring. Add remaining ingredients and simmer, covered, 30 minutes. Makes about 6 cups.

New England Fish Chowder

Ask at the fish market for chowder fish. These are smaller pieces left from cutting up big fish and generally sell for much less money. Check for bones, however, and remove any before adding to chowder. Fish should be cooked quickly to retain its best flavor and texture.

Cook the bacon or salt pork in a large saucepan with onion and celery until bacon is crisp and onion tender. Add potatoes and boiling water, bay leaf, thyme, and salt and cook, covered, until potatoes are tender, about 15 minutes. Add milk. Cream flour and butter together to make a roux and stir into chowder. Bring to a boil, stirring, and simmer one minute. Add fish and simmer one minute longer. Remove from heat and let stand covered about 10 minutes. Serve with pilot crackers. Makes 10 cups.

4 slices bacon, cut up, or ¼ cup
 diced salt pork
½ cup chopped onion
½ cup chopped celery
2 cups cubed potatoes (2 to 3
 medium)
1½ cups boiling water
1 bay leaf (optional)
¼ teaspoon dried thyme
1 teaspoon salt
4 cups milk
¼ cup flour
¼ cup butter or margarine
1 pound chowder fish or
 boneless white fish fillets cut
 in 1-inch pieces
Pilot crackers

Fish Chowder #2

This is my version of fish chowder for those on lower caloric diets.

Cook bacon with onion until bacon is crisp and onion tender. Add potatoes, water, and salt and cook, covered, until potatoes are tender, about 15 minutes. Mix dry milk with flour and stir into potatoes. Bring to a boil and simmer, stirring, 1 minute. Add fish and simmer 1 minute. Remove from heat and let stand, covered, 10 minutes before serving. Serve with a sprinkling of paprika. Makes 6 cups.

3 slices bacon, cut up
½ cup chopped onion
1½ cups cubed potatoes (2
 medium)
2 cups boiling water
½ teaspoon salt
½ cup nonfat dry milk powder
 or granules
2 tablespoons flour
½ to ¾ pound chowder fish, cut
 up
Paprika

Oyster Stew

1 pint shelled fresh oysters
¼ cup butter
Oyster liquor
3 cups milk, scalded
1 cup cream, scalded
½ teaspoon salt
Dash white pepper
Oyster crackers

It was always our custom to have oyster stew on Christmas Eve. I probably was intrigued by the oyster crackers as much as by the stew—since Mother would buy the oyster crackers for the Christmas Eve stew and when they were gone, that was it until next year.

Drain and reserve oyster liquor. Check oysters and remove any pieces of shell. Heat butter. Add oyster liquor and oysters and heat just until oysters begin to curl on the edge. Combine with hot milk, cream, salt, and pepper. Serve with oyster crackers. Makes about 5 cups or 4 servings.

Corn Chowder

¼ cup diced salt pork or 4 slices
    bacon, diced
1 medium onion, chopped
4 cups diced, peeled potatoes
1 cup water
3 cups milk
2 cups corn (fresh, canned
    whole kernel, or frozen,
    thawed)
¾ teaspoon salt
Freshly ground pepper to taste
2 tablespoons chopped fresh
    parsley

New England has always been famed for its corn chowder. It can be made with canned or frozen corn, or with corn freshly cut from the cob. It is a hearty chowder, which with a sandwich and fruit would make a satisfactory lunch or supper.

Fry salt pork or bacon about 2 minutes. Add onion and continue to fry until onion is soft but not browned. Add potatoes and water and simmer, covered, about 20 minutes or until potatoes are tender. Add milk, corn, salt, and pepper and continue cooking over low heat for 10 minutes. Serve sprinkled with fresh parsley. Makes 6 servings.

Lamb Barley Soup

Lamb barley soup can be the centerpiece for a luncheon or supper meal. Add lots of bread and butter, milk to drink, and fruit for dessert.

Combine lamb breast in a saucepan with water, salt, peppercorns, 1 small onion, and 1 stalk celery. Bring to a boil and simmer, covered, for about 2 hours. Do this the day before making the soup. Strain broth and refrigerate lamb breast and broth separately.

To make soup, remove fat from broth. Measure broth and add water if necessary to make 4 cups. Cook broth and barley together, covered, for 1 hour. Meanwhile, remove lamb meat from bones and dice. Add with all remaining ingredients to lamb broth and barley and cook, covered, another 30 minutes. Makes 6 to 7 cups.

1½ pounds breast of lamb
1 quart water
1 teaspoon salt
6 peppercorns
1 small onion
1 stalk celery
¼ cup regular barley
½ cup chopped onion
½ cup chopped celery
½ cup chopped carrots
1 cup stewed tomatoes
¼ cup chopped fresh parsley
Salt to taste

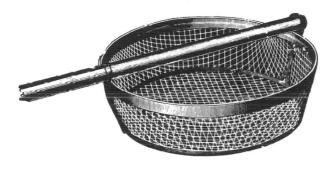

Tuna Chowder

Here is a way to "take a can of tuna" for a quick luncheon or supper soup.

Heat oil in a saucepan and saute onion and celery until tender but not browned. Peel and dice potato. Add with all remaining ingredients to cooked vegetables. Cover and simmer 20 minutes. Taste for seasoning. Makes 4 cups.

* *Vegex is an all vegetable flavoring extract which can be purchased in health food stores.*

1 tablespoon oil
1 medium onion, chopped
2 stalks celery, chopped
1 large potato
1 can (6½ ounces) chunk light tuna
2 cups water
½ cup chopped tomatoes, canned or fresh
2 teaspoons Vegex*
Salt and freshly ground pepper to taste

Split Pea Soup

1 smoked pork hock
6 cups water
1 cup dried green split peas
1 carrot, peeled and diced
1 stalk celery, diced
1 medium onion, chopped
¼ teaspoon ground thyme
Salt and freshly ground pepper
    to taste

Whenever I buy a smoked pork shoulder, I ask the meat man to cut off the hock end which I save for soup. It makes wonderful split pea or bean soup. A good home-made soup is always better if you follow this two-day process.

The day before you plan to make the soup, cover the pork hock with the water and simmer several hours until tender. (If you wish, put an onion, a stalk of celery, a few peppercorns, and a piece of bay leaf in with the pork hock.) Drain liquid into a container and refrigerate overnight so that the fat can be taken off. Cool the pork hock enough to handle. Remove skin and fat and cut any meat on bone into fine dice and refrigerate to add to soup.

Next day, skim fat from the broth and strain it. Sort and wash split peas and combine with broth, carrot, celery, onion, and seasonings. Bring to a boil and simmer, covered, about 1 hour or until split peas are tender. Add diced ham to soup. This makes about 1½ quarts of soup. Can be stored for several days in the refrigerator.

This soup freezes well, so if the quantity is too large, freeze a container for future use.

Variation
Bean Soup: Omit split peas. Sort and soak 1 cup dried pea beans in water overnight. Cook in broth for about an hour before adding vegetables; then proceed as directed.

Black Bean Soup

This makes a particularly good soup with which to start a meal. This recipe can be halved or it freezes well.

Wash and sort beans, cover with double their volume of water, and soak overnight.

Next day, drain beans. Saute onion and green pepper lightly in butter. Add to beans with ham hock, 7 cups water, bouillon cube, lime juice, and bay leaves. Bring to a boil and simmer, covered, about 1½ hours or until beans are tender. Remove ham hock and bay leaves and let soup cool slightly. (Use any meat on ham hock for sandwiches or other use; discard bay leaves). Puree soup in small quantities until smooth. When all soup is pureed, taste for seasoning, reheat, and add sherry. Chop hard cooked egg fine and use as a garnish. Makes about 2 quarts.

1 pound dried black beans
Water to soak
½ cup chopped onion
½ cup chopped green pepper
2 tablespoons butter or
  margarine
1 ham hock (about 1 pound)
7 cups water
1 beef bouillon cube
2 tablespoons lime juice
2 bay leaves
¼ cup dry sherry
Salt and freshly ground pepper
  to taste
1 hard cooked egg

Lentil Soup

Lentil soup is really heartwarming. Serve it with pita bread sandwiches and hot tea.

Heat butter in a 6-cup saucepan and saute onion and carrot until tender but not browned. Add lentils, beef stock, salt, pepper, and cumin. Bring to a boil, cover, and simmer over low heat until lentils are tender, about 1 hour. If desired, puree soup in a blender or processor. Add lemon juice. Reheat to serve. Makes 1½ quarts.

3 tablespoons butter
¾ cup chopped onion
1 medium carrot, peeled and
  chopped
½ pound (1 cup) dried lentils,
  washed
4 cups beef stock, or 3 beef
  bouillon cubes dissolved in 4
  cups water
½ teaspoon salt
Freshly ground pepper to taste
½ teaspoon ground cumin
1 tablespoon lemon juice

Onion Soup

2 tablespoons butter or olive oil
2 cups sweet onion slices
2½ cups beef stock
½ teaspoon sugar
1 long thin loaf French bread
6 to 8 tablespoons grated
   Parmesan cheese

One of the real treats of the soup world is onion soup. As a starter you need a strong, well-flavored beef stock and plenty of onions. If you haven't time or the ingredients to prepare a homemade beef stock, buy canned condensed beef bouillon and dilute it only half strength. For onions, use either sweet Spanish onions or the red Italian.

The classic service for onion soup is in a 1-cup earthenware casserole dish which can go into the oven. The absence of such service wouldn't stop me from making onion soup, though.

Heat butter or oil in a heavy 6-cup saucepan. Add onions which have been cut on the bias so they are not full rings. Cook and stir until onions are limp but not browned. Add beef broth and sugar. Bring to a boil and simmer, covered, about 10 minutes.

Meantime, cut French bread in about 1-inch-thick slices and toast on both sides in a broiler.

To serve, put a ladle of soup in dish, add a piece of toasted bread and sprinkle liberally with cheese. Fill the dish with soup and put in another piece of toast and pile on the cheese. Either bake at 375° F for about 15 minutes or run under the broiler until cheese is melted. Serve with remaining bread and additional Parmesan cheese. Makes 1 quart soup.

Quick Supper Soup

2 slices bacon, finely cut
1 medium onion, chopped
1 can (13¾ ounces) chicken
   broth
1 medium potato, peeled and
   diced
1 tablespoon uncooked rice
½ cup water
1 cup chopped raw cabbage
Chopped fresh parsley

A hearty soup that can be quickly made. Served with ham sandwiches on rye bread, with fresh fruit for dessert, it's a nice supper or luncheon.

Saute bacon and onion in a saucepan until bacon is crisp. Add remaining ingredients except parsley and simmer covered 15 minutes. Serve with chopped parsley. Makes 3½ cups.

Celery Soup

A cup of this soup, well chilled and perhaps sprinkled with chopped chives or parsley, would be a pleasant start to a meal.

Dice celery, onion, and potato and cook in 2 cups water with vegetable extract until vegetables are tender. Add carrot and cook a few minutes longer. Mix milk powder, water, and yogurt. Stir into vegetables and reheat. Taste and add salt, if necessary. Serve hot or chilled. Makes about 4 cups.

4 stalks celery
1 medium to large onion
1 medium potato, peeled
2 cups water
2 teaspoons Vegex*
1 carrot, peeled and shredded
⅓ cup nonfat dry milk powder or granules
1 cup water
1 tablespoon plain yogurt
Salt to taste

* *Vegex is an all vegetable flavoring extract which can be purchased in health food stores.*

Herbed Beef Soup

When there is a bargain in ground beef or some in the freezer you wish to use up, herbed hamburger soup is one delicious answer. It is hearty for lunch or supper.

In a 2½-quart saucepan, fry crumbled ground beef until lightly browned. Pour off accumulated fat.

In a food processor or grinder, process onion, celery, carrots, potato and parsley until chopped fine (or chop fine by hand). Also chop up any large pieces of tomato. Add vegetables to ground beef along with water, herbs, and salt. Bring to a boil and simmer, covered, for about 2 hours. This makes 8 cups of thick soup. It freezes very well.

½ to ¾ pound ground beef
1 large onion, chopped
2 or 3 stalks celery
2 large peeled carrots
1 potato, peeled
Several sprigs fresh parsley
1 can (1 pound) stewed tomatoes
2 tomato cans water
½ teaspoon each dried basil, oregano, and thyme; or 1½ teaspoons Italian seasoning
1 teaspoon salt

Baked Bean Soup

2 cups Boston baked beans
1 stalk celery cut in 1-inch
    pieces
½ small onion
4 cups water
1 cup canned tomatoes
1 tablespoon flour
1 teaspoon prepared mustard
3 tablespoons water
2 beef bouillon cubes
Salt and freshly ground pepper
    to taste

This recipe, found in an old Cape Cod cookbook, makes use of leftover Boston baked beans. It is a good soup for a cold night. Hot dogs on buns and cole slaw would go well with it.

Combine beans, celery, onion, 4 cups water, and tomatoes in a 2½-quart saucepan. Cover and simmer 30 minutes. Put through a food mill or puree in a processor or blender. Mix together flour, mustard, and 3 tablespoons water and stir into bean mixture. Add bouillon cubes and reheat, stirring, until bouillon cubes are dissolved and mixture boils. Taste and add salt and pepper as needed. Makes 5½ cups.

Chilled Zucchini Soup

2 large zucchini
1 medium onion
½ green pepper
1½ cups chicken broth
¼ teaspoon dried basil or ¾ tea-
    spoon fresh basil
¼ teaspoon dried rosemary or ¾
    teaspoon fresh rosemary
1½ cups milk
½ teaspoon salt
Freshly ground pepper to taste
Lime wedges

A summer treat when zucchini is plentiful. Serve with cold chicken sandwiches made on whole wheat bread and radishes.

Scrub and cut off stem end of zucchini. Slice zucchini, onion, and green pepper. Cook in chicken broth until tender. Cool slightly and puree in processor or blender. Add herbs, milk, and salt and pepper; chill. Serve with a wedge of lime. Makes 4½ cups.

Gazpacho

Of Spanish origin, Gazpacho is cool and refreshing in the summer. Serve it to start a seafood salad luncheon.

Cut bread into small pieces and put into a bowl. Add water, oil, garlic pushed through a press, and salt. Stir and let stand several hours. Put tomatoes through a food mill or strainer into bread mixture. Add onion, pimento, and vinegar and blend or process until smooth. Chill well. Serve garnished with thin slices of cucumber. Makes 1 quart.

2 slices soft white bread
½ cup water
¼ cup oil
1 clove garlic
½ teaspoon salt
1 quart peeled and diced fresh tomatoes (about 2 pounds)
¼ cup chopped onion
¼ cup diced pimento
2 tablespoons wine vinegar
Cucumber slices

Vichyssoise

Vichyssoise is the French name for cold potato soup. There are richer versions made with heavy cream, but this recipe is delicious without being too caloric.

Clean leeks carefully of sand. Use only the white part and cut crosswise into thin slices. Saute leeks and onion in butter in a 2-quart saucepan until tender but not browned. Peel potatoes and cut into thin slices. (There should be 2 cups or more.) Add potatoes and chicken broth to leeks and onions in saucepan and cook, covered, until potatoes are very tender, about 30 minutes. Cool slightly and puree in processor or blender until smooth. Add cream and salt and pepper to taste. Chill. Serve very cold in soup cups garnished with snipped chives. Makes about 1¼ quarts.

4 leeks
1 small onion, chopped
¼ cup butter or margarine
3 or 4 potatoes
3 cups chicken broth
¾ cup half-and-half
Salt and white pepper to taste
Snipped chives

Quick Soup Pick-Ups

There are times when soup is welcomed, but there's no time to fuss. Here are some quickly made soups.

Calico Chowder

1 medium onion, sliced thin
3 tablespoons butter
1 can (8 ounces) tomatoes, mashed
1 can (10¾ ounces) condensed beef noodle soup
1 can (10½ ounces) condensed pepper pot soup
1 soup can water
Additional butter
Oyster crackers

Cook onion slices in butter until tender but not browned. Add tomatoes, condensed soups, and water, and heat. To serve, top each serving with about a teaspoon of butter and some oyster crackers. Makes about 5 cups.

from A Fireman's Wife
Confidential Chat Column

Tomato Soup De Luxe

2 tablespoons chopped onion
2 tablespoons butter or margarine
1 ripe tomato, peeled and diced
1 can (10¾ ounces) condensed tomato soup
1 soup can water

If you prefer a creamier soup, use 1 soup can milk instead of water.

Saute onion in butter until tender but not browned. Add fresh tomato and cook 3 or 4 minutes. Add soup, blend in water, and heat. Makes about 2½ cups.

Cold Weather Soup

1 can (11½ ounces) condensed bean with bacon soup
1 can (10¾ ounces) condensed tomato soup
1 can (10½ ounces) chili con carne without beans
2 soup cans water
Hot bread

Combine all soups and water and serve piping hot with hot breads. Makes about 6 cups.

from A Fireman's Wife
Confidential Chat Column

Beef Potage

Saute mushrooms and green pepper in butter. Do not brown. Add soups and water and heat to boiling. Makes about 3½ cups.

from A Fireman's Wife
Confidential Chat Column

½ cup sliced mushrooms, fresh or canned
½ cup thin green pepper strips
1 tablespoon butter
1 can (10¾ ounces) condensed beef noodle soup
1 can (11 ounces) condensed beef soup
½ soup can water

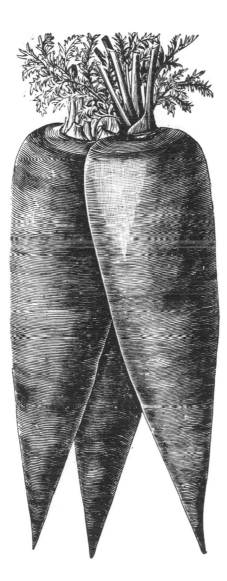

Sauces

Numbers refer to pages where recipes appear in this book.

Mustard Sauce for Fish 122
Devil Sauce 122
Make Your Own Mustard 122
English Style Mustard 123
Hollandaise Sauce 123
Bearnaise Sauce 124
Green Sauce 124
Polly's Savory Apple Jelly Sauce 124
Horseradish Cream Sauce 125
Fresh Horseradish Sauce 125
Mint Sauce for Lamb 125
Fresh Tomato Sauce 126
Orange Raisin Sauce 126
Yogurt Cucumber Sauce 127

Sauces

Today sauces do not take such a prominent part in our cooking, since many are high in calories and difficult to prepare. According to hearsay, sauces reached such a high accord in classic cookery because they were used to enhance the slightly gamy flavor of meat, fish, and fowl that was necessarily stored without refrigeration.

But I've included a few easy-to-prepare sauces which you might like to have in your cooking repertoire.

Mustard Sauce For Fish

**1 tablespoon prepared brown
  mustard**
**¼ cup butter or margarine,
  melted**

When you are broiling or pan frying fish with no additions, serve this mustard sauce on the side. It is particularly good with mackerel and bluefish.

Mix mustard with a small amount of melted butter. Gradually add remaining butter and heat. Makes ⅓ cup.

Devil Sauce

½ tablespoon dry mustard
**2 tablespoons Worcestershire
  sauce**
¼ teaspoon Tabasco sauce
2 teaspoons lemon juice
1 can (10¾ ounces) beef gravy

Serve devil sauce with steak, roast beef, hamburgers, or even hot dogs, if you like. It is hot two ways.

Combine mustard, Worcestershire, Tabasco, and lemon juice in a small saucepan. Stir in a small amount of gravy to blend, then add remaining gravy. Bring to a boil and simmer, covered, about 10 minutes. Makes 1¼ cups.

Make Your Own Mustard

6 tablespoons dry mustard
**3 tablespoons water, white
  wine, or stale beer**

If you love hot mustard, make your own from dry mustard. Either this or English style mustard, below, is good with Chinese dishes.

Blend mustard with liquid to make a paste. If you like a little thinner mustard, add more of the chosen liquid. Makes about ⅓ cup.

English Style Mustard

Mix mustard, salt, and sugar. Add hot water and blend in remaining ingredients. Chill. Store, covered, in refrigerator. Makes ⅓ cup.

½ cup dry mustard
¼ teaspoon salt
½ teaspoon sugar
1 tablespoon hot water
2 tablespoons cider vinegar
1 teaspoon oil
½ teaspoon horseradish

Hollandaise Sauce

Used for green vegetables such as asparagus or broccoli, this sauce is also one of the ingredients in eggs Benedict (page 91). A blender or a food processor makes this adaptation of the classic hollandaise sauce easy to prepare. Use the variations suggested below for compatible meat dishes.

3 egg yolks
2 tablespoons fresh lemon juice
¼ teaspoon salt
Dash white pepper
½ cup butter, softened
½ cup boiling water

Put egg yolks, lemon juice, salt, pepper, and butter in blender or processor. Whirl or process to mix. Keep machine running and slowly add boiling water until blended. Remove to a small bowl or pan and cook over hot water, stirring constantly, until thick and custard-like. Makes 1½ cups.

Variations
Mint: Add 1 tablespoon chopped fresh mint or 1 teaspoon crushed dried mint.
Chive: Add 2 tablespoons finely chopped chives.
Dill: Add 2 teaspoons chopped fresh dill weed or 1 teaspoon crushed dried dill weed.

Bearnaise Sauce

3 egg yolks
1 tablespoon fresh lemon juice
1 tablespoon tarragon vinegar
½ teaspoon onion salt
Dash freshly ground pepper
½ cup butter, softened
½ cup boiling water
3 teaspoons chopped fresh
   tarragon or 1 teaspoon
   crushed dried tarragon
2 teaspoons chopped fresh
   parsley

Bearnaise sauce is one of the components of Chateaubriand steak. This recipe is an adaptation of the classic French bearnaise. It is a variation of hollandaise, so if you master one, it is easy to make the other. Bearnaise is good with roast beef, lamb, or veal, too.

Put egg yolks, lemon juice, vinegar, onion salt, pepper, and butter in blender or processor. Whirl or process to mix. Keep machine running and slowly add boiling water until blended.

Remove to a small bowl or pan and cook over hot water, stirring constantly, until thick and custard-like. Stir in tarragon and parsley. Makes 1½ cups.

Green Sauce

1 cup mayonnaise
¼ cup chopped fresh parsley
½ cup finely chopped chives
½ cup finely chopped
   watercress
1 tablespoon grated onion
1 tablespoon tarragon vinegar

Serve well chilled with cold shellfish or meat.

Mix mayonnaise lightly with all remaining ingredients. Store, covered, in the refrigerator. Makes about 2 cups. Will keep for about 2 weeks in refrigerator.

Polly's Savory Apple Jelly Sauce

½ teaspoon dry mustard
¼ teaspoon ground cloves
½ teaspoon cinnamon
2 tablespoons vinegar
1 jar (8 ounces) apple or
   crabapple jelly

A delicious spicy sauce to serve with ham, lamb, or roast duck or goose.

In a small saucepan mix spices and vinegar. Blend in jelly and cook over low heat until jelly is melted and flavors blended, stirring constantly. Makes about 1 cup.

Horseradish Cream Sauce

A natural to serve with ham, pork, or cold roast beef.

Combine sour cream with horseradish and lemon juice. Mix lightly and store, covered, in refrigerator. Makes ¾ cup.

½ cup dairy sour cream
4 tablespoons drained horseradish
1 teaspoon lemon juice

Fresh Horseradish Sauce

Fresh horseradish is tangy as all get out, and really clears your head while you are making this sauce.

Grate enough peeled horseradish root to make ⅔ cup. (I recommend either a food processor or a blender.) Combine horseradish with sugar and vinegar. Keep refrigerated in a covered container. Makes ⅔ cup.

⅓ cup grated fresh horseradish
½ teaspoon sugar
4 tablespoons cider vinegar

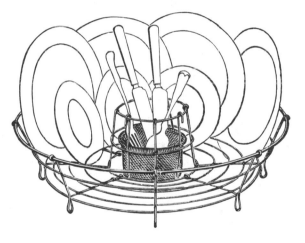

Mint Sauce For Lamb

Mint sauce is traditional for lamb, although some prefer mint jelly. This version is simple to make, but it does need fresh mint leaves to be really good.

Combine vinegar with water and brown sugar. Bring to a boil and pour over mint leaves. Let stand for at least 1 hour to develop flavor of mint before using. Makes 1 cup.

½ cup wine vinegar or cider vinegar
¼ cup water
¼ cup firmly packed light brown sugar
¼ cup chopped fresh mint leaves

Fresh Tomato Sauce

2 pounds ripe fresh tomatoes
3 tablespoons butter or
    margarine
½ cup finely chopped onion
½ cup chopped green pepper
1½ tablespoons finely chopped
    shallots or green onions
1 clove garlic, chopped
½ teaspoon salt
Freshly ground pepper to taste

About 12 years ago a new way of cooking called cuisine minceur *was developed in France. Basically, this type of cooking did away with the heavy cream and egg sauces which were integral to French cooking. Many vegetables were used, more than in previous cooking styles. Fresh tomato sauce would be one example of a* cuisine minceur *sauce.*

Remove core from tomatoes and cut remaining tomatoes into cubes. Heat butter and saute onion, pepper, shallots, and garlic until onion is soft. Add tomatoes, salt, and pepper and continue cooking about 10 minutes.

Puree in blender or food processor until smooth. Push through sieve with wooden spoon to remove seeds. Reheat to serve. Makes about 2 cups. This sauce could be served on fish, pasta, over poached eggs, or with shellfish.

Orange Raisin Sauce

1 cup seedless raisins
1 cup orange juice
½ cup water
6 tablespoons brown sugar
1 tablespoon cornstarch
1½ tablespoons grated orange
    rind
¼ teaspoon salt
1 tablespoon cider vinegar

Good to serve with baked ham or roast duck or goose.

Combine raisins, orange juice, and water in a 1-quart saucepan. Cover and simmer 10 minutes. Mix brown sugar, cornstarch, orange rind, and salt. Stir into raisin mixture and cook and stir until thickened and clear. Mix in vinegar. Serve hot. Makes about 1½ cups.

Yogurt Cucumber Sauce

Serve with cold lamb or roast beef or as a garnish for chilled soups or sliced tomatoes.

Mix cucumber with yogurt, garlic, dill, and salt and pepper. Store, covered, in refrigerator for several hours before using. Makes about 3 cups. Will keep several weeks under refrigeration.

1 cup seeded and finely
   chopped cucumbers
2 cups plain yogurt
1 clove garlic, finely chopped
   (optional)
¾ tablespoon chopped fresh dill
   weed or ½ teaspoon crushed
   dried dill weed
Salt and freshly ground pepper
   to taste

Seafood

Numbers refer to pages where recipes appear in this book.

Shellfish   130
Easy Souffled Clams   131
Clam Pie   132
Baked Stuffed Lobster   132
Boiled Lobsters   133
Steamed Lobster   133
Broiled Scallops and Bacon   134
Scallop Salad Plate   134
Scallops with Linguine   135
Steamed Mussels   135
Curried Shrimp   136
Shrimp and Mushrooms   136
Scalloped Oysters   137
Pan Fried Oysters   137
Finfish   138
Broiled Fish   139
Pan Fried Fish   139
Steamed Fish   139
Poached Fish   140
Bluefish with Tomato Sauce   140
Baked Stuffed Striped Bass   141
Stuffed Fillet of Flounder   142
Baked Sole or Flounder Fillets   142
Rosy Fish Fillets   143
Codfish Provincetown   143
Cod Boiled Dinner   144
Baked Cod with Vegetables   144
Batter Fried Fish   145
Quick n' Easy Fried Fish   145
Tartar Sauce   145
Haddock with Curried Tomatoes   146
Mustard Broiled Atlantic Mackerel   146

Broiled Pan Dressed Whiting   147
Spaghetti with Fish Sauce   147
Salmon Rice Casserole   148
Tuna Kidney Bean Salad   148

Seafood

We in New England are blessed with an abundance of seafood, both shellfish and finfish. It is both good and good for us, since most seafood is low in calories and cholesterol. A prudent diet suggestion is finfish at least three times a week, preferably cooked in a plain manner.

Shellfish

In our area, the most popular shellfish are lobster, clams, oysters, bay and sea scallops, shrimp, and mussels. Crabs and conch are sometimes available, particularly the crabs which are found in the lobster traps.

Shellfish, like finfish, are fragile and must be bought and stored with great care. Lobsters should be alive and wiggling when purchased, clams and mussels tightly closed. Always purchase shellfish at a reliable source. If you are purchasing any kind of finfish or shellfish that cannot be gotten to your refrigerator within a reasonable time, say an hour, bring along a simple ice chest with ice in it to protect the fish en route.

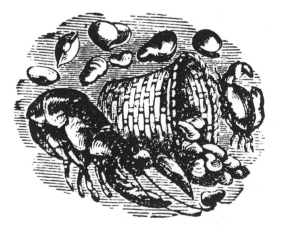

Easy Souffled Clams

If you go clamming and have good luck, it is sometimes hard to think of ways to use the clams other than chowder and fried clams. This recipe is simple to make and very good. Serve sliced tomatoes and lettuce with it and fresh blueberries and cream for dessert.

Put ⅓ of bread crumbs in bottom of a well-buttered 1-quart casserole. Mix clams with onion and spoon in ½ clams. Repeat layers, ending with crumbs. Pour over melted butter and clam juice. Bake at 375° F for 45 minutes. Makes 4 servings.

2 cups soft whole wheat bread crumbs (about 3 slices)
2 cups chopped fresh clams
2 tablespoons grated onion
½ cup melted butter or margarine
1 cup clam juice

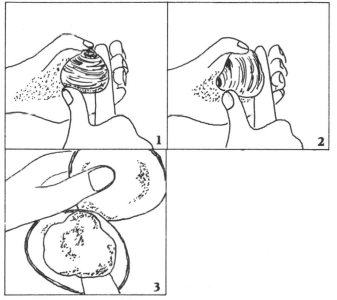

Scrub clam shells to remove mud and dirt. Place clams in the freezer for an hour to relax the muscle that holds the two shells closed. Hold the clam firmly in one hand. Insert the side of the blade of a clam knife next to the hinge. Turning the clam, work the knife around the shell to the opposite side of the hinge. Pry open the shell, scrape the meat from the top shell and slip the knife underneath the meat to release it from the bottom shell.

Clam Pie

Pastry for a 2-crust 9-inch pie
3 cups ground raw quahog or
    sea clams
½ cup finely chopped onion
1 cup fine cracker crumbs
½ cup evaporated milk
¼ teaspoon freshly ground
    pepper
¼ teaspoon dried thyme

Had I not read a clam pie recipe in a national magazine in which the clams were (1) steamed 8–10 minutes to open them; (2) cooked by themselves for 15 minutes; (3) cooked 15 minutes more *with* vegetables *(carrots and potatoes); and finally (4) baked 35 to 40 minutes at 425° F, this recipe might not have appeared. Those poor clams. Okay, so here is mine.*

Line a 9-inch pie plate with pastry. Mix clams, onion, cracker crumbs, evaporated milk, and seasonings. Spoon into pie shell. Cover with pastry and seal edges. Cut several slits in top.

Bake at 425° F for about 50 minutes or until nicely browned. Serve hot or cold. Makes one 9-inch pie.

Baked Stuffed Lobster

2 lobsters, 1½ pounds each
30 round crackers, finely
    crushed (1 cup of cracker
    crumbs)
¼ cup butter, melted
2 teaspoons Worcestershire
    sauce
Lobster liver or tomalley
Additional melted butter
Lemon wedges

Perhaps because the first time I ate lobster on Cape Cod it was a baked stuffed lobster, it is still my favorite way to prepare it at home. This recipe was given to me years ago by a friend who is a native of Massachusetts. I have made it many times with no failures—and that is important since lobster has become a special occasion luxury. This recipe is for 2 lobsters. It is easily multiplied for 4, but the number is qualified by how many you can get into your oven. Eight is my limit.

Ask at the fish market to have lobsters split and cleaned. ("Cleaned" means only that they will take out the stomach, which is near the front feelers.) The liver, a grayish green, goes into the stuffing. Wash the lobsters and place, cut side up, in a baking pan.

Mix crumbs, butter, Worcestershire sauce, and lobster liver until well blended. Divide between body shells. Bake at 400° F for 25 minutes. Serve with additional melted butter and lemon wedges.

Boiled Lobsters

When boiling lobster, it is okay to leave the little wooden pegs in the claws, and if the fish market has used rubber bands to keep the lobster from pinching, leave them on, too. Remove both before serving the lobster.

For each 1½-pound lobster use about 3 quarts water and about 2 tablespoons salt. Many people living near the shore swear by ocean water to use in boiling lobster.

Bring the water to a boil, catch the lobster from behind the head and plunge it into the water. Cover and let simmer about 8 minutes. Remove from water and place lobster on its back on a cutting surface. Use a large heavy knife and a mallet and split the lobster from end to end. Remove the stomach (which is at the claw end), and the intestinal vein. Do not discard either the liver (or tomalley) or, if the lobster is female, the roe, called coral because of its color. They are delicious eating. If desired, the coral can be saved for later use. It freezes well.

Serve the lobster with plenty of melted butter and lemon wedges. Accessories are small forks for picking the lobster out of small crevices, nut crackers for cracking the claws, and lightly dampened guest towels for sticky fingers.

A "bone" plate, platter, or any suitable large container where everyone can reach it is good for parking the shells.

Boiled lobster meat can be chilled to use for any number of lobster dishes as well.

Steamed Lobster

Some prefer to steam rather than boil lobster, so we include the directions for steaming.

Put 2 to 3 inches of water in a pot large enough to hold the lobsters. Bring the water to a boil, put in lobsters, cover, reduce heat and steam as follows:

1 pound	18 minutes
1¼ pounds	20 minutes
1½ pounds	25 minutes
2 to 3 pounds	30 minutes

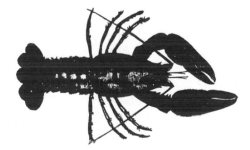

Broiled Scallops and Bacon

1 pound sea scallops, fresh or
frozen and thawed
¼ cup honey
¼ cup soy sauce
¼ cup lemon juice
8 slices bacon
4 cherry tomatoes

New Bedford fishermen bring in sea scallops from George's Bank. When they are plentiful, dip in lemon juice and freeze.

Remove any shell pieces from scallops. Rinse and drain. Mix honey, soy sauce, and lemon juice and marinate scallops in mixture for several hours in the refrigerator. Drain off sauce and reserve. Meanwhile, cook bacon slices over moderate heat about 4 minutes. Remove from fat.

Put scallops and bacon on 4 skewers, stringing bacon around and between scallops. Top each skewer with cherry tomato. Grill about 3 inches from heat for 5 to 7 minutes, basting with sauce and turning to brown all sides. Makes 4 servings.

Scallop Salad Plate

1 pound sea scallops
2 cups dry white wine
2 sprigs parsley
1 small onion, sliced
2 sprigs fresh thyme or ½ teaspoon dried thyme
½ cup oil
2 tablespoons lemon juice
½ teaspoon salt
Freshly ground pepper to taste
Crisp lettuce
Sliced cucumbers
Sliced fresh tomatoes
Mayonnaise

Cold scallops are very good and when marinated in an oil and vinegar sauce, they are delicious. If you like, add deviled eggs to this cold plate. Serve with bread sticks.

Cut sea scallops into 3 or 4 pieces; wash and drain. Combine wine with parsley, onion, and thyme in a skillet. Bring to a boil, cover, and simmer 10 minutes. Add scallops and simmer 3 to 5 minutes. Let cool in liquid. When cooled, drain and mix with oil, lemon juice, salt, and pepper. Chill in refrigerator for several hours.

Drain and arrange on crisp lettuce. Garnish with sliced cucumbers and tomatoes and serve with a bowl of mayonnaise for those who wish it. Makes 4 servings.

Scallops with Linguine

With a tossed green salad, crisp hot bread, and cheese and crackers, a good meal.

If sea scallops are used, cut each in 4 pieces. Wash scallops and dry. Heat butter in skillet and add garlic and salt. Cook until garlic is lightly browned. Add scallops, pepper, basil, and parsley and cook, stirring, about 5 minutes. Serve with hot cooked linguine. Makes 4 servings.

1 pound cape or sea scallops
¼ cup butter or margarine
1 clove garlic, minced
½ teaspoon salt
Freshly ground pepper to taste
1 tablespoon chopped fresh
    basil or 1 teaspoon dried basil
½ cup chopped fresh parsley
1 pound cooked linguine

Steamed Mussels

Mussels have gained new popularity. They are a product of our East Coast waters and as tasty as steamers according to some. Serve with lots of Italian or French bread.

Scrub mussels well with a stiff brush to remove the pieces of eel grass and seaweed which might be attached to them, as well as their own fibrous "beards." Discard any that feel heavy as they are probably filled with dirt. Rinse well.

Put wine, thyme, and parsley in a large saucepan. Add mussels and cover. Bring to a boil and cook 2 to 3 minutes or until mussels are opened. Discard any that do not open.

Serve mussels and broth in flat bowls with melted butter and lemon wedges. Makes 4 servings.

2 quarts mussels
¼ cup dry white wine
2 sprigs fresh thyme or ½ tea-
    spoon dried thyme
2 sprigs parsley
Melted butter or margarine
Lemon wedges

Curried Shrimp

1 pound raw shrimp in shell
4 tablespoons butter or
　margarine
1 clove garlic, finely chopped
1 medium apple, cored, peeled,
　and diced
2½ tablespons flour
1 tablespoon curry powder
½ teaspoon chopped fresh
　ginger root
¼ teaspoon sugar
1⅔ cups chicken broth
Salt and freshly ground pepper
　to taste
2 to 3 cups hot cooked rice

This shrimp is actually better if prepared in advance, refrigerated, and reheated at serving time. Serve chopped peanuts, toasted coconut, chutney, mandarin oranges, and chopped green onions in small bowls. Each person helps themselves to whatever accompaniment they wish.

Peel, devein, and wash shrimp. Drain well.

Heat butter in a 1½-quart saucepan and slowly saute garlic, onion, and apple until tender but not browned, about 10 minutes. Stir in flour, curry powder, ginger root, and sugar and cook for 1 minute.

Slowly stir in chicken broth and continue stirring until mixture boils and is thickened. Taste and add salt and pepper as needed. Add shrimp and cook 3 to 5 minutes. Serve over hot cooked rice. Makes 4 servings.

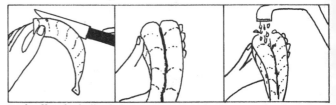

Peel off soft shell of shrimp. Using a sharp paring knife make a shallow cut down the back of the shrimp, exposing the black vein. Hold shrimp under running water to wash the vein away. You may need to use the tip of your knife to scrape the vein away.

Shrimp and Mushrooms

1 pound raw shrimp in shell
¾ pound fresh mushrooms
4 green onions
4 tablespoons butter
1 tablespoon oil
¼ cup chopped fresh parsley
¼ cup dry sherry
½ teaspoon salt
Freshly ground pepper to taste
1 cup plain yogurt
2 cups hot cooked rice

Steamed snow peas would go well with the shrimp and mushrooms. Serve a sherbet for dessert.

Peel, devein, and wash shrimp. Drain well. Rinse mushrooms, if necessary, and cut off stem ends. Slice onions.

Heat butter and oil in a 10-inch skillet and cook onions for several minutes. Add mushrooms and cook and stir about 10 minutes over moderate heat. Add parsley, sherry, salt, and pepper and bring to a boil. Stir in shrimp and cook a few minutes longer until shrimp turns pink. Add plain yogurt and heat, but do not boil. Serve with hot cooked rice. Makes 4 servings.

Scalloped Oysters

Scalloped oysters make a lovely winter supper dish. Serve with noodles, broccoli, and a grape and apple salad.

1 pint fresh oysters
½ cup butter or margarine
1 teaspoon grated onion
  (optional)
Freshly ground pepper to taste
Freshly ground nutmeg to taste
2 cups soft bread crumbs
¼ cup oyster liquor
¼ cup cream

Drain oysters, saving liquor. Take out any shell pieces that might be present.

Melt butter in a saucepan and add onion, pepper, and nutmeg and mix well. Stir in the bread crumbs.

Put half of crumb mixture in a buttered 1-quart flat baking dish. Spread oysters on crumbs and top with remaining crumbs. Mix oyster liquor and cream and pour over all. Bake at 375° F for 30 to 35 minutes. Makes 2 to 4 servings, depending on appetites.

Pan Fried Oysters

If you wish to stretch the pan fried oysters, serve with soft scrambled eggs, toasted English muffins, and lots of coffee, for a brunch or breakfast meal.

1 pint fresh oysters
1 large egg
2 tablespoons light cream
¾ to 1 cup freshly rolled saltine
  cracker crumbs
½ cup (about) butter
Salt
Freshly ground pepper
Lemon wedges

Drain oysters and remove any shell. Beat egg lightly with cream. Dip oysters in egg, then in cracker crumbs. Let air dry on wax paper about 10 minutes.

In a large skillet, melt butter to about ¼ inch deep. When hot, add oysters and cook quickly until nicely browned. Sprinkle with salt and pepper and serve with lemon wedges. Makes 2 to 4 servings depending on appetites.

Finfish

When buying fish remember that fresh fish has no odor. The amount to buy per person depends on the amount of bones and other waste matter in the fish. This guide may help.

Whole	¾ pound
Dressed or pan dressed	½ pound
Fillets or steaks	⅓ pound
Portions	⅓ pound
Canned	⅙ pound

Fish may be purchased fresh, frozen, or canned. **Fresh fish** should have firm flesh, not separating from the bone. Eyes should be bright and clear on a whole fish.

Frozen fish should be adequately wrapped and have been held at 0° F or below while in storage. It should have no odor.

Canned fish includes tuna, salmon, mackerel, and sardines. Tuna comes in "fancy" or solid form, the most expensive, and used where appearance is important, such as on a cold fish plate; chunk, smaller pieces ideal for salads or casseroles; and flaked or grated, great for sandwiches or canapes. Salmon is canned by species. The differences are in color, texture, and flavor. In order of price, the grades are red or sockeye; Chinook or king salmon; medium red, coho, or silver salmon; pink salmon; chum or keta salmon. Mackerel and sardines are each one species.

The basic ways to cook fresh or frozen fish are to bake, broil, pan fry, poach, or steam. I recommend that frozen fish always be thawed before cooking. Let the frozen fish stand in the refrigerator overnight or for 4 to 5 hours, depending on thickness of fish. Thawing can be hastened under cold, running water.

The sign of doneness of fish is when it flakes easily with a fork. Try separating the flesh of raw fish into flakes; it is impossible. But when the fish is cooked, the flesh separates easily; and regardless of the method of cooking, this test will always be true. The cardinal sin in fish cookery is overcooking.

These facts may help you if you are new to purchasing and cooking fish.

Fillets of sole or flounder are interchangeable in recipes. Cod, haddock, pollock, ocean catfish, and hake are interchangeable in recipes. Schrod (or scrod) is young cod or haddock. Bluefish and mackerel can be substituted for each other. When you go into the fish market and see "whitefish" on sale, ask the fish man what kind of fish it is. There is no fish called whitefish, except a small freshwater fish, so varieties of less known fish are sold as whitefish. Often, for example, it is ocean catfish, which is one of my very favorite fish. So then I buy extra and freeze it.

Broiled Fish

Fish cooks so quickly that you should have all the rest of the meal ready before the fish goes in the broiler to cook.

Place fillets, skin side down, on greased broiler pan. Dribble lemon juice generously over fish; spread with softened or melted butter. Sprinkle with bread crumbs. Broil 8 minutes or until fish flakes. Makes 4 servings.

1½ to 2 pounds fillets of cod, haddock, bluefish, mackerel, or flounder
3 to 4 tablespoons lemon juice
2 to 3 tablespoons butter, softened or melted
½ cup plain or seasoned dry bread crumbs

Variation
Omit butter and crumbs. Broil fish for 4 minutes. Spread with ½ cup mayonnaise and broil 4 minutes longer.

Pan Fried Fish

Pan fried fish is still one of the most popular methods of cooking fish. My mother always used bacon fat in which to fry fish. It's very good.

Wash fish and cut in serving size pieces. Beat together milk, egg, and salt. Dip fish in egg and then in crumbs. Let fish air dry 10 or 15 minutes on wax paper. Heat fat (about ⅛ inch deep) in large skillet. Fry fish over moderate heat, turning carefully to brown both sides, about 6 to 8 minutes in all. Makes 4 servings. Serve with lime or lemon wedges.

1½ to 2 pounds skinless, boneless fillets of cod, haddock, pollock, ocean catfish, flounder, or hake
2 tablespoons milk
1 egg
½ teaspoon salt
1 cup dry bread or cracker crumbs or cornmeal
Fat for frying (about ¼ cup)
Lime or lemon wedges

Steamed Fish

Steamed fish can be served as is with parsley butter or used in fish casseroles or salads.

Put the fish in a steamer rack with enough water below it to create a good steam. Cover and bring to a boil and steam fish 5 to 8 minutes depending on thickness.

Poached Fish

2 cups water or dry white wine,
   or 1 cup each
½ lemon, sliced
1 small onion, thinly sliced
½ teaspoon salt
3 peppercorns
2 sprigs parsley
2 pounds fillets or steaks of cod,
   flounder, haddock, or other
   fish

Poaching fish is one of the better ways to cook it, to my mind. The cooked fish can be served with lemon butter and parsley; it can be chilled to make into fish salad; a whole poached fish can be skinned, covered with mayonnaise, and decorated with sliced stuffed olives, parsley, lemon slices, radish slices, or any compatible decoration you choose and be the centerpiece of a buffet supper; or the cooked fish can be flaked and creamed.

Combine liquid, lemon, onion, salt, peppercorns, and parsley in a skillet large enough to hold fish in a single layer. Simmer, covered, 10 minutes. Add fish. Simmer, covered, 5 to 10 minutes depending on thickness of fish. Remove to platter and serve in any way desired. Makes 4 servings.

Bluefish with Tomato Sauce

Bluefish fillets for 4 (about 1½
   to 2 pounds)
2 tablespoons all-purpose flour
½ teaspoon salt
Freshly ground pepper to taste
1 egg, beaten
1 tablespoon water
½ cup seasoned dry bread
   crumbs
¼ cup oil
4 to 5 medium fresh
   mushrooms, sliced
4 whole green onions, chopped
2 ripe tomatoes, peeled and
   diced (about 1½ cups)
2 teaspoons Italian seasoning
Additional seasoned bread
   crumbs
3 tablespoons grated Parmesan
   cheese

You might want to serve spaghetti with butter with the bluefish. Mixed green salad and Italian bread would be good, too.

Wash and dry fillets. Dip in flour which has been mixed with salt and pepper, then in egg beaten with water, and finally in seasoned bread crumbs. Let breaded fillets air dry about 10 minutes on wax paper. Heat oil in a 10-inch skillet and pan fry fillets quickly to brown both sides, 4 to 5 minutes. Place in an oiled flat casserole.

In same skillet, saute mushrooms and green onions for about 5 minutes. Add tomatoes and Italian seasoning and cook until tomatoes are soft and sauce begins to reduce a little. Pour over fish in casserole. Measure any seasoned crumbs left from breading fish and add enough to make ⅓ cup. Sprinkle over tomato sauce. Sprinkle cheese over crumbs. Run dish under broiler and heat until cheese melts and is nicely browned. Makes 4 servings.

Baked Stuffed Striped Bass

The striped bass was here when the Pilgrims arrived and helped keep them going. It's really quite a sight to bake one whole (head and all), but even if you have the head cut off, it's still a beauty to serve.

Wash fish inside and out and pat dry. Sprinkle inside of fish with ½ teaspoon of the salt, and pepper. If you have a bake-and-serve platter, grease it well and place fish on that. If you do not, choose a pan long enough to hold fish, grease well, and lay a double strip of heavy duty foil down the pan so that the ends of the foil extend up over the ends of the pan. (The foil folded in half lengthwise should be a wide enough strip.) Grease foil and place fish on that.

Saute the celery and onion in 4 tablespoons of the butter until tender. Add the remaining salt and all the rest of the ingredients (if egg is used the stuffing is softer and clings together; without egg, it is drier) and mix well. Stuff inside of fish, but put any leftover stuffing in bottom of pan and bake with fish. Spread fish with remaining 2 tablespoons butter. Bake at 350° F for 45 to 55 minutes or until fish flakes easily with a fork. If an aluminum foil strip was used, lift fish by ends of foil and transfer to platter. Carefully remove foil from under fish. To serve, cut fish down to backbone and serve some fish and stuffing. Then turn fish and cut from other side. Makes 4 servings.

1 dressed striped bass (about 3 pounds)
1 teaspoon salt
Freshly ground pepper to taste
½ cup chopped celery
¼ cup chopped onion
6 tablespoons butter or margarine
1 quart dry bread cubes
1 egg, beaten (optional)
½ teaspoon dried rosemary
¼ teaspoon dried thyme

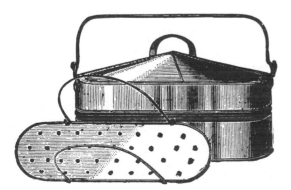

Stuffed Fillet of Flounder

1 small onion, finely chopped
4 tablespoons butter or
    margarine
3 cups soft bread crumbs
3 tablespoons chopped fresh
    parsley
1 can (4 ounces) mushroom
    stems and pieces
1 tablespoon lemon juice
½ teaspoon salt
2 pounds fillet of flounder
Melted butter or margarine

Tastily stuffed flounder fillets are company fare. Serve with a green vegetable, a lettuce and tomato salad, French bread, and chilled pineapple with creme de menthe for dessert.

Saute onion in butter until tender. Mix in crumbs, parsley, the mushrooms and their liquid, lemon juice, and salt, stirring to blend well.

If the fillets are large enough so that 1 makes a serving, pile ¼ of stuffing on half the fillet and fold fillet over stuffing. If smaller, put stuffing on one fillet and top with another. Place on a well-greased baking pan. Brush with melted butter and bake at 400° F for 25 to 30 minutes. Makes 4 servings.

Baked Sole or Flounder Fillets

1 can (10¾ ounces) condensed
    cream of mushroom soup
½ soup can milk
½ cup grated cheddar cheese
1½ pounds fillet of sole or
    flounder
½ cup minced fresh clams or
    mussels
2 tablespoons butter or
    margarine
3 tablespoons lemon juice
Freshly ground pepper to taste
2 hard cooked eggs, chopped
2 tablespoons chopped fresh
    parsley

Baked potatoes put in the oven ahead of the fish and oven-baked broccoli will go well with this casserole; for dessert, fresh fruit.

Combine mushroom soup with milk and cheese and stir over low heat until cheese is melted. Arrange half of fish in a shallow buttered baking dish and scatter half the clams or mussels on top of fish. Add half sauce. Repeat. Dot top with butter, pour over lemon juice, and add pepper to taste.

Bake at 350° F for 20 to 25 minutes or until fish flakes easily. To serve, garnish with chopped hard cooked eggs and parsley. Makes 4 servings.

Rosy Fish Fillets

This unusual combination of two New England products—fish and cranberries—is good as well as pretty. Serve with boiled parslied potatoes, celery slaw, and hot bran muffins.

Thaw fillets, if frozen, and cut into 4 serving size portions. In a 10-inch skillet combine apple juice with celery, onion, bay leaf, peppercorns, and salt. Bring to a boil, cover, and simmer 10 minutes. Add fish and poach about 5 minutes or until fish flakes easily with a fork.

Remove fish carefully to a platter and keep warm. Strain poaching liquid and cook to reduce to 1 cup. Serve fish with cranberry sauce. Makes 4 servings.

Cranberry Sauce: Combine the 1 cup poaching liquid with the cranberries, sugar, lemon juice, and cinnamon. Cook for about 5 minutes or until berries' skins pop. Makes 2 cups. Serve in a bowl with fish.

1½ to 2 pounds fresh or frozen haddock, cod, sole, flounder, or other fish fillets
4 cups apple juice
1 stalk celery, cut up
1 small onion, sliced
1 small bay leaf
4 peppercorns
½ teaspoon salt
Cranberry sauce (recipe below)

Cranberry Sauce

2 cups fresh cranberries
¼ cup sugar
¼ cup lemon juice
¾ teaspoon cinnamon

Codfish Provincetown

The combination of ingredients here makes a fine sauce with the fish. Serve rice baked in the oven with the fish, a lettuce salad, and lots of Portuguese bread.

If frozen codfish is used, thaw. Place fish in a flat buttered casserole. Mix all remaining ingredients except crumbs, and spoon over fish. Sprinkle crumbs on top. Bake at 350° F for 30 minutes or until fish flakes easily. Makes 2 or 3 servings.

1 pound fresh or frozen codfish
2 tablespoons softened butter or margarine
1 clove garlic, finely chopped
1 medium onion, finely chopped
1 medium tomato, peeled and chopped
½ teaspoon salt
½ teaspoon dried tarragon
Freshly ground pepper to taste
¼ cup dry white wine
½ cup bread crumbs

Cod Boiled Dinner

2 pounds cod or haddock fillets
1 cup water
12 small potatoes
6 small onions
6 medium carrots, peeled and
  cut into 1-inch pieces
1 medium cabbage, cut into 6
  wedges
1 teaspoon salt
Water to cover vegetables
½ cup butter or margarine,
  melted
2 tablespoons chopped fresh
  parsley
¼ pound salt pork, diced
2 tablespoons flour
1 cup milk
Freshly ground pepper to taste

A codfish boiled dinner served with plenty of whole wheat bread and butter is delicious. Add grape-nuts pudding (page 270) for dessert and you've a real New England meal.

Steam fillets in cup of water until fish flakes when tested with a fork (about 8 to 10 minutes depending on thickness of fillets). Remove fish from water and keep warm.

Cook potatoes, onions, carrots, cabbage, and salt in water just to cover until done, 15 to 20 minutes. Drain. Toss potatoes with melted butter and parsley.

While vegetables are cooking, make gravy. Fry salt pork slowly until crisp. Remove from pan and reserve. Pour off all but 2 tablespoons fat. Add flour and milk and cook and stir until mixture comes to a boil and is thickened.

To serve: Arrange on each plate a piece of cod, 2 potatoes, 1 onion, some carrots, and 1 wedge of cabbage. Ladle gravy over cod fillet and sprinkle with salt pork. Makes 6 servings.

from Prefix
Confidential Chat Column

Baked Cod with Vegetables

1 green pepper
1 medium onion
1 ripe tomato
1½ pounds cod fillets
½ teaspoon salt
Freshly ground pepper to taste
½ cup tomato juice
2 tablespoons butter or
  margarine
½ teaspoon paprika
1 cup plain yogurt

Serve with steamed cracked wheat and a fresh pineapple salad.

Remove seeds from green pepper and slice. Slice onion and tomato. Place half of vegetable slices in a well-buttered 9×9×2-inch flat casserole. Arrange cod fillets on top of vegetables and sprinkle with salt and pepper. Place remaining vegetables on top of fish, pour over tomato juice, dot with butter, and sprinkle with paprika. Bake at 350° F for 15 to 20 minutes; then cover with yogurt and continue baking until yogurt is heated through. Makes 4 servings.

Batter Fried Fish

Use any white fish fillets except flounder or sole which are too delicate for batter frying. The English use dogfish for fish and chips. You can fry enough frozen French fries to serve 4 in the hot fat before you fry the fish, if you wish. Drain on paper towels and keep hot.

¾ cup all-purpose flour
½ cup flat beer or lemon-lime
    carbonated beverage
2 teaspoons oil
1 egg, separated
1 pound boneless fish fillets
    (cod, haddock, ocean catfish,
    hake)
Oil or fat for frying
Lemon wedges

Mix flour, liquid, and oil. Let stand in refrigerator for several hours. Beat egg yolk and white separately and fold first yolk, then white into flour mixture.

Cut fish fillets into serving pieces and dip in batter. Fry in about 2 inches oil or fat heated to 375° F in an electric skillet or heavy skillet. Turn to brown both sides. Total frying time about 5 minutes. Drain on paper towels. Serve at once with lemon wedges. Makes 4 servings.

Quick n' Easy Fried Fish

If you like to fry fish this way, strain and save oil in a separate container, covered, in the refrigerator. By adding a little new oil each time, it can be reused several times before discarding. (Use cod, haddock, ocean catfish or hake)

1½ to 2 pounds fish fillets about
    ¾ inch thick
Water
½ teaspoon salt
Lemon pepper
1½ cups (about) dry pancake
    mix
Oil or fat for frying
Tartar sauce (recipe below)

Tartar Sauce

1 cup mayonnaise
¼ cup drained pickle relish
1 tablespoon lemon juice

Cut fish into serving size pieces. Dip in cool water. Sprinkle with salt and lemon pepper and roll in dry pancake mix. Heat enough oil or shortening to cover the bottom of a heavy skillet or electric skillet to 1½ to 2 inches in depth to 375° F. Add prepared fish and fry, turning to brown both sides, for a total of 4 to 5 minutes. Drain on paper towels. Serve with tartar sauce. Makes 4 servings.

Tartar Sauce: Mix mayonnaise with drained pickle relish and lemon juice. This makes 1¼ cups. Store unused portion, covered, in the refrigerator.

Haddock with Curried Tomatoes

1½ cups instant rice, uncooked
1½ to 2 pounds haddock fillets
4 tablespoons butter
1 cup chopped onion
½ cup chopped celery
1 cup canned tomatoes
¼ cup lemon juice
¾ teaspoon curry powder
1 teaspoon salt
Freshly ground pepper

Since haddock and cod are related, recipes for either are interchangeable with the other. Buttered green beans and a fruit salad dessert could round out the meal.

Put rice in bottom of a flat casserole (about 6-cup capacity) and arrange haddock fillets on top.

Heat butter in saucepan and cook onion and celery until tender but not browned. If tomatoes are whole, chop and add with juice to onions. Stir in lemon juice, curry powder, salt, and pepper and bring to a boil. Pour over fish and rice. Bake at 350° F for 30 minutes or until fish flakes with a fork. Makes 4 servings.

Mustard Broiled Atlantic Mackerel

1 large mackerel (2 pounds) or
   two 1-pound mackerel,
   dressed
1 tablespoon oil
½ teaspoon salt
4 tablespoons lemon juice
Freshly ground pepper to taste
1 teaspoon prepared mustard
2 tablespoons butter, softened
2 tablespoons chopped fresh
   parsley

This fish is found in the waters off New England and the middle Atlantic Ocean. Mackerel is an oily fish, which if given a good shot of lemon juice, lots of freshly ground pepper, and just a dash of salt is quite good when broiled. It is abundant in June, August, and September and is in fairly good supply in July, October, and November. Its size varies from ½ to 2½ pounds and the flesh is dark. Any recipe that is good for mackerel is good for bluefish and vice versa.

Split fish in middle of back and lay, skin side down, on greased broiler rack.

Mix oil, salt, 2 tablespoons of the lemon juice, and pepper and rub on flesh side of fish. Broil, 4 inches from source of heat, about 5 minutes.

Meanwhile, cream mustard, butter, 2 tablespoons lemon juice, and parsley together. Spread on broiled fish and place under broiler another 2 minutes or until topping is melting and beginning to brown. Makes 4 servings.

Broiled Pan Dressed Whiting

Whiting is a long narrow fish that ranges from ¼ to 4 pounds. It is native to New England and the middle Atlantic Ocean waters. It can be purchased whole, dressed, or as fillets. It is most abundant in June, July, and August and is in fairly good supply in September, October, and November. It is a lean fish, with white flesh and a mild flavor. When in season, it can be frozen for later use. Always thaw before cooking.

2 pounds pan dressed whiting (4 fish about ½ pound each)
3 tablespoons melted butter or oil
3 tablespoons lemon juice
½ teaspoon salt
½ teaspoon paprika
Freshly ground pepper to taste

Clean, wash, and dry fish. Place in a single layer on a well-greased baking pan. Combine remaining ingredients and brush fish inside and out with sauce.

Broil 4 inches from source of heat, 5 to 8 minutes. Turn fish carefully, brush again with sauce and broil about 5 minutes longer or until fish flakes easily with a fork. Pour any sauce in pan over fish to serve. Makes 4 servings.

Spaghetti with Fish Sauce

A nice change from the usual sauce for spaghetti. A green salad and crusty bread will go well with this main dish.

1 pound boneless white fish fillets
1 sprig fresh thyme or ¼ teaspoon dried thyme
3 sprigs fresh parsley
1 cup (about) dry white wine
½ teaspoon salt
Freshly ground pepper to taste
¼ cup oil
1 large clove garlic, finely minced
4 tablespoons chopped fresh parsley
1 tablespoon lemon juice
1 pound thin spaghetti or linguine, cooked al dente

Put fish in a pan that will hold it neatly. Add thyme, parsley sprigs, wine, salt, and pepper. Bring to a boil and simmer about 5 minutes. Cool fish in wine. When cool, remove skin, if any, and break into pieces. Reserve ¼ cup cooking liquid.

Heat oil in a skillet and cook garlic over low heat, stirring, for a minute. Do not brown. Add chopped parsley, lemon juice, and ¼ cup cooking liquid. Add fish to sauce and reheat. Serve over drained spaghetti. Makes 4 servings.

Salmon Rice Casserole

1 can (15½ ounces) salmon*
2 cups cooked rice
1 cup thinly sliced celery
¼ cup chopped fresh parsley
¼ cup sliced pitted ripe olives
½ cup mayonnaise
2 tablespoons French dressing
2 tablespoons lemon juice
½ teaspoon salt
½ cup buttered dry bread
    crumbs

Serve buttered peas and a salad of greens tossed with grapefruit sections with the casserole. For dessert: raspberry sherbet.

Drain salmon and break into large pieces. Remove bones. Mix together rice, celery, parsley, olives, mayonnaise, French dressing, lemon juice, and salt. Add salmon and toss lightly. Spoon into a buttered 6-cup casserole and sprinkle with buttered crumbs. Bake at 400° F for 25 to 30 minutes or until hot through. Makes 4 servings.

* *Chinook or king, medium red, coho or silver, or pink salmon—any would be suitable for this casserole.*

Tuna Kidney Bean Salad

1 can (6½ or 7 ounces) tuna in oil
1 cup cooked kidney beans,
    drained
¼ cup chopped sweet pickle
¼ cup chopped celery
2 tablespoons chopped onion
2 hard cooked eggs, chopped
2 tablespoons pickle liquid
1 teaspoon prepared mustard
½ cup mayonnaise
Salad greens

Buttered whole wheat bread and crisp red radishes, would add to this good salad.

Drain tuna and flake. Combine all ingredients except salad greens, and toss lightly. Chill well. Serve on salad greens. Makes 4 servings.

Meats and Poultry

Numbers refer to pages where recipes appear in this book.

Roasting Meats   152
Roast Beef   152
Roast Pork   152
Roast Leg of Lamb   152
Broiling Meats   153
Beef Pot Roast   154
Company Steak   155
New England Boiled Dinner   155
Meat Balls with Mushrooms and
    Sherry   156
Beef and Noodles Port   156
Beef Casserole Superb   157
Stretch Burgers   157
Beef Patties   158
Eggplant Casserole   158
Family Meat Loaf   159
Gravy   159
White Veal Stew   160
Veal Casserole   160
Chopped Veal Parmigiana   161
Irish Lamb Stew   161
Savory Lamb Chops   162
Lamb and Vegetable Hotpot   162
New England Baked Ham
    Slice   163
Scalloped Potatoes and Ham   163
Ham Steak   164
Curried Ham Dinner   164
Boiled Cured Pork Shoulder
    Dinner   165
Pork Chops with Wine   165
Pork Cutlets   166

Pork Chops and Sauerkraut   166
Stuffed Pork Shoulder   167
Orange Pork Chops   168
Roast Chicken   168
Stuffing for Roast Chicken   169
Fried Chicken   169
Broiled Chicken   169
Coating for Oven Baked
    Chicken   170
Oriental Chicken Casserole   170
Chicken and Vegetable Pie   171
Baked Chicken Pieces
    Piquante   171
Chicken Birds   172
Chicken with Vegetables, Chinese
    Style   173
Cornish Game Hens with Vegetables and
    Rice   173
Turkey Scallopini   174
Turkey Breast with Sour
    Cream   175

Meats and Poultry

One of the ways to keep from having a heart attack over meat prices when you shop is to calculate mentally the cost per serving. Very often, even an expensive prime rib is not so expensive if the number of servings is divided into the price. On the other hand, oxtails at $1.25 a pound are actually costing $2.50 a pound because of the amount of bone. But again, even with 25% fat, the cheaper ground beef is generally less expensive per ounce of meat than the lean with 18% fat. You really have to learn your mathematics to stay ahead of the game, but it is possible.

The oft given advice of planning your menus around markets' weekly specials is still a truism. If you have freezer space for any unused portion, the "family packs" may save money.

Learning to bone and disjoint chickens can save you considerably in the long run. Using every last piece of meat and bone of the purchase is another way of husbanding your money. Some examples: When suet is trimmed from beef cuts, it goes into the suet bag in the freezer for the birds. All bones left from carving meat go into the soup pot bag. Small pieces of cooked meat, if enough, make hash; if not, meat sandwich filling—stretch with hard cooked egg, if necessary. Or heat in leftover or canned gravy and serve over mashed potatoes.

Steaks for the whole family are usually seven-bone chuck. Use seasoned meat tenderizer, as directed, for flavor and more tender meat. And before broiling, spread on a little butter or margarine and a dollop of Worcestershire sauce. You'll be surprised how good they taste. One caution: These steaks usually are thin, so don't broil them more than 8 minutes altogether.

Don't be afraid to ask the meat man for assistance. I've not run into an impolite one yet. That includes such things as having a couple of chops cut off a loin roast, or the hock off a picnic shoulder, or a steak off a cured or fresh ham, to give the purchase auxiliary uses.

Commercial meat stretchers are not nearly as good as ones you can prepare yourself, but much more expensive. It makes more sense to spend the money on more meat, since so-called "helpers" are not inexpensive.

Another thing to avoid is overbuying. Chickens keep a couple of days in the meat keeper and beef three days, likewise pork, but be prepared to wrap and freeze them if they are going to be around much longer. Cured hams and canned hams should be refrigerated. Bacon can be frozen for at least two months and keeps in the refrigerator after the package is opened about a month. Frankfurters don't keep in the refrigerator much longer, but can be frozen.

It is my preference that all meats should be thawed before cooking, preferably in the refrigerator. If you have a microwave oven, follow the defrosting directions given with it.

By thawing meat before it is to be cooked, one has control of the timing of the preparation, whether it is broiling, pot roasting, roasting, or frying.

Roasting Meats

Roasting is cooking meats with dry heat and is a method usually reserved for tender cuts that do not need any aid in tenderizing.

Roast Beef

4- to 6-pound standing rib of beef

Place rib bone side down in a roasting pan. Roast at 300° F for 25 minutes per pound for rare, 30 minutes per pound for medium, and 35 minutes per pound for well done. Allow meat to stand at room temperature for 15 minutes before carving. If using a meat thermometer, place it so it does not touch bone or fat. The temperatures are:

Rare	110°–120° F
Medium	130°–140° F
Well done	150°–160° F

A rolled rib weighing 5 to 7 pounds should be roasted at 300° F, 32 minutes per pound for rare, 38 minutes per pound for medium, and 48 minutes per pound for well done.

Roast Pork

3- to 5-pound center cut loin

Place bone side down in a roasting pan. Roast at 350° F for 30 to 35 minutes per pound. Pork should always be well done. The internal temperature with a meat thermometer should be 170° F. Be certain the thermometer is not touching bone or fat.

Roast Leg of Lamb

3- to 8-pound leg of lamb

Place lamb on rack in roasting pan. Roast at 325° F for 25 minutes per pound for rare, 30 minutes per pound for medium, and 35 minutes per pound for well done. The internal temperature with a meat thermometer should be:

Rare	140° F
Medium	150° F
Well done	170° F

Be certain the thermometer does not touch fat or bone.

Broiling Meats

Before energy prices went sky high, we were always told to preheat the broiler 10 minutes. Now we learn that it is not necessary. For the past 5 years, I've not preheated the broiler—and it works.

Place the meat (steaks or chops) on a greased or oiled broiler rack set over the drip pan to catch any fat. The surface of the meat should be about 3 inches from source of heat.

1-inch steaks	medium	20
	rare	15
1½-inch steaks	medium	30
	rare	25
2-inch steaks	medium	45
	rare	35

If there is ever any question of the steak overcooking (or undercooking) never hesitate to cut into the center to check.

Beef Pot Roast

3 tablespoons flour
1 teaspoon salt
Freshly ground pepper to taste
4 pounds beef bottom round
2 to 3 tablespoons beef
    drippings or butter
1 can (10½ ounces) condensed
    consomme
1 medium onion, cut up
1 carrot, peeled and cut up
2 stalks celery, chopped

Gravy

Liquid from pot roast
3 tablespoons flour
½ cup water
½ cup dry white wine
Salt and freshly ground pepper
    to taste

Pot roast is a great favorite and this recipe is one of the best. A 3- or 4-quart heavy pan with a tight lid will pay for itself over and over again through use in cooking good meat recipes. If you like a smooth gravy, force the cooked vegetables through a sieve or puree them in the food processor before making the gravy. The trivet or rack called for in this recipe is part of its success.

Mix 3 tablespoons flour, salt, and pepper. Rub into beef. Heat drippings or butter in a Dutch oven or casserole large enough to hold meat comfortably. Brown roast on all sides in drippings. Remove meat from pan and pour off excess fat. Put a trivet or rack in bottom of pan and return meat. Add consomme, onion, carrot, and celery and bring to a boil. Cover, reduce heat so liquid will just simmer, and cook about 3 hours or until meat is tender.

Remove meat to a platter and keep hot. Slightly mash vegetables in liquid.

To make gravy: If there seems to be an excess of fat on liquid remove as much as possible. Mix the additional 3 tablespoons flour with ½ cup water until smooth. Add with wine to liquid in pan and cook and stir until mixture boils and is thickened. Taste and season with salt and pepper if needed. Slice beef and serve with gravy. Makes 8 servings.

Company Steak

A 7-bone chuck steak does nicely for this recipe. Put 4 potatoes in to bake the last hour and fifteen minutes, and a casserole of sliced zucchini with butter, salt, and pepper. Heat some rolls—and for dessert, icy cold pears with Camembert cheese.

Put 1 tablespoon oil in bottom of large shallow baking dish which can be covered. Trim excess fat from steak and place in dish. Spread remaining oil over steak and sprinkle with salt, pepper, and garlic.

Spoon tomatoes over steak, crushing with fork. Add mushrooms, oregano, and basil. Cover and bake at 350° F for 1½ hours. Test with fork, and when tender, remove cover, sprinkle with crumbs and bake for 30 minutes longer, uncovered. Makes 4 servings.

2 tablespoons oil
2 pounds (about) bone in chuck
  steak
½ teaspoon salt
Freshly ground pepper to taste
1 large clove garlic, chopped
1 can (14½ ounces) whole
  tomatoes in juice
1 can (4 ounces) mushroom
  stems and pieces
1 teaspoon dried oregano
½ teaspoon dried basil
½ cup seasoned dry bread
  crumbs

New England Boiled Dinner

Real New England corned beef has no saltpeter used in the curing so it cooks grey and not red. Some people prefer turnips to onions, and some stick a clove or two in the onion that cooks with the brisket, so you see there are a number of options.

Wash brisket and put into an 8-quart Dutch oven. Cover with cold water and add the onion. Bring to a boil. Reduce heat and simmer, covered, until meat is tender, 3 to 3½ hours. Remove meat to platter. Add carrots, potatoes, and small onions or turnips. Cook 15 minutes. Trim cabbage and cut into 6 wedges. Add to vegetables and continue cooking 15 minutes longer. Slice corned beef crosswise of the grain and serve 2 slices corned beef with a potato, carrot, onion (or turnip), and cabbage wedge. Always serve mustard, horseradish, and vinegar with a New England boiled dinner. Makes 6 servings with corned beef left over.

1 corned brisket of beef (about 4
  pounds)
Water to cover
1 onion
6 carrots, peeled
6 potatoes, peeled
12 small onions or 6 small
  turnips, peeled
1 medium head cabbage
Prepared mustard
Horseradish
Vinegar

Meat Balls with Mushrooms and Sherry

4 slices bacon, cut up
1 medium onion, chopped
1 clove garlic, chopped
¼ cup dry bread crumbs
1 egg
½ teaspoon salt
1 teaspoon soy sauce
1 pound ground beef
1 can (4 ounces) mushroom
    stems and pieces
1 can (10½ ounces) condensed
    cream of mushroom soup
½ cup dry sherry

To accompany these nicely flavored meat balls, good enough to be a company dish, rice and frenched green beans would be good. For a salad, serve fresh pear and endive salad.

Fry bacon until crisp. Remove from skillet and reserve. Pour off and reserve all but one tablespoon of bacon fat. Saute onion and garlic until tender. Mix with bread crumbs, egg, salt, soy sauce, and ground beef and shape into 12 meat balls. Return 2 tablespoons of bacon fat to skillet and brown meat balls on all sides. As they are browned, transfer to a shallow 6-cup casserole. Heat mushrooms and their liquid, soup, and sherry in skillet, scraping to remove brown crust from bottom. Pour over meat balls in casserole and sprinkle with bacon. Bake at 375° F for 30 minutes. Makes 4 servings.

4 slices bacon, cut up
1 pound stew beef
2 tablespoons flour
1 teaspoon salt
Freshly ground pepper to taste
1 large onion, chopped
1 clove garlic, chopped
    (optional)
1½ cups tawny port
2 cups uncooked fine noodles
1 beef bouillon cube
1 cup water
4 medium carrots, peeled and
    diced
1 cup soft bread crumbs
½ cup diced American process
    cheese

Beef and Noodles Port

With a one-dish meal such as this, serve a green salad and French bread. Apples for dessert could be baked while the beef is cooking.

Pan fry bacon until crisp. Remove from skillet. Coat meat cubes with flour, salt, and pepper and brown in bacon fat. Transfer to a 2-quart casserole. Fry onion and garlic until tender and place in casserole with meat. Add port, noodles, bouillon cube, water, carrots, and bacon and stir gently to mix. Cover and bake at 300° F for 1½ hours. Uncover and sprinkle with bread crumbs and cheese and bake 30 minutes longer. Makes 4 servings.

Beef Casserole Superb

With its delicately balanced herbs this casserole is a great dish. Serve with hot buttered noodles, crusty bread, and hearts of lettuce. It's a good way to make use of your slow cooker and have the meal ready without last minute fuss.

Mix flour with ½ teaspoon salt and freshly ground pepper. Roll meat pieces in flour. Heat butter in skillet and brown meat, transferring to slow cooker as browned. When all meat is browned, heat tomato sauce in skillet and scrape browned crust from bottom. Pour over meat in cooker. Add to cooker the wine, 1 teaspoon salt, Worcestershire, herbs, small onions, and mushrooms. Cover and set on low. Cook for 7 hours. Thirty minutes before end of cooking time add artichokes. Serve with hot buttered noodles. Makes 6 servings.

If you do not have a slow cooker, brown floured meat in butter in a 2-quart Dutch oven over low heat, add tomato sauce, wine, salt, Worcestershire sauce, rosemary, basil, dill, onions, and mushrooms and cook, covered, over low heat for 1½ to 2 hours or until meat is tender. Add artichokes the last 15 minutes of cooking.

¼ cup flour
½ teaspoon salt
Freshly ground pepper to taste
2 pounds boneless stew beef
¼ cup butter or margarine
2 cans (8 ounces each) tomato sauce
1 cup dry red wine
1 teaspoon salt
2 teaspoons Worcestershire sauce
½ teaspoon dried rosemary
1 tablespoon chopped fresh basil or 1 teaspoon dried basil
¼ teaspoon dried dill weed
1 cup small whole onions
2 cups (10 to 12) sliced medium mushrooms
1 jar (6 ounces) marinated artichoke hearts, drained
Hot buttered noodles

Stretch Burgers

If you prefer, these burgers can be broiled. Three inches from source of heat, they take about the same length of time as pan fried. French fries would be good with them.

Combine bread, garlic salt, pepper, Worcestershire, and wine in a bowl and blend well. Add ground beef and lightly mix with bread and seasonings. Shape into 4 patties. Heat butter in skillet and pan fry patties, about 8 minutes for medium, turning to brown both sides. Makes 4 servings.

1 slice white bread, crumbled
½ teaspoon garlic salt
Freshly ground pepper to taste
½ teaspoon Worcestershire sauce
3 tablespoons dry red wine
¾ pound ground beef
1 tablespoon butter or margarine

Beef Patties

⅓ cup uncooked oatmeal
½ cup milk
1 tablespoon soy sauce
½ teaspoon salt
3 tablespoons chopped fresh
    parsley
¾ pound ground beef

Another way to add a tasty stretch to beef. For a quick supper serve these with frozen French Fries heated on top of range, sliced tomatoes, and hard rolls.

Combine oatmeal with milk, soy sauce, salt, and parsley. Let stand a few minutes to absorb milk. Lightly mix in ground beef until well blended. Shape into 4 patties and pan broil over moderate heat, turning to brown both sides, about 4 minutes on each side for medium. Makes 4 servings.

Eggplant Casserole

1 medium eggplant
½ cup (about) butter or
    margarine
¾ pound ground beef
1 teaspoon salt
Freshly ground pepper to taste
½ teaspoon nutmeg
¼ teaspoon cinnamon
2 cloves garlic, chopped
2 medium onions, chopped
2 tomatoes, peeled
Paprika

This eggplant casserole can be prepared in advance, refrigerated, and baked when needed. If refrigerated, add about 10 minutes to the baking time in the recipe. Served with parslied rice, crusty hot bread, and grape and celery salad it would make a tasty meal.

Peel eggplant, cut in half lengthwise, and cut into ½-inch slices. Heat part of butter in a skillet and saute eggplant slices until nicely browned on both sides. Transfer to paper towels to drain, as browned. Add additional butter as needed.

When eggplant is all browned, put ground beef in skillet and cook, stirring, until all red color is gone. Mix salt, pepper, spices, and garlic into beef. Spoon beef from skillet into another dish. Add remaining butter and brown onions lightly.

To assemble casserole: In a buttered flat 5-cup casserole arrange half the eggplant slices. Spoon in meat. Slice tomatoes and arrange on top of meat. Put in remaining eggplant and top it with onions. Sprinkle with paprika. Bake at 350° F for 30 minutes. Makes 4 servings.

Family Meat Loaf

The only outstanding thing about this meat loaf is that it is good. Sweet potatoes and a casserole of sliced carrots and celery can go into the oven to bake at the same time.

Combine onion, bread, egg, Worcestershire sauce, parsley, salt, water, and chili sauce. Mix to blend well. Add to ground beef and mix with a fork or fingers until evenly distributed. Pack lightly into a 9×4-inch loaf pan. Lay bacon slices lengthwise along top. Bake at 350° F for 1 hour. Remove meat loaf to platter. Plenty for 4 with leftovers.

To make gravy: Pour 3 tablespoons of the fat accumulated in the bottom of the pan into a saucepan. Skim off remaining fat and discard. Pour meat loaf juices into a measuring cup and add water to make 2 cups.

Add all-purpose flour to saucepan and stir over moderate heat until bubbly. Gradually add water and juices, stirring, and cook and stir until gravy boils and is thickened.

Taste and if gravy seems to need more flavor, add 1 or 2 beef bouillon cubes. Stir until dissolved. Taste again and add salt and pepper to taste. Makes 2 cups gravy.

Variations

Omit bread and add ½ cup uncooked oatmeal.

Omit bacon and spread top of loaf with additional catsup or chili sauce.

Omit ½ pound of beef and grind or chop ½ pound kielbasa and add to meat loaf.

1 medium onion, chopped
2 slices bread (caraway rye is good), cut up
1 egg
1 teaspoon Worcestershire sauce
2 to 3 sprigs parsley, chopped
1 teaspoon salt
¼ cup water
3 tablespoons chili sauce or catsup
1½ pounds ground beef
2 slices bacon (optional)

Gravy

3 tablespoons fat from meat loaf
Juices from meat loaf
Additional water
3 tablespoons all-purpose flour
1 or 2 beef bouillon cubes (optional)
Salt and freshly ground pepper to taste

White Veal Stew

3 to 4 pounds veal neck bones
   with meat
2 cups water
½ teaspoon salt
6 peppercorns
Good sized sprig of tarragon or
   ½ teaspoon dried tarragon
½ cup dry white wine
Additional water if needed
½ cup frozen small white
   onions
1 medium carrot, peeled and
   diced
2 medium potatoes, peeled and
   cut in half
¾ cup cooked peas, drained
3 tablespoons butter or
   margarine
3 tablespoons flour
Salt and freshly ground pepper
   to taste

Sometimes one exchanges time for money, and making a veal stew from veal neck bones is one of those times. But it is an excellent stew.

The day before you wish to serve the white veal stew, cook neck bones with 2 cups water, ½ teaspoon salt, peppercorns, and tarragon until meat is tender, about 2 hours. Cool enough to handle, then remove meat from bone and cut into dice. Discard bones. Strain liquid. Refrigerate veal and liquid overnight.

Before serving time, measure liquid, add liquid from peas (if any) and wine and if necessary, water to make 2½ cups. Put into a saucepan and cook onions, carrots, and potatoes until tender. Add peas and veal. Cream butter and flour together to make a roux. Add to stew and cook until mixture boils and is thickened, stirring carefully. Taste and add salt and freshly ground pepper, if necessary. Makes 3 to 4 servings.

Veal Casserole

3 tablespoons flour
¾ teaspoon salt
½ teaspoon paprika
¼ teaspoon dried sage
¼ teaspoon dried rosemary
Freshly ground pepper to taste
1½ pounds cubed boneless veal
4 tablespoons butter or
   margarine
2 tablespoons oil
½ cup milk
1 can (10¾ ounces) condensed
   cream of mushroom soup
1 cup soft bread crumbs
¼ cup chopped fresh parsley

Serve green noodles and julienned carrots with this veal.

Mix flour with seasonings and herbs, and coat veal cubes. Heat 2 tablespoons of the butter with the oil in skillet and brown veal. Transfer veal as browned to a buttered 6-cup casserole. Add milk and soup to skillet and cook and stir to scrape brown crust from skillet. Pour over veal in casserole. Melt remaining 2 tablespoons butter and mix with bread crumbs and chopped parsley. Sprinkle over soup and veal. Bake at 350° F 45 to 50 minutes or until veal is tender. Makes 4 servings.

Chopped Veal Parmigiana

One of my friends who is a great cook persuaded me to try the frozen chopped veal, since regular veal is expensive. I did and this recipe resulted. When you eat it, it's obviously chopped veal, but good. The secret is for once not to thaw the meat before cooking.

1 package (16 ounces) frozen chopped veal "steak"
3 tablespoons flour
1 egg
1 tablespoon water
¼ teaspoon salt
Freshly ground pepper to taste
¾ cup plain dry bread crumbs
3 tablespoons grated Parmesan cheese
3 tablespoons oil
1 cup tomato sauce
4 slices mozzarella cheese

Do not thaw veal steaks. Coat all over with flour. Beat egg, water, salt, and pepper together lightly. Dip coated steaks in egg mixture, then in bread crumbs which have been mixed with Parmesan cheese, coating both sides and edges.

Heat oil in a large skillet over high heat and brown veal quickly on both sides. As browned, remove to a greased flat baking pan. Spoon tomato sauce over browned steaks and top each with a slice of mozzarella cheese. Bake at 350° F for 25 to 30 minutes. Makes 4 servings.

Irish Lamb Stew

The late Maura Laverty, of Irish cookery fame, says of Irish Lamb Stew, "the potatoes should be cooked to a pulp." You can make more than one layer of meat and potatoes and onion, if you wish, but always end with potatoes.

3 pounds lamb stew meat with bones or 2 pounds boneless
1 cup frozen small white onions
1 tablespoon chopped fresh parsley
1½ tablespoons chopped fresh thyme or 1½ teaspoons dried thyme
1 teaspoon salt
4 potatoes
Water to cover

Put lamb in a 2½-quart saucepan. Add onions, parsley, thyme, and salt. Peel potatoes, cut in halves, and place on meat and onions. Put in water just barely to cover meat. Bring to a boil, reduce heat, and simmer for about 1½ hours or until meat is tender. Makes 4 servings.

Savory Lamb Chops

4 shoulder lamb chops
¼ cup all-purpose flour
½ teaspoon salt
Freshly ground pepper to taste
1 tablespoon Worcestershire
    sauce
2 tablespoons tomato paste
½ cup plain yogurt
4 tablespoons chopped fresh
    parsley

Serve buttered orzo and steamed broccoli with the chops. Bake pears for dessert while the chops are baking.

Rub chops with flour, salt, and pepper which have been mixed. Place in a buttered flat baking dish. Mix Worcestershire sauce, tomato paste, and yogurt and pour over chops. Bake at 350° F for one hour or until tender. Serve with sauce and sprinkle with chopped parsley. Makes 4 servings.

Lamb and Vegetable Hotpot

1½ pounds lamb cubes
2 large onions, thinly sliced
½ pound green beans, sliced
2 large potatoes, peeled and
    sliced
2 large carrots, peeled and
    sliced
2 ripe tomatoes, peeled and
    sliced
2 large green peppers, seeded
    and cut into strips
1½ teaspoons salt
Freshly ground pepper to taste
½ cup butter or margarine
½ cup hot water

A marvelous combination of lamb and vegetables. Serve with plenty of crusty bread, and cheese for dessert.

Fill a 2½-quart Dutch oven with 2 layers each of meat and vegetables in the order listed, sprinkling with salt and pepper and dotting with butter between the layers. Pour over the hot water. Cover tightly and cook over low heat for about 1¼ hours or until meat and vegetables are tender.

To serve, dig down into the pot so that something of everything is in each serving. Makes 4 servings.

New England Baked Ham Slice

Put sweet potatoes in the oven to bake with the ham. Rolls—heated during the last part of the baking time— and apple salad could finish up the menu.

1 inch-thick center cut ham slice (1½ pounds)
10 cloves
1 tablespoon prepared brown mustard
½ cup white grape juice or apple cider
¼ cup pure maple syrup

Put ham slice into a greased flat casserole and stud fat on edges with cloves. Spread mustard over ham slice. Mix grape juice and maple syrup and pour over ham. Bake at 400° F for about 45 minutes or until ham is browned and bubbly. Serve sliced with pan juices. Makes 4 servings.

Scalloped Potatoes and Ham

A good way to use up a small amount of leftover ham. A canned cranberry, banana, and peanut salad and whole wheat bread and butter are good accompaniments.

3 medium potatoes
Water to cover
1 cup diced cooked ham
2 medium onions, sliced
1 stalk celery, sliced

Cook potatoes in water 20 minutes. When cool enough to handle, peel and slice. Layer potatoes, ham, onions, and celery in a buttered 6-cup casserole.

To make sauce: Melt butter in saucepan and stir in flour, mustard, salt, and pepper. Gradually add milk and cook and stir until mixture boils and is thickened. Pour over food in casserole, digging down with a fork so sauce gets to bottom. Bake, covered, at 350° F for 30 minutes. Uncover, sprinkle with crumbs, and bake 10 minutes longer. Makes 4 servings.

Sauce

2 tablespoons butter or margarine
2 tablespoons flour
½ teaspoon dry mustard
1 teaspoon salt
Freshly ground pepper to taste
1½ cups milk

½ cup buttered dry bread crumbs

Variation

Omit sauce and use 1 can (11 ounces) condensed cheese or condensed cream of mushroom soup diluted with ½ soup can milk.

Ham Steak

1 ham steak, 1½ pounds
3 tablespoons cider vinegar
½ teaspoon dry mustard
2 teaspoons sugar
¼ cup water

The ham cooks quickly, so be ready with the rest of the dinner—which might be French fries, zucchini, and a pineapple salad.

Trim fat from ham and fry the fat slowly in a large skillet at medium heat until skillet is well greased. Remove fried fat. Add ham and cook at medium high heat until nicely browned, turning to brown both sides. Remove ham to platter and add vinegar, mustard, sugar, and water. Cook and stir to remove brown crust from skillet. Pour at once over ham. Makes 4 servings.

Curried Ham Dinner

1 canned ham (about 3 pounds)
4 to 6 canned pear halves with juice
4 to 6 canned peach halves with juice
6 maraschino cherres
½ cup brown sugar
2 teaspoons curry powder
1 can (18 ounces) sweet potatoes, unsweetened
2 large firm bananas

A delightfully easy way to serve up a spectacular meal. With an iced bowl of crisp vegetables, French bread, and a tart sherbet for dessert, it will be one to remember.

Remove fat from ham (and gelatin if it has been refrigerated). Place on a flat baking dish large enough to hold ham, fruit, and potatoes.

Combine pears, peaches, and maraschino cherries in bowl. Pour off ½ cup juice and mix with brown sugar and curry powder.

Bake ham and sweet potatoes at 350° F for 30 minutes, basting often with curry mixture. Place pears and peaches around ham and bake 15 minutes longer, basting often. Peel bananas and cut into quarters. Arrange around ham and bake 5 minutes longer. To serve, slice ham and serve with fruits and potatoes. Makes 4 to 6 servings.

Boiled Cured Pork Shoulder Dinner

A boiled dinner is one of my favorite meals, and very often a cured pork shoulder can be bought at a good price, which makes it an even stronger favorite. I ask the meat man to cut off the hock end and use it for split pea soup (page 112).

Put pork shoulder in a saucepan and cover with cold water. Use a pan in which the shoulder fits neatly so it won't drown in the water. If necessary, turn it from time to time. If you like a more spicy flavor, add an onion with two whole cloves stuck in it. Bring to a boil, reduce heat, and simmer, covered, 2½ to 3 hours or until meat is tender when pierced with a fork.

Remove meat (and onion, if used) from broth and keep warm. Discard onion.

Put potatoes, carrots, and small onions in broth. Cover and boil 15 minutes. Place cabbage wedges on top of vegetables and continue cooking 15 minutes longer or until potatoes and carrots are tender.

If meat has cooled, slice and place slices on top of cabbage long enough to reheat.

Serve with mustard, horseradish, and vinegar. Makes 4 servings, with bone for soup and pieces of meat left over for salad and for sandwiches.

4¾ pounds (about) cured pork shoulder
Water to cover
1 onion stuck with 2 whole cloves (optional)
4 whole potatoes, peeled
4 carrots, peeled and cut in half lengthwise
1 cup small whole onions
4 cabbage wedges
Prepared mustard
Horseradish
Vinegar

Pork Chops with Wine

Mashed sweet potatoes and fried green tomatoes would taste good with these pork chops.

Trim fat from pork chops. Heat oil in a 10-inch skillet and brown chops on both sides. Add remaining ingredients. Cover and cook over low heat for about 45 minutes or until chops are tender. Check occasionally to see that there is enough liquid. If not, add more wine or water. Makes 4 servings.

4 pork chops (about 1 pound in all)
1 tablespoon oil
1 clove garlic, chopped
1 beef bouillon cube
½ teaspoon dried tarragon
½ cup dry sherry

Pork Cutlets

1 pound boneless pork steak
¼ cup flour
1 egg
1 tablespoon water
½ cup plain dry bread crumbs
½ teaspoon poultry seasoning
½ teaspoon salt
Freshly ground pepper to taste
2 tablespoons butter or
    margarine
2 tablespoons oil
1 can (10½ ounces) turkey gravy

Serve pork cutlets with mashed potatoes and a vegetable combination of steamed carrots, celery, and onions. Chilled applesauce would make a nice side dish. Cookies and tea for dessert.

Pound pork steak between two pieces of plastic wrap until very thin, and cut into 4 pieces. Dip in flour. Mix egg with water in a flat pan. Combine bread crumbs with poultry seasoning, salt, and pepper. Dip floured pork in egg and then in crumb mixture. (If you want to do this ahead, pork cutlets can wait as long as 30 minutes before frying.) Heat butter and oil in a large skillet and brown pork over moderately high heat, turning to brown both sides. Remove from skillet and keep hot. Add gravy to skillet, heat quickly to boiling, and serve with cutlets. Makes 4 servings.

Pork Chops and Sauerkraut

4 pork chops
1 tablespoon prepared brown
    mustard
1 small clove garlic, finely
    chopped
1 teaspoon caraway seed
½ teaspoon salt
Freshly ground pepper to taste
1 can (20 ounces) sauerkraut

Buttered noodles and cranberry sauce along with rye bread will round out the menu for these spicy pork chops.

Trim fat from pork chops and fry slowly to grease skillet; when fat is crisp, discard. Mix mustard, garlic, caraway, salt, and pepper and spread on pork chops. Brown in pork fat in skillet over medium heat, about 30 minutes, turning to brown both sides. Pork should be completely cooked. Remove from skillet and quickly heat sauerkraut in same skillet. Serve with pork chops. Makes 4 servings.

Stuffed Pork Shoulder

If you like to make your own soup, it really pays to learn to bone meat; and the bones from a pork shoulder make delicious broth for soup. In any event, this stuffed pork shoulder is a good main dish. Bake sweet potatoes and a casserole of broccoli at the same time.

If you bone the pork shoulder yourself, leave it flat. If it has been boned at market, cut string and unroll.

Saute onion in butter until tender. Add poultry seasoning, salt, and bread crumbs and mix well. Stir in egg. Spread on pork and roll up. Either retie or fasten with skewers.

Place on rack in a pan and roast at 325° F for 2½ to 3 hours or until meat thermometer registers 170° F. Remove meat from oven and let stand 10 minutes. Meanwhile, make gravy.

To make gravy: Stir 2 tablespoons flour into pork's pan juices. Add 1½ cups water and cook and stir until mixture boils. Season to taste. (If gravy does not have enough flavor, add a chicken bouillon cube.)

To serve pork, carefully remove skin and as much fat as possible. Cut crosswise into slices. Makes 6 servings, with leftovers.

4 pounds (about) fresh pork
   shoulder, boned
1 large onion, chopped
¼ cup butter or margarine
1 tablespoon poultry seasoning
½ teaspoon salt
3 cups soft bread crumbs
1 egg, beaten

Gravy

2 tablespoons flour
1½ cups water
Salt and freshly ground pepper
   to taste
1 chicken bouillon cube
   (optional)

Orange Pork Chops

4 pork chops
1 medium onion, chopped
¾ cup orange juice
2 teaspoons grated orange rind
2 tablespoons honey
½ teaspoon salt
Freshly ground pepper to taste

Serve steamed rice, peas and celery, lettuce wedges, and rolls with these perky chops.

Trim fat from pork chops and slowly fry in skillet until there is enough fat in which to brown chops. Remove fat pieces and brown chops on both sides, cooking onion at the same time. Add remaining ingredients and cook, covered, over low heat until chops are tender, about ½ to 1 hour. Serve chops with any juices in pan. Makes 4 servings.

Roast Chicken

1 roasting chicken (about 4 pounds)
1 tablespoon butter or margarine
1 teaspoon dried tarragon
Salt and freshly ground pepper
¼ cup butter or margarine
3 tablespoons fresh lemon juice

An unstuffed chicken cooks more quickly than one which is stuffed. Peel potatoes, cut in half, and roast in the pan with the chicken the last 45 to 50 minutes. Creamed carrots and a fruit salad can be served with the chicken.

Wash and dry chicken. Mix 1 tablespoon butter and tarragon and put inside chicken. Season inside and out with salt and pepper.

Place chicken on rack in roasting pan, breast side down. Melt ¼ cup butter and mix with lemon juice. Brush chicken all over with the mixture. Roast at 350° F for 1 hour, brushing every 15 minutes. Turn chicken breast side up and continue roasting another hour, brushing as before, using pan juices as they accumulate. Chicken should be roasted about 30 minutes per pound. The leg joint should move easily when done; another test for doneness is to prick chicken to see if the juices are running clear and yellow with no trace of pink or red.

Remove chicken, breast side up, to a platter and let stand 15 minutes before carving. Reduce pan juices about ⅓ and serve in a separate dish.

A 4-pound chicken should serve 6.

Stuffing for Roast Chicken

If you prefer to stuff the chicken (some people think it gives the meat a better flavor) this is a good basic recipe.

Heat butter in a large skillet and saute celery and onion until tender, but not browned. Add remaining ingredients and toss over low heat until they are well mixed and bread is lightly toasted. This makes enough stuffing for a 4-pound chicken. Double this recipe for a medium sized turkey.

½ cup butter or margarine
¾ cup chopped celery
¼ cup chopped onion
4 cups soft bread crumbs
½ teaspoon salt
1 teaspoon poultry seasoning
½ teaspoon dried sage

Fried Chicken

This is one way to fry chicken. There are many, but this is a simple recipe which brings out the chicken flavor.

Disjoint chicken. Save bony pieces such as back and neck for soup. (I also cut the third joint off the wings.) Wash chicken pieces and dry. Mix flour, salt, and pepper and dip chicken in mixture. Heat butter and shortening in a large skillet and fry chicken over moderate heat 30 minutes, turning with tongs once or twice. Do not crowd pieces; use 2 skillets, if necessary. Makes 4 servings.

1 broiler-fryer chicken (2½ to 3 pounds)
¼ cup all-purpose flour
½ teaspoon salt
Freshly ground pepper to taste
¼ cup butter or margarine
¼ cup shortening

Broiled Chicken

Chicken quarters or halves are usually broiled. Wash and dry well. Cut off the third joint (wing tip) and place on a greased or oiled broiler rack. Brush your chosen seasoning on chicken. Broil skin side up first. Surface of chicken should be at least 4 inches from source of heat. Broil 15 minutes, turn, and broil 15 minutes on other side.

If broiling pieces, surface of pieces should be 3 inches from source of heat. Brush pieces with butter or marinade and turn frequently. Broil about 20 minutes altogether.

Coating for Oven Baked Chicken

½ cup flour
½ cup very fine dry bread
crumbs
2 tablespoons cornstarch
2 teaspoons sugar
2 teaspoons instant chicken
bouillon granules
½ teaspoon salt
1 teaspoon garlic salt
1 teaspoon dried minced onion
1 teaspoon paprika

A make-your-own coating for chicken which is very good.

Mix all ingredients very well. Store in a covered container. This makes about 1⅓ cups, or enough for two 2½- to 3-pound cut-up chickens.

To use, coat the pieces of a 2½- to 3-pound chicken with 2 to 3 tablespoons oil. Put about ⅔ cup of the coating (half of this recipe) in a plastic bag and add 2 pieces of chicken at a time. Shake to coat. Continue to coat all pieces. Place in a single layer in a greased shallow pan. Bake at 400° F for 20 minutes. Turn and bake 25 minutes longer. Makes 4 servings.

Oriental Chicken Casserole

2 cups diced raw chicken*
1 cup sliced onions
2 tablespoons butter
½ cup bean sprouts
½ cup thinly sliced celery
1 cup peas, fresh or frozen (and
thawed)
½ cup chicken broth (or more if
needed)
1 cup half-and-half
2 tablespoons soy sauce
1 can (3 ounces) chow mein
noodles

Serve with baked rice and pineapple-carrot slaw. Cut chicken from bones and then cook bones and skin with a little water to get the chicken broth called for in the recipe.

Carefully cut chicken from bones. (Do not use skin in casserole; it can be used to make broth.) Saute onions in butter until tender. Combine with chicken, bean sprouts, celery, and peas and mix lightly. Spoon into a buttered 6-cup casserole. Mix broth with half-and-half and soy sauce and pour over casserole. Cover and bake at 350° F for 45 minutes. If dry, add additional chicken broth during cooking. Serve topped with Chinese noodles. Makes 4 servings.

* *1 small broiler or 1½ whole chicken breasts.*

Chicken and Vegetable Pie

A really easy main dish. If canned chicken, chicken broth, and pastry mix are used, it is even easier. It is ever so good, however.

Heat butter in saucepan. Add flour and cook until bubbly. Drain vegetable liquid into measuring cup and add chicken broth so total liquid is 2 cups. Stir liquid into flour mixture and cook and stir until sauce boils and is thickened. Add nutmeg, vegetables, and chicken. Taste and add salt and pepper, if needed. Spoon into a flat 1-quart casserole. Roll pastry to fit and mark into 4 triangles with knife or pastry cutter. Place on chicken mixture. Bake at 425° F for 30 minutes or until crust is lightly browned and filling is bubbly. Makes 4 servings.

3 tablespoons butter or margarine
¼ cup flour
1 can (16 ounces) mixed vegetables
Chicken broth
¼ teaspoon nutmeg
2 cups diced cooked chicken
Salt and freshly ground pepper to taste
Pastry for 1 crust (page 263)

Baked Chicken Pieces Piquante

Put 4 baking potatoes in the oven and a casserole of green beans to cook with the chicken.

Wash and dry chicken pieces. Place in a single layer in a buttered flat pan, skin side down.

Melt butter with sugar and salt. Stir in flour and all remaining ingredients except paprika. Brush half sauce on chicken.

Bake at 375° F for 30 minutes. Turn chicken, spread with remaining sauce and sprinkle with paprika. Continue baking for 15 minutes or until chicken is done. Serve hot. Makes 4 servings.

1½ pounds chicken pieces
¼ cup butter or margarine
1 tablespoon sugar
½ teaspoon salt
1 tablespoon flour
⅓ cup water
2 teaspoons Worcestershire sauce
1½ tablespoons lemon juice
¼ cup vinegar
Dash Tabasco sauce
Paprika

Chicken Birds

8 chicken legs, boned
½ cup chopped mushrooms
¼ cup chopped celery
1 green onion, chopped
2 tablespoons butter or
  margarine
1 cup cooked rice
½ teaspoon salt
Freshly ground pepper to taste
½ teaspoon crushed dried
  tarragon
3 tablespoons butter or
  margarine, softened
½ cup Chablis

It's easier to bone a leg than a breast and these birds are nifty. You might want to try your favorite bread stuffing, too. And cold, they make good picnic fare.

To bone chicken legs, use a sharp knife and cut along one side of chicken from thigh end down. With knife, work around bone to release flesh. Cut loose at bottom.

Put leg meat between two pieces of plastic wrap and flatten with a mallet.

Saute mushrooms, celery, and onion in 2 tablespoons butter until tender. Mix with rice, salt, pepper, and tarragon. Spread a layer of the rice mixture on the flesh side (not skin side) of chicken and roll up. Put seam side down in a buttered casserole. Spread chicken with softened butter and pour Chablis into pan. Bake at 350° F for 1 hour or until chicken is tender and lightly browned. Baste with wine several times during baking. Makes 4 servings.

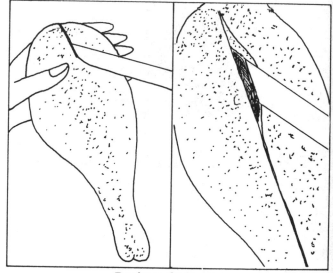

Boning a chicken leg

Chicken with Vegetables, Chinese Style

Whenever you have a stir-fry dish, be sure everything is ready before you start to cook.

Skin chicken, remove meat from bone, and cut into 1-inch dice. (Use skin and bones to make chicken broth.) Mix chicken pieces with cornstarch. Heat oil in a large skillet or wok. Stir fry chicken quickly to brown. Sprinkle with garlic powder. Stir in vegetables. Sprinkle with soy sauce. Cover and cook 5 minutes. Serve over hot cooked rice. Makes 4 servings.

* *3 boneless breast halves could be used instead of thighs. Cut into thin strips.*

8 broiler-fryer chicken thighs*
¼ cup cornstarch
¼ cup oil
⅛ teaspoon garlic powder
1 large ripe tomato cut into chunks
⅓ cup sliced water chestnuts
1 can (4 ounces) sliced mushrooms, drained
1 cup bean sprouts
1 cup coarsely chopped green onion, both green and white
1 cup celery sliced on the bias
¼ cup soy sauce
2 to 3 cups hot cooked rice

Cornish Game Hens with Vegetables and Rice

A meal in itself. Heat garlic bread with hens the last 15 minutes. Serve cranberry sauce, and for dessert fresh or frozen peaches and ice cream.

Split hens in half. Wash and dry. Dice onion; seed and dice pepper. Combine with mushrooms and their liquid, salt, pepper, rosemary, rice, wine, and broth and mix well. Spoon into a buttered flat casserole. Lay hens, skin side up, on top of rice and vegetables. Spread hens with 1 tablespoon of the butter. Bake at 350° F, covered, for 45 minutes. Uncover, brush hens again with additional butter and bake 15 minutes longer. Fluff rice with fork before serving with hens. Makes 4 servings.

2 Cornish game hens (about 1½ pounds each), thawed
1 medium onion
1 small green pepper
1 can (4 ounces) sliced mushrooms
1 teaspoon salt
Freshly ground pepper to taste
½ teaspoon dried rosemary
¾ cup uncooked rice
¾ cup dry white wine
¾ cup chicken broth
2 tablespoons butter or margarine, softened

Turkey Scallopini*

4 turkey scallopini (about ¾
    pound altogether)
Salt and freshly ground pepper
    to taste
3 tablespoons (about) flour
1 egg, beaten
1 tablespoon water
1 cup (about) dry bread crumbs
2 tablespoons oil
4 tablespoons butter or
    margarine
1 tablespoon lemon juice
¼ cup dry white wine

Occasionally one can buy turkey already cut for scallopini. If you cannot, with a sharp knife, cut thin slices on the bias from a skinless, boneless raw turkey breast. A 1½-pound turkey breast will cut into about 8 scallopini slices. If this is too many, separate each with plastic wrap, overwrap, seal, date, and freeze. They will keep 6 months at 0° F. Or cut off the number of scallopini needed and braise the remainder for turkey salad the next day.

Place scallopini between pieces of wax paper or plastic wrap and flatten with a mallet until thin, but do not break the flesh. Season to taste with salt and pepper and dip in flour. Mix egg with water and dip floured scallopini in egg mixture and then in crumbs, coating both sides well. Let air dry on paper 10 minutes.

Heat oil and butter in a large skillet and quickly saute breaded scallopini on both sides to brown nicely. Remove to platter and keep warm as they are browned. When all are browned, pour off most of fat in skillet, add lemon juice and wine, and swirl in skillet until hot. Pour over scallopini to serve. Makes 4 servings.

Scallopini slices can also be made from boneless chicken breast. Both turkey and chicken breast cut more easily if allowed to stand in freezer one hour. Cut chicken down side of breast. Pieces will not be as large as turkey, but handle in the same manner.

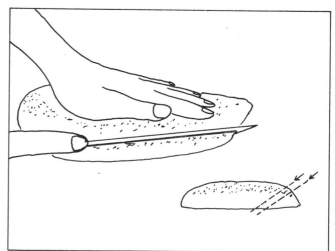

Hold turkey breast flat on cutting surface. With a sharp knife, cut slices on a bias.

Turkey Breast with Sour Cream

Brown rice, green beans amandine, grapefruit and cranberry sauce salad, and a meringue pie shell (page 264) filled with ice cream make up a special menu built around this turkey.

Bone and remove skin from turkey. Cut turkey meat into 6 equal pieces. Saute onion in butter until tender. Add soup, mushrooms with their liquid, wine, and herbs and seasonings. Stir to blend.

Place turkey pieces in a flat buttered casserole and cover with soup mixture. Bake, covered, at 325° F for 60 minutes. Remove cover, gently stir in sour cream, sprinkle with paprika, and bake 20 minutes longer. Makes 6 servings.

1 turkey breast (about 3 pounds)
2 tablespoons butter or margarine
1 can (10¾ ounces) condensed cream of mushroom soup
1 can (3 ounces) sliced mushrooms
½ cup dry white wine
¼ teaspoon dried oregano
¼ teaspoon dried rosemary
Freshly ground pepper to taste
1 cup dairy sour cream
Paprika

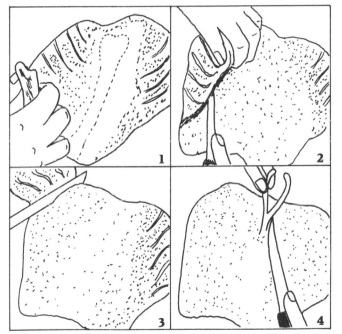

Place turkey breast skin side down. Cut along both sides of breast bone to loosen it. Pull up on the breast bone to remove. Work your knife underneath the rib bones on one side while pulling up on them. Cut rib bones off at outside edge. Repeat on other side. Remove wish bone near center of breast. Turn breast over and pull skin off with your fingers.

Dried Legumes and Cereals

Numbers refer to pages where recipes appear in this book.

Dried Legumes (Beans)   178
Cooking Time & Yields for Beans   179
Boston Baked Beans   179
Baked Rice and Beans   180
Baked Beans with No Molasses   180
Chick Pea and Vegetable Stew   181
Netta's Southern Baked Beans   181
Refried Beans   182
Bean Tostados   182
Soybean Casserole   183
Lentil and Tomato Salad   183
Barley with Lentils   184
Lentil Curry   184
Baby Lima Beans in Tomato Sauce   185
Split Peas with Lamb Chops   185
Cannellini with Tomatoes   186
Cereals   187
Cooking Time & Yields for Grains   187
Homemade Tomato Soup   188
Sweet Rice   188
Fried Rice   189
Bulgur Pilaf   189
Brown Rice Medley   189
Rice Pilaf   190
Mideast Salad Appetizer   190
Spoon Bread   191

Dried Legumes and Cereals

These thrifty products are ages old in usage. They offer variety in taste, combine well with any number of other foods, and are an excellent buy nutritionally.

Dried Legumes (Beans)

In this category you will find a great variety of beans, some carried in the supermarket, others at specialty food stores. They include beans such as navy beans, also known as California or Michigan pea beans; red kidney beans; pinto beans; black turtle or just plain black beans; cranberry beans; lima and baby lima beans; pinto beans; blackeye beans, also known as black-eyed peas; garbanzo beans, also called chick peas; Great Northern (a larger variety of navy beans); red beans; soybeans; white kidney beans, also known as cannellini; green or yellow split peas; and lentils.

After purchasing, the dried beans will keep almost indefinitely in a tightly covered container in a dry place.

If buying canned beans, keep them in a cool place (below 70° F) and mark date of purchase on can in order to use first, just as you would with any canned product.

Cooked beans should be stored in refrigerator, covered; they will keep four to five days. Cooked beans can also be frozen in a covered, vapor proof container, as long as six months.

With the exception of split peas and lentils, dried beans should be soaked before cooking to restore water lost in drying. There is a long soak method and a quick soak.

Long soak method: To 1 pound dry beans add 6 cups water and 2 teaspoons salt. Let stand overnight. Drain. Beans soaked this way cook more quickly and retain their shape better. A rule of thumb is to use 2 to 3 cups water for each 1 cup beans.

Quick soak: To 1 pound dry beans add 6 to 8 cups hot water. Bring to a boil, cover, and cook 2 minutes. Remove from heat and let stand an hour or so. Drain, then cook.

To cook 1 pound soaked beans, place in a large saucepan. Cover with 6 cups hot water. Simmer with the lid tilted until beans are tender. Add additional hot water if needed. Test beans frequently during cooking. They are done when fork tender. One pound dry navy beans equals 6 cups cooked. As a rule of thumb, 1 cup dry beans equals 2 to 3 cups cooked beans.

Cooking Time & Yields For Beans *(based on pre soak)*			
1 Cup Dry Measure	**Water**	**Cooking Time**	**Yield**
Black beans (turtle beans)	4 cups	1½ hours	2 cups
Black-eyed peas	3 cups	½ hour	2 cups
Chick peas (garbanzo)	4 cups	2 hours	2 cups
Great Northern beans	3½ cups	1½ hours	2 cups
Kidney beans	3 cups	1½ hours	2¼ cups
Lentils & split peas	3 cups	¾ hour	2¼ cups
Limas	2 cups	1 hour	1¼ cups
Baby limas	2 cups	1 hour	1¾ cups
Pea beans	3 cups	1½ hours	2 cups
Pinto beans	3 cups	2 hours	2 cups
Red beans	3 cups	3 hours	2 cups
Soybeans	4 cups	3 hours or longer	2 cups

Boston Baked Beans

This recipe comes from Boston's Durgin-Park restaurant. I have made these baked beans many times and they are delicious. If this quantity is too much for your family, baked beans freeze nicely in covered containers. Thaw completely before heating.

1 pound dried pea (navy) beans
12 cups cold water
2 teaspoons salt
½ pound salt pork
1 medium whole onion
4 tablespoons brown sugar
⅓ cup molasses
1 teaspoon dry mustard
½ teaspoon salt
¼ teaspoon freshly ground pepper
2 cups boiling water, or more if needed

Sort beans to remove any stones or dirt. Wash. Soak beans overnight in 6 cups cold water to which 2 teaspoons salt have been added. In the morning drain. Add about 6 cups water, bring to boil, and parboil 10 minutes.

Drain in a colander and rinse well with cold water. Cut piece of salt pork in half through its rind and cut each half into 1-inch squares. Put onion and half of the salt pork in bottom of a 2-quart bean pot. Spoon in beans. Mix sugar, molasses, dry mustard, ½ teaspoon salt, and pepper with the 2 cups boiling water. Pour over beans. Press remaining salt pork into beans. If necessary, add additional boiling water to make liquid come just to top of beans. Bake in a 300° F oven for 5 hours, adding water as necessary. Makes 1½ quarts.

Baked Rice and Beans

3 slices bacon, cut in half
½ cup chopped onion
6 tablespoons catsup
2 tablespoons brown sugar
1 teaspoon Dijon mustard
½ teaspoon salt
Freshly ground pepper to taste
1½ cups cooked rice
1 can (15 ounces) pinto beans

Sauteed cherry tomatoes, spinach salad, and rye bread could finish the menu.

In a 10-inch skillet, cook bacon until about half done. Remove bacon. Add onions to skillet and cook until soft but not browned. Mix in remaining ingredients. Spoon into a buttered 6-cup casserole. Arrange bacon strips on top. Bake, uncovered, at 350° F for 30 to 35 minutes. Makes 4 servings.

Baked Beans with No Molasses

1 cup dried pea (navy) beans
Water to cover
1 medium onion, chopped fine
1 teaspoon salt
1 teaspoon dry mustard
½ box (1 firmly packed cup) dark brown sugar
¼ pound salt pork scored on one side
½ cup catsup

Beanpot Barbie sent this recipe in to Chatters at the request of Hoppy.

Wash and sort beans. Soak overnight in water to cover. In the morning, drain and add fresh water. Cover and simmer until soft, about 30 to 40 minutes. Pour into a 1-quart bean pot; add just enough water to cover beans; then stir in all the remaining ingredients. Cover and bake at 300° F for 5 to 7 hours. Uncover the last hour to let liquid thicken. If you have a crockery slow cooker, cook on low for about 8 hours. Makes 8 servings.

from Beanpot Barbie
Confidential Chat Column

Chick Pea and Vegetable Stew

Served with a tossed green salad and whole wheat French bread, this skillet dinner is good fare.

Heat oil in a 3-quart Dutch oven and fry onions until soft. Drain chick peas and add with the garlic to the onions. Fry until garlic is lightly colored. Add potatoes and fry, turning, until they are lightly browned. Mix in the tomatoes. Mix Italian seasoning, tomato paste, salt, and pepper in 2 cups hot water. Add to food in Dutch oven. Bring to a boil and simmer gently, covered, until potatoes are soft, about 20 minutes. Stir from bottom occasionally and add additional hot water, if necessary, just to cover. Makes 4 servings.

* To use dried chick peas soak 1 cup overnight and cook as directed until tender.

¼ cup oil
2 medium onions, thickly sliced
1 can (20 ounces) chick peas (garbanzos)
2 cloves garlic, sliced
3 medium potatoes, peeled and thinly sliced
2 large ripe tomatoes, peeled and coarsely chopped
1 teaspoon Italian seasoning
1½ tablespoons tomato paste
½ teaspoon salt
Freshly ground pepper to taste
2 cups hot water, or more if needed

Netta's Southern Baked Beans

This version of baked beans is a real man-pleaser. Prepare in advance, refrigerate, and bake when needed.

Seed and chop green pepper. Chop onion; peel and chop tomato. Mix pepper, mustard, and paprika with corn syrup, Worcestershire sauce, and bacon fat. Combine all ingredients with beans and spoon into a buttered 6-cup casserole. Bake at 300° F for 1 hour. Makes 4 to 6 servings.

1 small green pepper
1 small onion
1 fresh tomato
½ teaspoon each freshly ground pepper, dry mustard, and paprika
1½ tablespoons dark corn syrup
1 tablespoon Worcestershire sauce
1½ tablespoons bacon fat
1 can (28 ounces) pork and beans

Refried Beans

1 pound dried pinto beans
6 cups water
2 teaspoons salt
1½ cups chopped onion
2 cloves garlic, crushed
½ cup bacon drippings, lard, or oil
Salt to taste

You can make your own refried beans, as here, or buy them canned. Either way they make a delicious addition to a tortilla, as you will see in Bean Tostados.

Wash and sort beans. Soak overnight in 6 cups water and 2 teaspoons salt. Drain, wash, and simmer in water to cover, about 2½ hours, until fork tender. Drain, saving ¾ cup cooking liquid.

In a large skillet, cook onion and garlic in bacon drippings until tender, but not browned. Add beans and the reserved cooking liquid. Mash beans with potato masher until beans and fat form a creamy liquid. (Beans and reserved cooking liquid can be pureed in a blender or food processor and then added to onion-garlic mixture.) Cook over low heat for 10 minutes, stirring often. Serve as a side dish or use as a filling for Bean Tostados. Makes 4 cups. Will store, covered, in refrigerator for several days.

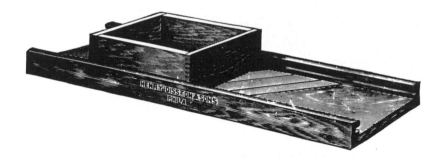

Bean Tostados

12 6-inch tostados or tortillas, fried crisp and flat
4 cups refried beans or 2 cans (15 ounces each) refried beans
3 cups shredded cheddar or Monterey jack cheese
1 cup shredded iceberg lettuce
1 large tomato, peeled and chopped
1 medium avocado, peeled and cut into 12 wedges
Tabasco sauce

Mexican food has a well-deserved popularity. Try this American version of bean tostados for supper.

On 2 cookie sheets, arrange tostados in a single layer. Spoon ⅓ cup refried beans on each tostado. Sprinkle with cheese and bake at 350° F for 10 minutes or until cheese is melted. Top each tostado with lettuce, tomato, and avocado. Serve immediately. Makes 6 servings.

Soybean Casserole

Soybeans take a lot of cooking but they are good. A carrot slaw and whole wheat bread would taste good with the beans, with cheese for dessert to help the protein.

½ pound dried soybeans
3 cups water
1 teaspoon salt
3 tablespoons finely minced chutney, preferably mango
1 can (6 ounces) tomato paste
1½ teaspoons prepared mustard
16 frozen small white onions
3 tablespoons molasses

Wash and sort soybeans. Cover with 3 cups water and salt and soak overnight. In the morning, pour off the soaking water and cover with water to about 2 inches above the beans. Heat to boiling and simmer 3 to 4 hours or until beans are tender. Drain, reserving 2 cups of the liquid. Mix the chutney, tomato paste, mustard, onions, and molasses with the reserved liquid. Simmer with the beans until the sauce has slightly thickened. Spoon into a 1-quart bean pot or casserole and bake at 325° F for 1½ hours. Makes 4 servings.

Lentil and Tomato Salad

Hot pita bread and butter would complement this salad, and orange sherbet with creme de menthe would be fine for dessert.

1 large Spanish onion, finely chopped
2 tablespoons oil
1 clove garlic, finely chopped
1 bay leaf
5 cups water
½ pound dried lentils, washed
2 tablespoons lemon juice
¼ cup oil
1 teaspoon salt
1 teaspoon Dijon mustard
Freshly ground pepper to taste
1 medium tomato, chopped
½ green pepper, seeded and chopped
1 medium tomato, sliced
2 tablespoons chopped fresh parsley

In a 2-quart saucepan, saute onion in 2 tablespoons oil until tender but not brown. Add garlic, bay leaf, water, and lentils and simmer, covered, until lentils are tender but not mushy, 35 to 40 minutes. Drain and remove bay leaf.

Mix together lemon juice, ¼ cup oil, salt, mustard, and pepper. Mix with drained warm lentils and chill. When ready to serve, mix in chopped tomatoes and green peppers.

Put in a bowl and garnish top with sliced tomatoes and chopped parsley. Makes 4 servings.

Barley with Lentils

¼ cup butter or margarine
¾ cup chopped celery
1 cup chopped onion
4 cups water
¾ cup dried lentils, washed
2 cans (1 pound each) tomatoes
    in puree
¾ cup barley
½ teaspoon dried basil
1½ teaspoons salt
Freshly ground pepper to taste
½ teaspoon garlic salt
½ cup shredded zucchini

A very filling dish which combines a popular legume and cereal. Serve whole wheat bread, and fruit for dessert.

Heat butter in a 3-quart Dutch oven and saute celery and onion until tender but not browned. Add water and lentils and simmer, covered, for 20 minutes. Add tomatoes, barley, basil, and seasonings and simmer, covered, for about an hour. Stir often and add additional water if needed. Add zucchini and cook 5 minutes longer. Makes 6 servings.

Lentil Curry

½ pound dried lentils
4 cups water
3 tablespoons butter or
    margarine
2 medium onions, chopped
1 tart cooking apple, peeled,
    cored, and diced
1 tablespoon flour
1 tablespoon curry powder
1 teaspoon sugar
½ teaspoon salt
Freshly ground pepper to taste
1 teaspoon apricot jam
2 teaspoons lemon juice
2 cups hot cooked rice

Serve with cherry tomatoes, celery sticks, chopped peanuts, and whole wheat rolls. For dessert, broiled canned peaches with sour cream.

Wash lentils and soak in water for 6 hours. Simmer them in the soaking water until just soft and still whole, about 20 minutes. Heat butter and fry onions and apple until just soft. Stir in flour and curry powder. Add lentils and liquid, sugar, salt, pepper, apricot jam, and lemon juice, and cook 10 minutes longer. Serve at once over rice. Makes 4 servings.

Baby Lima Beans in Tomato Sauce

This dish could be a main course; with it you might serve broccoli and a Waldorf salad. The salad could double for dessert.

Wash and sort lima beans and soak overnight in 6 cups of water with salt. Drain. Cover with water about 1 inch over beans and simmer, covered, about 1 hour, until tender. Drain.

Fry bacon until crisp. Remove from skillet and drain on paper towels. Add all remaining ingredients, including beans, to pan and simmer about 25 minutes or until thickened. Serve sprinkled with bacon. Makes 4 servings.

2 cups dried baby lima beans*
6 cups water
1 teaspoon salt
3 slices bacon, finely chopped
1 can (1 pound) tomatoes
½ green pepper, chopped
¼ cup firmly packed brown sugar
¼ cup chopped onion
¼ teaspoon chili powder, or to taste
1 tablespoon vinegar

* If dried baby lima beans are not available, use regular dried limas.

Split Peas with Lamb Chops

You might want to bake some apples for dessert while the chops are baking. A bowl of crisp celery and radishes in lieu of salad and rye bread and butter go with the main dish.

Sort and wash split peas. Combine with water, salt, pepper, onion, carrots, and rosemary in a saucepan. Cover and simmer 15 minutes. Spoon into a buttered flat casserole.

Trim fat from chops and dredge chops in flour. Heat butter in skillet and brown chops on either side. Place chops on top of peas and bake at 350° F for 45 minutes or until chops are tender. Makes 4 servings.

1½ cups dried split peas
4 cups water
½ teaspoon salt
Freshly ground pepper to taste
1 medium onion, sliced
4 medium carrots, peeled and sliced
½ teaspoon dried rosemary
4 shoulder lamb chops
3 tablespoons flour
2 tablespoons butter or margarine

Cannellini with Tomatoes

2 cans (20 ounces each)
  cannellini (white kidney
  beans)*
2 medium tomatoes, peeled
1½ tablespoons chopped fresh
  basil or 1½ teaspoons dried
1 medium onion, chopped
2 tablespoons olive oil
Salt and freshly ground pepper
  to taste

Serve these delicious beans with almost any dinner. They are truly good.

Drain beans. Chop tomatoes and combine with basil, onion, and olive oil in a saucepan. Cook over low heat, stirring, until tomatoes are slightly cooked. Add beans and mix lightly. Heat until beans are hot. Makes 4 to 6 servings.

* *If you can purchase dried cannellini beans, about 1½ cups dry beans, soaked and cooked, are needed.*

Cereals

All important civilizations were founded on the cultivation and use of one or another of the cereal grains. The Mideast cultivated wheat, barley, and millet. The ancient cultures of the Orient were based on rice. The Inca, Maya, and Aztec civilizations depended on corn.

Cultivation of cereal grains began so long ago that its early history is lost. But we do know that cereals have been man's most important food plants since the dawn of history.

They include rice, wheat, oats, barley, corn, rye, sorghum grain, and millet. Whole grains are concentrated sources of needed nutrients.

We buy them in varying forms, such as cracked wheat or bulgur, oatmeal, cornmeal, rye flour, and many other products. Rice probably comes in as many variations at the consumer level as any of the cereals: white milled rice, brown rice, converted rice, parboiled or instant rice, and innumerable combinations of rice and seasoning, some dried, some frozen, and some in cans.

Brown rice is particularly popular because it retains the bran layer which gives it a nutlike flavor and higher nutritive value.

Oatmeal, long a popular cereal and ingredient for everything from meat loaf to cookies, can be ground in a blender or food processor for 1 minute to make oat flour, which has all the nutrition of oatmeal. It takes 1½ cups uncooked quick or old fashioned oatmeal to make 1¼ cups oat flour. Oat flour can be substituted for white flour spoon for spoon as a thickening agent in sauces and gravies.

Cereals are sources of protein, but not complete protein; so without some other protein to balance, they should not be considered a substitute for meat. Small amounts of cheese, eggs, fish, or meat can complete the protein cycle of cereals. Or cereal-legume combinations such as lentils and barley or brown rice, or split peas with cracked wheat or bulgur, will be suitable substitutes for meat.

Whatever natural cereals you choose will add interest to the menu and be healthful.

Cooking Time & Yields for Grains

1 Cup Dry Measure	Water	Cooking Time	Yield
Barley	3 cups	1¼ hour	3½ cups
Brown rice	2 cups	1 hour	3 cups
Buckwheat	2 cups	15 minutes	2½ cups
Bulgur wheat	2 cups	15–20 minutes	2½ cups
Cracked wheat	2 cups	25 minutes	2⅓ cups

For milled, converted, parboiled, or instant rice, follow directions on package. Generally rice doubles in quantity in cooking.

Homemade Tomato Soup

5 tablespoons chopped onion
2 tablespoons butter or
    margarine
3 tablespoons ground oat flour*
¼ teaspoon salt
2¼ cups milk
1 can (16 ounces) whole
    tomatoes, undrained
1 can (15 ounces) tomato puree
1 teaspoon sugar
1 bay leaf

Until you make homemade tomato soup, you've forgotten how good it tastes. Serve it with a grilled cheese sandwich and a tossed green salad.

Saute onion in butter in a 3½-quart Dutch oven or saucepan until tender. Blend in oat flour, and salt. Remove from heat. Gradually stir in milk, tomatoes, and puree. Add sugar and bay leaf. Break up tomatoes with a wooden spoon. Cook over medium heat, stirring occasionally, until thickened. Remove bay leaf to serve. Makes 6 cups. If soup becomes too thick on standing, add additional milk.

*About 5 tablespoons uncooked oatmeal ground in the blender for about a minute should make 3 tablespoons oat flour for the soup. If you make a larger amount of oat flour, store unused portion in a tightly covered container in a cool place up to 6 months.

Sweet Rice

1 cup uncooked rice
3½ cups milk
½ teaspoon salt
5 tablespoons butter or
    margarine
¼ cup raisins
¾ cup chopped dates
½ teaspoon almond extract

Rice is such a versatile grain that it works equally well for main dishes, salads, or desserts. If you prefer to chill this dessert, you may.

Combine rice, milk, salt, and 2 tablespoons of the butter in a 2-quart saucepan. Bring to a boil. Stir once. Cover and cook over low heat until milk has been absorbed, about 50 minutes, stirring occasionally. Heat 3 tablespoons butter in a skillet and saute raisins and dates for a few minutes. Stir into rice with almond extract. Serve warm with additional milk, if desired. Makes 4 servings.

Fried Rice

Fried rice makes a good accompaniment to almost any meat or chicken or fish. Keep the ingredients on hand as it is a favorite.

1 egg, lightly beaten
1 tablespoon butter or
  margarine
3 slices bacon
3 tablepoons chopped onion
2 cups cooked rice
1½ tablespoons soy sauce
Salt and freshly ground pepper
  to taste
3 tablespoons thinly sliced
  green onions

Scramble egg in butter and reserve. Fry bacon until crisp and reserve. In fat in pan, fry chopped onions until tender but not browned. Add rice to onions and fry until lightly brown. Add seasonings and green onion and mix well. Crumble bacon and slice egg into thin slices and lightly stir both into rice. Makes 4 servings.

Bulgur Pilaf

Pilaf made from cracked wheat or bulgur fits nicely into menu including lamb or chicken.

2 tablespoons oil
1 small onion, chopped
1 cup cracked wheat or bulgur
½ teaspoon salt
2 cups chicken broth

Heat oil in a 1-quart saucepan and saute onion nd cracked wheat until onion is tender and wheat ghtly browned. Add salt and broth and simmer, overed, 20 to 25 minutes or until broth is ab- orbed. Makes about 2½ cups or 4 servings.

Brown Rice Medley

A rice dish nice for a buffet table.

2 medium carrots
3 tablespoons oil
¾ cup sliced green onions
2 cups sliced, cored unpeeled
  apples
2 cups cooked brown rice
½ teaspoon salt
⅓ cup raisins
1 tablespoon sesame seeds

Peel and thinly slice carrots. Saute in oil, stirring, or about 10 minutes. Add onions and apples and ontinue cooking 10 minutes. Add rice, salt, and aisins and cook and stir until rice is hot. Lightly nix in sesame seeds. Makes 4 servings.

Rice Pilaf

Rice pilaf is good with lamb or chicken.

1 cup rice
1 medium onion, chopped
3 tablespoons oil
2 ripe tomatoes, peeled and
    diced
2 cups water
2 beef bouillon cubes
Salt and freshly ground pepper
    to taste

Cook rice and onion in oil until rice is lightly browned, about 10 minutes, stirring constantly. Add all remaining ingredients and simmer, covered, over low heat about 20 minutes or until all liquid is absorbed. Let stand, covered, another 20 minutes over very low heat until rice is dry and fluffy. Stir from bottom 2 or 3 times with a fork. Makes 4 to 6 servings.

Mideast Salad Appetizer

Serve as an appetizer to a meal that might include roast lamb, assorted vegetables, and whole wheat rolls.

1 cup cracked wheat or bulgur
Cold water
1½ cups chopped fresh parsley
½ cup chopped fresh mint
    leaves
¾ cup chopped green onion
2 ripe tomatoes, peeled and
    chopped
½ cup lemon juice
¼ cup olive oil
1 teaspoon salt
Freshly ground pepper to taste
Romaine lettuce

Combine cracked wheat with cold water to cover and let stand 1 to 2 hours. Drain and press out all liquid possible.

Mix lightly with parsley, mint, green onion, tomatoes, lemon juice, olive oil, and salt and pepper. Chill. Serve on romaine lettuce leaves. Makes 6 servings.

Spoon Bread

Spoon bread is aptly named since it is souffle-like and is served and eaten with a spoon. Asparagus tips with cheese sauce and sliced tomatoes would go along nicely with spoon bread.

1 cup white or yellow cornmeal
3 cups milk
2 tablespoons butter or
   margarine
1 teaspoon salt
1 teaspoon baking powder
3 eggs

Combine cornmeal and milk in top of double boiler and cook over boiling water about 30 minutes or until thickened. Stir in butter, salt, and baking powder.

Separate eggs and beat whites until stiff. Beat egg yolks until light. Fold a little of hot cornmeal into yolks and return to cornmeal. Fold in egg whites. Pour into a buttered 2-quart casserole and bake at 375° F for 30 minutes. Serve hot with butter. Makes 4 to 6 servings.

Salads and Salad Dressings

Numbers refer to pages where recipes appear in this book.

Salad Greens   194
Bean Sprouts   196
Salad Bar in a Bowl   197
Layered Salad   197
Potato Salad   198
Tossed Dinner Salad   199
Cucumber Salad   199
Mashed Potato Pepper Salad   200
Baby Lima Bean Salad   200
Green Beans Vinaigrette   201
Chef's Salad   201
Chicken Barley Salad   202
Roast Beef Salad   202
Molded Summer Vegetable Salad   202
Seven Layer Salad   203
Nicoise Salad   203
Salmon Salad   204
Marinated Beans   204
Fruits for Salad   205
Apple Salad   205
Molded Cranberry Orange Relish   206
Orange Cole Slaw   206
Summer Salad   206
Blender Mayonnaise   207
Thousand Island Dressing   207
Russian Dressing   207
Seasoned Blender Mayonnaise   208
Basic French Dressing   208
Creamy Dressing   208
Roquefort Dressing   208
Herb Dressing   208

Tarragon Dressing   208
Another French Dressing   209
Cream Cheese Honey Dressing   209

Salads and Salad Dressings

Today my favorite salad is a mixed green salad—any greens from beet to spinach, although despite the disapproval of the haute cuisine experts, I still like iceberg lettuce. But it wasn't always so. I was brought up on Jell-O salads, particularly when we had company. My mother's favorite was lime flavored gelatin with crushed pineapple and cottage cheese, or the ubiquitous jellied "perfection salad."

From a background like this, I'll try to give you a varied salad section, to suit all tastes.

Salad Greens

Salad greens come in such a variety that it seems one eventually chooses a few favorites and goes farther afield only when spurred by a new recipe or a major price differential. Here are some of those available:

ESCAROLE: A curly green, best used in mixed salads.

CHICORY: A slightly bitter taste—a nice addition to a green salad bowl.

ENDIVE (French or Belgian) has white straight leaves, can be used as a base for a salad or cut crosswise into a green salad or other recipes. It is not actually a "green" but fits into that category.

BOSTON LETTUCE—known in the trade as Butterhead—is a soft-leafed lettuce that makes a good salad base or can be torn into pieces for a mixed green.

ICEBERG, actually Crisphead lettuce, is by far the most popular and widely used lettuce. The leaves are good for a base or in mixed greens; also served in wedges with dressing.

ROMAINE: A long, loose head with green leaves, romaine can be used as a base, is excellent in mixed green, or can stand alone as a green salad.

BIBB LETTUCE, a soft-leafed lettuce, has a tinier head than Boston. Generally available only if locally grown, bibb is delicate and can be served with a light oil and vinegar dressing.

SPINACH: When buying fresh spinach, save the smaller center leaves for salad. A nice color and flavor contrast.

BEET GREENS can be used in tossed salads, where they add a piquant flavor.

DANDELION LEAVES are good mixed into a green salad.

WATERCRESS: Its rather peppery flavor is a nice addition to a mixed green salad, or it can be served by itself with thin mild onion and orange slices and an oil and vinegar dressing. It is a delightful salad.

Other things to go into green salads include red or Spanish onions; green onion; fresh mushrooms; radishes; raw broccoli, asparagus, cauliflower, or snow peas; avocado; tomatoes; leeks; all kinds of fresh herbs; parsley; orange and grapefruit sections; chives; carrots; or cooked green beans.

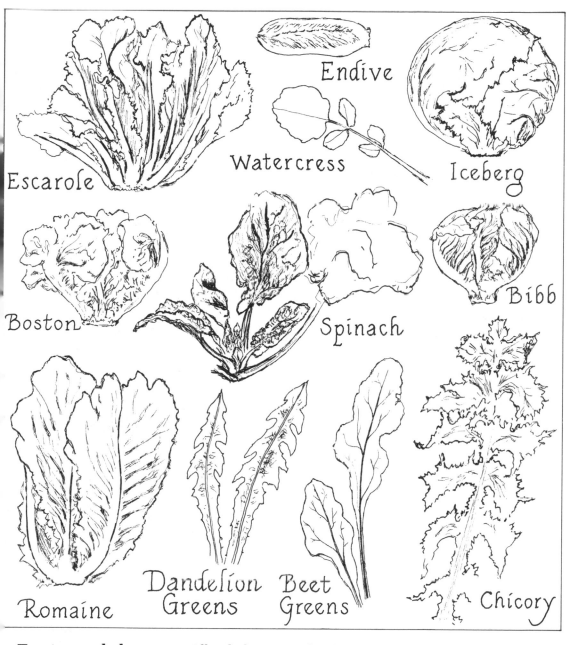

To store salad greens: All salad greens should be stored in plastic bags in the hydrator section of the refrigerator. Do not wash until ready to use. Then wash, cut off any rust spots, and dry in a salad spinner or in clean towels. Some greens, such as watercress, are very perishable, so buy only when they can be used in a day or two.

To cut or tear: As a rule I cut greens, mostly because it seems to work faster for me. For iceberg lettuce use a knife, for the leafier greens the kitchen scissors. It is a matter of personal preference.

Bean Sprouts

Bean sprouts are so easy to grow that they're about the only thing I (being no gardener) grow successfully.

You need a quart jar with a ring lid (actually two jars are better, because you can start the second jar before the other runs out); some cloth to cover the top—any thin, clean white cloth will do; I use pieces of a white t-shirt that gave up the ghost—water, and mung beans.

Put ⅓ cup mung beans in the jar, cover with water, and let them soak overnight. The next morning drain them and wash in a couple of waters right in the jar. Cover the top of the jar with a piece of the white cloth and screw on the ring lid. You're in business.

The theory behind the cloth cover is that you can water the beans through the cloth each day, but I find it quicker to take off the lid and fill up the jar with water and drain it through my fingers. Put the cloth and lid back on to keep the sprouts clean.

Almost at once the beans will begin to grow. As you water them each day, shake well so they won't become too compactly grown in the bottom of the jar. In the summer, you'll have bean sprouts in about three days—in the winter it may take four. I keep the jar right by the kitchen sink so I won't forget to water it. After the jar gets full, it goes in the refrigerator to stop the growing.

I eat beans and sprouts without picking off the sprouts. If you don't like the beans, you'll have to pick off the sprouts.

Salad Bar in a Bowl

A pretty salad to serve at a small buffet or for the hostess to serve at the table as a first course. The vegetables suggested can be varied to suit your taste.

Put greens in bottom of a large salad bowl, about 12 inches across; use more than 1 quart greens if a large base is needed. Put peas, eggs, beans, beets, radishes, and sliced green onions in a pattern over the greens—such as in parallel rows or any other attractive way. Cover and chill in refrigerator.

Cut cucumber and onion into chunks. Whirl in blender with garlic until finely chopped. Drain well. (The best way is to put a piece of cheesecloth in a strainer. Drain off as much juice as will come out naturally and then squeeze to remove most of the rest of the liquid.) Mix with mayonnaise, lemon juice, sugar, and Worcestershire. Chill before serving. Makes 2 cups. Serve in a separate bowl with salad. Store any leftover dressing, covered, in refrigerator. Will keep a week or 10 days.

1 quart (about) cut-up mixed greens
1 cup cooked peas, drained
2 hard cooked eggs, sliced
1 cup cooked garbanzo beans, drained
1 can (1 pound) sliced beets, drained
1 cup sliced radishes
½ cup sliced green onion
1 medium cucumber, peeled
1 small onion
1 small clove garlic
1 cup mayonnaise
1 tablespoon lemon juice
1 tablespoon sugar
1½ teaspoons Worcestershire sauce

Layered Salad

Serve this salad with rolled slices of deli ham, hard rolls, and mint iced tea.

Wash and dry greens before cutting into pieces.
Layer spinach, tomatoes, romaine, onion, zucchini, eggs, and sprouts in salad bowl in order given. Cover bowl with plastic and chill.

Combine yogurt with cheese, chives, and mayonnaise. Chill. Pour over salad and toss when ready to serve. Makes 4 to 6 servings.

3 cups bite-size raw spinach pieces
1 or 2 ripe tomatoes, sliced
3 cups romaine lettuce pieces
1 medium red onion, sliced
1 medium zucchini, thinly sliced
2 hard cooked eggs, sliced
1 cup alfalfa sprouts
1 cup plain yogurt
3 ounces blue cheese, crumbled
2 tablespoons chopped chives
1 tablespoon mayonnaise, or more to taste

Potato Salad

2 medium large potatoes
3 eggs
Water
2 tablespoons grated onion
½ teaspoon salt
Freshly ground pepper to taste
3 tablespoons oil
2 tablespoons vinegar
½ cup chopped dill pickles
½ cup chopped celery
½ cup mayonnaise
Radishes
Parsley

This is a potato salad I've been making for years. If there are any secrets to my potato salad, they might include marinating the potatoes immediately after cooking, while they are still warm; using grated onion (a personal dislike for little pieces of onion in potato salad started this habit); and sticking to a particular local commercial mayonnaise which I find enhances the flavor. (For other uses I normally make my own mayonnaise, which is quite mildly flavored.) This salad is also a nice base for adding other things, which I'll suggest at the end of the recipe.

Scrub potatoes and rinse. Put in a pan large enough to hold eggs as well. Cover with water and bring to a boil. Cover and let simmer 15 minutes. Remove eggs. Continue cooking potatoes another 10–15 minutes or until tender; do not overcook. Peel at once and dice into a bowl. There should be about 3 cups. Add onion, salt, pepper, oil, and vinegar and toss lightly. Peel eggs and tuck them in whole, with potatoes; chill both thoroughly in a covered bowl. Some time before serving, remove eggs and add pickles, celery, and mayonnaise to potatoes. Chop two of the cooked eggs back into bowl. Toss all together.

Place in a decorative bowl. Slice remaining egg and radishes and garnish bowl with egg slices radish slices, and parsley sprigs. Makes about 5 cups.

Variations

Add chopped cucumbers to taste.

Add chilled cooked fresh or frozen peas or cut up peapods to taste.

Add about 2 cups diced cooked chicken or turkey, 2 tablespoons capers, and an additional ¼ to ½ cup mayonnaise.

Honey Glazed Vegetable
(recipe on page 22

Tossed Dinner Salad

When time comes for getting dinner, I bring out all the plastic bags with salad items from the refrigerator and have a ball. Generally there are 2 or 3 kinds of greens and I mix them up. Then either Spanish or green onions, radishes, cucumbers, and bean sprouts. If there are any odds and ends of raw or cooked vegetables, I might put them in, and sometimes there are raw mushrooms which are added. You can see from this that it is hard to give a recipe for a tossed salad, and I think anyone who makes salads regularly has his or her own ideas about how they want to do it. But here is a formula from which to work. For dressing, I use lemon or lime juice and seasoned salt, but I include here a simple oil and vinegar dressing.

2 cups shredded lettuce or your favorite green, or a mixture
½ cup shredded raw spinach
½ cup diced celery
½ cup diced cucumber
1 or 2 green onions, cut in ½-inch pieces
¼ cup radish slices
3 tablespoons oil
2 tablespoons wine vinegar or cider vinegar
½ teaspoon salt
Freshly ground pepper to taste

Wash and dry greens before shredding. Put all vegetables in a salad bowl and toss lightly. Cover and chill in refrigerator until ready to serve. Then add oil, vinegar, salt, and pepper, sprinkling them over the vegetables, and toss lightly again. Makes 4 servings.

Note: If you want to get the salad ready in advance, it's okay. Just don't add the dressing until the last minute.

Variations

Tomato wedges or your favorite fresh herbs could be added to this basic formula. Bean sprouts add a nice texture, too.

Cucumber Salad

A wonderful summer accompaniment to cold chicken or ham.

Combine vinegar, yogurt, and onion in a 4- or 5-cup bowl. Slice in cucumbers. Add parsley flakes and salt and pepper to taste. Chill thoroughly. Makes 6 servings.

2 tablespoons vinegar
1 cup plain yogurt
2 tablespoons grated onion
4 medium cucumbers, peeled and thinly sliced
2 teaspoons dried parsley flakes or 2 tablespoons chopped fresh parsley
Salt and freshly ground pepper to taste

Mashed Potato Pepper Salad

4 large or 6 medium potatoes
Water
1 medium onion, finely
    chopped
6 tablespoons oil
2 or 3 4-inch green chili
    peppers, fresh or canned
1 tablespoon lemon juice
½ teaspoon salt
Additional whole chili peppers
    and pimento for garnish

*Hot with chili peppers and cold from the refrigerator,
this is good for a picnic or with cold cuts or roast chicken
at home.*

Use Idaho or long white (California) potatoes.
Peel potatoes and boil in water until tender. Drain
and reserve cooking water. Shake potatoes in pan
over heat for several minutes to dry. Mash potatoes and add a little of the potato water.

While the potatoes are cooking, saute onion in
oil until tender, but not brown. Remove seeds
from peppers and chop fine. Add onion, chili peppers, lemon juice, and salt to mashed potatoes.
Beat until light and fluffy, adding more potato
water if necessary to get the right texture. Cover
and chill. To serve, pile chilled potatoes in a bowl
and garnish with peppers and strips of pimento.
Makes 6 servings.

Baby Lima Bean Salad

1 package (10 ounces) frozen
    baby lima beans
2 stalks celery, finely chopped
2 tablespoons finely chopped
    onion
¼ teaspoon salt
4 tablespoons French dressing
    (page 208)
⅓ small head crisp lettuce
¼ cup mayonnaise
¼ cup chopped pimento

*The lima beans can be marinated overnight so that part
of the salad is out of the way the day before. This salad is
good with pork or beef or poultry.*

Cook lima beans as directed on package. Drain
and cool slightly. Mix with celery, onion, salt, and
French dressing. Chill well. When ready to serve,
chop lettuce coarsely and mix with mayonnaise
and pimento into lima beans. Makes 4 servings.

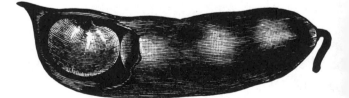

Green Beans Vinaigrette

Green beans vinaigrette are a nice addition to a tossed vegetable salad; they fit into a buffet menu; or they can be served by themselves as a salad.

Cut off stem ends of beans and wash well. Either steam or cook in a small amount of water until beans are tender-crisp, about 15 minutes. Drain and put beans in a bowl and cool. Mix seasonings with vinegar and oil to blend. Stir in olives and capers. Pour over beans and toss well. Cover and chill in refrigerator for several days, turning beans occasionally in vinaigrette sauce. Serve as a salad on shredded lettuce (or add to tossed vegetable salad). Makes 6 servings as a salad.

1½ pounds green beans
Water
2 teaspoons dry mustard
¾ teaspoon salt
Freshly ground pepper to taste
1 teaspoon paprika
1½ teaspoons sugar
6 tablespoons cider vinegar or wine vinegar
¾ cup oil
2 tablespoons chopped stuffed olives
1 teaspoon capers
Shredded lettuce

Chef's Salad

A chef's salad is a popular menu item and yet if you analyze it, it is primarily a base of salad greens topped with julienned ham, chicken, and Swiss cheese. Sometimes you get sliced hard cooked egg and tomato wedges. This recipe is a pattern on which to build your own chef's salad—it makes a good Sunday night supper when served with assorted breads and a beverage.

In a large salad bowl mix greens with onion rings and cucumber slices. Arrange on top of the greens the chicken, Swiss cheese, ham, tomatoes cut in wedges, and eggs, sliced or cut in lengthwise wedges. Serve the salad with coarse salt, the pepper mill, and Thousand Island dressing on the side. Makes 4 servings.

Note: If it is easier to make 4 individual salads, divide ingredients between 4 salad bowls.

1½ quarts cut-up greens
8 or 10 thin Spanish or red onion rings
½ cucumber, thinly sliced
1 cup julienned cooked chicken
1 cup julienned Swiss cheese
1 cup julienned ham or tongue
2 ripe tomatoes
2 hard cooked eggs
Salt and freshly ground pepper to taste
Thousand Island dressing (p. 207)

Chicken Barley Salad

⅓ cup barley
½ teaspoon salt
2 cups boiling water
1 cup chopped cooked chicken
¾ cup thin celery slices
¼ cup green onion slices
½ cup plain yogurt
1 tablespoon soy sauce
Dash garlic powder
Freshly ground pepper to taste
Lettuce

Even though I've always loved barley, the first time I saw a barley salad recipe I had to be convinced. Obviously, I was. Use this as a main dish with toasted bread. Garnish the salad with fresh tomato slices and serve canned apricots and cookies for dessert.

Cook barley in salted water, covered, on low heat for 1 hour, stirring occasionally. Drain and cool. (The barley can be cooked the day before.) Add all remaining ingredients except lettuce and toss to blend. Chill. Serve on lettuce. Makes 4 servings.

Roast Beef Salad

2 cups julienned cold roast beef
¼ cup French dressing (page 208)
1 cup diced celery
2 tablespoons chopped green
    onions
½ cup mayonnaise
1 teaspoon Dijon mustard
1 tablespoon horseradish
Lettuce

Get some deli beef sliced a little thicker than usual and cut it in julienne pieces as a change from cold cuts. Rye bread, cherry tomatoes, and dill pickles are easy additions to the menu.

Marinate roast beef in French dressing for several hours in refrigerator. Drain. Add celery and onion. Mix mayonnaise with mustard and horseradish and toss with beef. Serve in lettuce cups. Makes 4 servings.

Molded Summer Vegetable Salad

1 envelope unflavored gelatin
¼ cup cold water
1 cup boiling water
1 tablespoon lemon juice
3 tablespoons cider vinegar
½ teaspoon salt
2 tablespoons grated onion
½ cup grated raw carrot
½ cup thinly sliced celery
¼ cup diced cucumber
Salad greens
French dressing (page 208)

A light salad such as this goes with most any meal.

Soften gelatin in cold water. Dissolve in boiling water. Add lemon juice, vinegar, salt, and onion. Chill until mixture begins to thicken. Mix in carrots, celery, and cucumber, and spoon into a 3- or 4-cup mold. Chill until firm. Serve on salad greens with French dressing. Makes 4 to 6 servings.

Seven Layer Salad

It is a boon to be able to get the salad ready the day before, and this is a grand one for a picnic. Sandwiches and lemonade are good partners.

Cook macaroni in boiling water with salt for 6 minutes (until al dente). Rinse with cold water. Drain and set aside. Make a bed of lettuce in the bottom of a large bowl. Layer macaroni on top. Continue with cabbage, onion, celery, cheese, and peas, using each to form one layer. Pour salad dressing over all, but do not toss. Cover and refrigerate several hours or overnight. Just before serving, toss and season to taste with salt and pepper. Makes 8 servings.

1 cup uncooked elbow
   macaroni
1 quart boiling water
1 teaspoon salt
½ head lettuce
2 cups shredded red cabbage
1 medium red onion, sliced
1 cup sliced celery
1 cup shredded cheddar cheese
1 package (10 ounces) frozen
   peas, thawed
1 cup low-calorie creamy salad
   dressing
Salt and freshly ground pepper
   to taste

Nicoise Salad

A salad of vegetables and fish which originated in the Mediterranean, this is a meal in itself, served with crusty rolls and cheese for dessert.

Wash beans and cut off stem end. Cut into 1-inch pieces. Steam or cook in a very small amount of water until tender. Drain. Mix oil, vinegar, mustard, salt, and pepper and toss with beans. Chill. Toss all remaining ingredients with beans and dressing. Makes 4 servings.

½ pound green beans
½ cup oil
¼ cup red wine vinegar
1 teaspoon Dijon mustard
¼ teaspoon salt
Freshly ground pepper to taste
1 medium red onion, thinly
   sliced
1 medium tomato, cut in
   wedges
1 can (3½ ounces) pitted ripe
   olives, drained
1 can (2 ounces) anchovy fillets,
   drained and chopped
1 can (7 ounces) tuna, drained
   and flaked
3 hard cooked eggs, quartered
1 tablespoon chopped fresh
   basil

Salmon Salad

1 can (15½ ounces) salmon*
1 cup diced cucumber
1½ tablespoons grated onion
2 tablespoons lemon juice
½ cup chopped walnuts
3 tablespoons French dressing
    (page 208)
⅓ cup mayonnaise
Crisp salad greens

Serve a chilled vichyssoise to start, sliced tomatoes and hard rolls with the salmon salad, and ice cream roll for dessert.

Drain salmon. Break into medium size chunks. Remove bones. Add cucumber, onion, lemon juice, walnuts, French dressing, and mayonnaise and toss lightly. Chill well. Serve on salad greens. Makes 4 servings.

* For this recipe use the red or sockeye, or Chinook or king salmon.

Marinated Beans

1 pound dried navy (pea), red
    kidney, or cannellini beans
3½ to 4 cups water
6 tablespoons oil
2 cloves garlic, peeled, whole
1 bay leaf
1 teaspoon salt

Marinade

6 tablespoons oil
6 tablespoons tarragon vinegar
    or white wine vinegar
¼ cup chopped fresh parsley
½ teaspoon crushed dried oreg-
    ano or 1½ teaspoons chopped
    fresh oregano
½ teaspoon crushed dried basil
    or 1½ teaspoons chopped
    fresh basil
¼ teaspoon salt
Freshly ground pepper to taste

This is definitely a plan-ahead, but well worth it. Marvelous to have in the summer to add zip to fish or vegetable salad plates.

Sort and wash beans. Soak overnight in 3½ to 4 cups water. In the morning add oil, garlic, bay leaf, and 1 teaspoon salt to beans in soaking water and simmer until just tender. Do not overcook. Test first at 45 minutes. Drain, remove bay leaf and garlic, and put beans in a bowl.

Mix together the marinade ingredients and pour over beans. Refrigerate for several hours or overnight. Serve as a side dish, in salads, or over pasta. Makes 4 cups. Will keep under refrigeration for several weeks.

Fruits for Salad

Fruits served as salad make a very fine counterpoint to dinner. One of my favorites, and one which most men will always eat, is made as follows:

Put a bed of greens on the salad plate—chopped or shredded, if you want them to be eaten—then fruit of most any kind: canned pineapple rings, orange or grapefruit sections, banana slices, fresh or canned pears or peaches; whatever is in season or in the cupboard. Top it with about 3 tablespoons cottage cheese and over that a good spoonful of whole cranberry sauce—canned, broken up with a fork, or your own homemade. This good and pretty salad is a hit every time.

Use fruits mixed in with greens for a pleasant flavor. Orange and onion slices are good to serve with poultry. Banana chunks rolled first in lemon juice and then in finely chopped nuts, and served with a French or cream cheese honey dressing (page 209), tempt appetites. Pears with cream or cottage cheese and a tart French dressing on a bed of chicory are always pretty and good.

Use fruits in season with a free hand. Many times I serve a generous fruit salad to double as dessert.

Apple Salad

Apple salad is a good winter salad to accompany pork, ham, meat loaf, chicken—in fact about every main dish course.

Peel 2 apples and core and dice. Core and dice other apple unpeeled. Sprinkle with lemon juice or sherry. Toss with remaining ingredients except lettuce. Serve in large lettuce-lined bowl or on individual lettuce-lined plates. Makes 4 to 6 servings.

3 apples, such as Cortland, McIntosh, Delicious
1 tablespoon lemon juice or dry sherry
¾ cup chopped walnuts
⅓ cup chopped celery
½ cup mayonnaise
Lettuce

Molded Cranberry Orange Relish

1 package (4-serving size)
  orange flavor gelatin
1 cup boiling water
½ cup orange juice
1 orange
1 can (16 ounces) whole
  cranberry sauce
½ cup finely chopped celery

This versatile relish can be served on a buffet table or in individual servings with lettuce and mayonnaise. It can be made year round, which adds to its popularity.

Dissolve gelatin in boiling water and add orange juice. Chill until mixture begins to thicken. Wash orange and cut into pieces. Remove seeds, if any. Chop in a processor or a blender. Add to gelatin with cranberry sauce and celery. Spoon into a 1-quart mold and chill until firm. Unmold and serve as a relish with hot or cold poultry or ham. Makes 1 quart or 8 servings.

Orange Cole Slaw

1½ cups orange sections
2 cups shredded cabbage
½ cup chopped dates or raisins
⅓ cup mayonnaise
¼ teaspoon salt
1½ teaspoons sugar
¼ teaspoon celery seed

A nice change from regular cole slaw. Serve as a dinner salad or with sandwiches.

Cut orange sections in half. Mix with cabbage and dates. Combine mayonnaise with salt, sugar, and celery seed and stir into cabbage mixture until well blended. Chill. Makes 6 servings.

Summer Salad

Salad greens
3 cups grapefruit sections
2 cups melon balls (honeydew,
  watermelon, or cantaloupe)
1 cup blueberries
1 cup sliced strawberries
2 bananas, sliced
2 teaspoons lemon juice
½ cup mayonnaise
⅓ cup orange juice

Croissants and iced tea go with this combination of fruits.

Arrange salad greens on 4 luncheon size plates. Arrange fruits on each plate to form a design or pattern. Sprinkle bananas with lemon juice. Serve with mayonnaise thinned with orange juice. Makes 4 servings.

Blender Mayonnaise

This mayonnaise may also be made in a food processor. The recipe can be doubled in the processor, but unless you are planning to use it within a week homemade mayonnaise does not keep as well as commercial. It is so easy to make that small amounts are no problem. I whirl my oil and vinegar dressing in the blender to get the mayonnaise cleaned out and give a little new flavor to the French style dressing.

1 cup oil
2 tablespoons lemon juice or vinegar
½ teaspoon dry mustard
½ teaspoon salt
1 egg

Combine ¼ cup oil, lemon juice or vinegar, mustard, salt, and egg in blender. Run 15 seconds with the lid on, then remove lid and gradually add remaining oil. When thickened, put into a jar, cover, and store in refrigerator. Makes 1½ cups.

Variations

Add 2 tablespoons each chopped fresh chives and parsley.

To ½ cup mayonnaise add 6 tablespoons plain yogurt and stir to blend. Taste and add a few drops of Tabasco, if desired.

Thousand Island Dressing: To 1 recipe blender mayonnaise add ⅓ cup chili sauce, 2 tablespoons finely chopped green pepper, 5 tablespoons chopped and well-drained pimento, and 1 tablespoon chopped chives. Mix lightly to blend. Makes about 1⅔ cups. Store, covered, in refrigerator about 10 days.

Russian Dressing: To 1 recipe blender mayonnaise add ½ cup chopped green olives, 2 tablespoons chopped sweet pickle (or same amount pickle relish), 5 tablespoons chili sauce, and 1 hard cooked egg, chopped. Makes 1¾ cups. Store, covered, in refrigerator about 10 days.

Seasoned Blender Mayonnaise

1 egg
2 tablespoons lemon juice
½ teaspoon salt
½ teaspoon sugar
½ teaspoon vinegar
2 green onions, including tops,
   cut up
1 clove garlic, chopped
½ teaspoon dry mustard
1 sprig parsley, cut up
1 cup oil

The onions, garlic, and other seasonings in this tasty mayonnaise make it a natural to serve with cold cuts, salad greens, or tomatoes.

Put egg, lemon juice, salt, sugar, vinegar, onions, garlic, mustard, and parsley in blender and blend until smooth. Continue blending, adding oil slowly. If oil does not blend in easily toward end of addition, stop motor and push oil down into mayonnaise with spatula and blend until oil is incorporated and mixture is thick and smooth. Makes 1½ cups. Store, covered, in the refrigerator.

Basic French Dressing

⅓ cup cider vinegar or lemon
   juice
1 cup oil
½ teaspoon salt
Freshly ground pepper to taste
¼ teaspoon paprika
1 teaspoon dry mustard
1 clove garlic, peeled and cut in
   half

A good dressing for either vegetable or fruit salads.

Combine all ingredients and shake well. Shake before each use. Store, covered, in refrigerator. Makes 1½ cups.

Variations

Creamy Dressing: Add ⅓ cup mayonnaise to above mixture and stir or shake until blended. Makes 1⅔ cups.

Roquefort Dressing: Omit mustard and add 4 tablespoons Roquefort or blue cheese. Makes 1¾ cups.

Herb Dressing: Add ¼ teaspoon crushed dried rosemary *or* ¼ teaspoon crushed dried basil to basic dressing.

Tarragon Dressing: Omit cider vinegar (or lemon juice) and use same amount of tarragon vinegar.

Another French Dressing

This dressing, made with wine vinegar and olive oil, is good with the more flavorful greens.

Mix mustard with salt, pepper, and lemon juice to blend. Gradually beat in olive oil and vinegar. Makes 1½ cups.

2 teaspoons Dijon mustard
¼ teaspoon salt
Freshly ground pepper to taste
2 tablespoons fresh lemon juice
1 cup olive oil
½ cup red wine vinegar

Cream Cheese Honey Dressing

A sprightly combination for fruits.

Soften cream cheese in a small bowl and mix in salt and honey. Gradually beat in orange juice and lemon juice. Serve with fruit salad. Makes 1 cup.

1 package (3 ounces) cream
cheese
½ teaspoon salt
2 tablespoons honey
½ cup orange juice
2 tablespoons lemon juice

Vegetables

Numbers refer to pages where recipes appear in this book.

Buying and Storing Vegetables   212
Cooking Methods   213
Artichokes   214
Asparagus   214
Beans   214
Beets   214
Broccoli   214
Brussels Sprouts   215
Cabbage   215
Carrots   216
Cauliflower   216
Celery   217
Collard or Kale Greens   217
Corn   217
Cucumbers   217
Dandelion Greens   217
Eggplant   217
Endive   218
Garlic   218
Mushrooms   218
Mustard Greens   218
Okra   218
Onion Family   219
Parsnips   219
Peas   219
Peppers   220
Potatoes   220
Sweet Potatoes   221
Pumpkin   221
Rutabagas and Turnips   221
Spinach   221

Squash   221
Tomatoes   222
Herbs   222
Coriander Mushrooms   224
Cottage Cheese and Spinach
     Dumplings   224
Baked Stuffed Potatoes   225
Parsley Chive New Potatoes   225
Sherried Sweet Potato
     Casserole   226
Ratatouille   226
Hot Pepper Relish   227
Piquante Squash   227
Baked Yellow Squash   227
Honey Glazed Vegetables   228
Harvard Beets   228
Orange Beets   228
Lemon Beets   228
Ginger Marmalade Beets   228
Gingered Parsnips   228
Braised Escarole with Pine Nuts   229
Parsnip and Apple Casserole   229

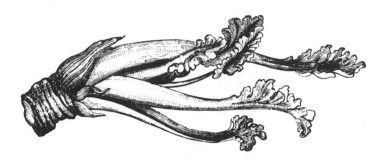

Vegetables

We are blessed with such a variety of fresh, frozen, and canned vegetables that we often tend to take them for granted. But both vegetables and fruits add valuable nutritional benefits to our diet. As well, they add variety and can make a dull meal shining bright. When some dietary change (such as that caused by an ulcer) occurs, and many fruits and vegetables are eliminated from the menu, one realizes the magnitude of the loss.

Remember that vegetables add vitamins A, B6, and C, among others—as well as iron, phosphorus, thiamine, niacin, and potassium. They also contain trace elements essential for health maintenance, an important factor, as well as providing bulk in the diet.

Buying and Storing Vegetables

When selecting vegetables from the fresh vegetable department, be certain they are fresh—no wilt, no brown or rust spots—and do not buy more than can be used in a reasonable time. Frozen vegetables come in such a variety, including some frozen straight from the vine, some partly cooked, or with a sauce or seasoning of some kind, or in combination with other vegetables. Choose the pack that suits the need. Often it is less expensive to buy the large bulk sacks of frozen vegetables. The amount needed can be taken out, the remainder resealed and returned to the freezer. Whatever you buy, check that the packages are in good condition and that they are solidly frozen; and get them from the store to your own freezer in jig time.

Canned vegetables also should be chosen by need. An example would be tomatoes. If they are to be used in soup, there is no need to buy a deluxe pack such as one might want to use in scalloped tomatoes. After buying canned vegetables (and fruits) store them in a cool place, no more than 70° F or less than 32° F year round. If you keep any size inventory, date the cans so that the first in will be used first. Canned products cannot be expected to maintain their optimum quality for more than a year.

Store fresh vegetables at home in the refrigerator hydrator. I prefer to put them in plastic bags and close with a tie. This keeps them separate and easier to find, if your hydrator is as full as mine. A week should be maximum storage, so buy accordingly.

When buying fresh vegetables, allow 3 to 4 servings per pound. Canned and frozen vegetables indicate servings on package.

Cooking Methods

The best way to cook vegetables is not more than necessary to make them tender-crisp. This can be accomplished by boiling in a small amount of water, steaming, stir frying, baking, or microwave. These rules apply to fresh or frozen. Canned vegetables have already been cooked done, so only need to be reheated with the seasoning you add.

In the case of both fresh and frozen vegetables, less water and shorter cooking are better for flavor, texture, and nutritive value.

Boiling

Prepare vegetables according to preference. Put 1 inch of water in saucepan, and always use a saucepan to fit amount of vegetables to be cooked. The pan should be about ⅔ full. Bring water to a boil, lower heat, and simmer, covered, until vegetables are just tender.

Steaming

An inexpensive expandable steamer that fits several sizes of pans is placed in a pan with about 1 inch of water (which should be below the level of the steamer). Put vegetables to be cooked in steamer and bring water to a boil. Cover pan, reduce heat, and steam until just tender.

Stir Frying

To stir fry, heat about 1 to 2 tablespoons of oil or butter in a heavy skillet or wok. Add vegetables—which should be thinly sliced, in any favorite combinations or singly—and stir and fry over medium to high heat until tender-crisp, about 2 minutes.

Baking

Potatoes, sweet potatoes, squashes, and pumpkin are good candidates for baking in their own skins, while other vegetables can be baked in a covered casserole. Slice or dice peeled vegetables, put in a casserole they fit, add butter and seasonings to taste, add 2 or 3 tablespoons liquid, cover, and bake anywhere from 350° F to 400° F.

Microwave Cooking

Check the owner's manual for directions. Most vegetables cook well and rapidly in a microwave oven.

Pressure Cooking

Almost all vegetables can be cooked in the pressure cooker, though there is hardly any need to do so except for the long cookers. Follow the manufacturer's directions.

Cooking Individual Vegetables

Artichokes

To prepare artichokes for cooking, cut off stem and 1 inch from top. With scissors, trim tips from larger leaves. Wash well. Put 4 artichokes in a saucepan into which they fit rather snugly. Add ¼ cup water, juice of 1 lemon, 2 stalks celery, 2 cloves garlic, 3 tablespoons olive oil. Cover and simmer about 45 minutes or until leaves are tender.

To eat, pull off leaves with fingers and scrape off flesh with teeth. When you get down to the center, you will find the choke which is not edible. Dig it out with a spoon and discard, before eating the heart.

Artichokes can be served hot with lemon butter or cold with a vinaigrette sauce or other dressing.

Asparagus

Break asparagus by holding stalk at each end and bending to break at tender spot. Wash well. Steam for about 5 minutes. Serve buttered, with hollandaise sauce, or cold in salad. Cut off woody ends and peel section remaining. Use for cream of asparagus soup or slice thinly into mixed green salad. Cook frozen asparagus as directed and serve the same as fresh.

Beans

Green or wax snap beans are the most common fresh bean. Cut off stem end and cook whole or cut into pieces. They can be boiled, steamed, microwaved, or stir fried. Depending on maturity of beans they take from 10 to 20 minutes. Served buttered or cooked with a little chopped bacon or some chopped onion, they are a popular vegetable. Cook frozen as directed.

Beets

Beets can be purchased in bunches with their greens. Cut greens off, leaving a 3-inch length of stem on beet. Scrub beets and boil, covered with water, until tender, 25 minutes or longer depending on maturity. Peel beets, slice, and serve with butter and vinegar or as Harvard beets. Or use canned beets.

Save beet greens. Cut off stems, wash well, and cut into bite-size pieces. Cook in the water that clings to leaves for 1 to 2 minutes. Serve with vinegar.

Broccoli

Buy broccoli with good green color. Cut off and steam heads for 8 to 10 minutes. Serve buttered, with lemon juice, or with hollandaise sauce. Trim stems, cutting away woody part. Slice thinly and marinate in French dressing. Use in green salads. Follow directions on package for frozen; manufacturer's instructions for cooking in microwave ovens.

Brussels Sprouts

Brussels sprouts are like tiny cabbages. Wash well. Steam, boil, or microwave. Cook quickly and test for tenderness at 10 minutes. Serve with lemon butter, sauteed sliced almonds, or poppy seed butter.

Cabbage

There are several varieties—Savoy, with yellowish crimped leaves; red cabbage; Chinese or celery cabbage; and regular cabbage, which is generally green in spring and white in winter. With the exception of Chinese cabbage (which is used mostly in salads and stir-fry combinations), cabbages are steamed, boiled, or microwaved. Cook shredded cabbage 5 to 10 minutes; wedges no longer than 15. Use all 4 types for cole slaw or cabbage salad.

Carrots

This is one of our most popular vegetables, served cooked or raw. To cook, prepare carrots as desired (whole, sliced, or julienned). Then steam or boil about 10 minutes, or microwave according to directions. Serve with butter, lemon juice, or honey glaze. Cook frozen carrots according to directions.

Cauliflower

Cauliflower, another cabbage related product, should have flowerets removed from stems and can be steamed, boiled, microwaved, or baked. It is good with butter and lemon juice or can be served with buttered bread crumbs and grated Parmesan cheese. Stems can be trimmed, sliced, and added to vegetable salads. Cook frozen cauliflower according to directions.

Celery

While celery is thought of primarily as a raw vegetable, it is delicious when braised. Cut outside stalks into thin slices and braise in a small amount of water and butter or margarine in a covered skillet. Season with salt and pepper. Allow about 1½ stalks per serving. Celery, finely chopped, also makes a delicious slaw. Use it as a substitute for cabbage in a slaw recipe.

Collard or Kale Greens

Collard and kale are very close relatives.

Wash and cut leaves in bite-size pieces. Saute chopped bacon in skillet; add washed greens; and simmer, covered, 8 to 10 minutes. Serve with vinegar. Cook frozen greens as directed. Follow microwave directions.

Corn

Sweet corn, white or yellow, on the cob has a year-round availability now though locally grown corn in season is best. Remove outer husks, plunge into a large pot of boiling water, and when water returns to boil, shut off heat. Let stand in water for 2 minutes and serve. Can also be microwaved; follow directions. Corn can be cut off the cob and sauteed in butter and a few spoons of water for no more than 5 minutes. Onions can be added for seasoning, or try a tablespoon or two of chili sauce. Corn also comes frozen and canned.

Cucumbers

Slicing, pickling, and English (the long ones) cucumbers are available. While cucumbers are primarily considered a raw vegetable, they are very good sauteed. Peel cucumber and cut in ¼-inch slices crosswise. Spread slices on paper towels to dry. Then dip in flour seasoned with salt and pepper. Saute in butter 3 to 4 minutes. Depending on size, allow ¾ to 1 cucumber per serving.

Dandelion Greens

Can be cooked or used raw in salads. Wash greens and cut up. Cook in water clinging to greens, about 1 minute. Serve with butter and vinegar.

Eggplant

Eggplants come small enough so that one might be an individual serving, particularly when stuffed; or in larger sizes up to 2 pounds. Do not peel unless the skin seems tough.

There is no need to soak in salt. Slice ¾-inch-thick slices, dip successively in flour, egg, and crumbs, and fry in butter until browned on one side. Turn and brown on other side until tender when pierced with fork. Season to taste with salt and pepper.

Endive

Belgian endive can be used as a salad vegetable, but is also delicious braised in butter and bouillon in a covered skillet until tender, about 10 minutes. Remove lid and allow bouillon to reduce to a very small amount. Allow about 1 head endive per person, depending on size.

Garlic

Garlic has many uses as a seasoning for meats, vegetables, fish dishes. Store away from onions and potatoes, in a covered jar. It can be chopped, squeezed through a garlic press, or used whole.

Mushrooms

Mushrooms have always been the prima donna of the vegetable world. Use as a vegetable in themselves or to accent another dish (vegetable, meat, or fish). Eat raw or broiled or in hors d'oeuvres—almost any way they are enchanting.

"Natural" mushrooms are brown and should be washed before use. It is not necessary to wash white mushrooms, though if it makes you feel better, do so, and pat dry. Cut only the dry end from the stem. Do not peel mushrooms.

Saute mushrooms in butter no longer than 4 to 5 minutes for serving as a vegetable. One pound will serve 4.

A 4-ounce can of mushrooms is equivalent to about 1 cup of sliced fresh. Use mushroom liquid as part of liquid in recipe, or save to use in soup.

Mustard Greens

Cut up, wash, and cook in the water that clings to leaves 1 to 2 minutes. Uncooked leaves can be added to salad.

Okra

May be boiled, baked, or fried. Also used in soups and stews. Cut off stems; if pods are large cut in half; boil 10 minutes in 1 inch water. Serve with butter and vinegar.

Onion Family

This versatile vegetable almost deserves a chapter of its own. You will find dry yellow and white cooking onions; red onions used mostly for salads; sweet Spanish onions, mild enough for salads, but also good for cooking; and Bermuda onions. Green onions are used primarily in salads but are also an ingredient in many cooked recipes. Leeks are large fresh bulb onions which are sold with their green tops, which may or may not be used in cooking. Shallots are also available.

Dry onions should be stored in a cool dry place, preferably dark. Once cut into, what is left of an onion should be wrapped in plastic wrap and stored in the refrigerator.

Green onions and leeks should be stored in the hydrator of the refrigerator. When green onions are in good supply, they can be steamed and served like asparagus.

Frozen whole and chopped onions are used like fresh. Whole onions are also available canned.

Parsnips

Parsnips are a hardy vegetable which may be creamed, sauteed, mashed, or deep fried. Steaming brings out their nutty flavor. Choose small to medium.

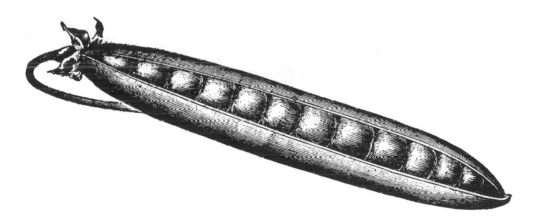

Peas

Peas in the pod are available fresh. Also peas come canned and frozen. There are the regular or English peas, which should be shelled, and the Chinese pea pods or snow peas (also called sugar peas) which are cooked in the shell or can be eaten fresh in salads. Snow peas are much used in stir-fry cooking. Buy bright green pea pods which are fresh looking and store in the refrigerator; the same goes for snow peas. Allow about ¾ pound of English peas per serving. Snow peas can serve 4 to the pound.

Peppers

Red and green bell peppers are used in cooking and salads. To skin a pepper, char under the broiler, and under running water, scrape off the skin. If you have a gas flame, the pepper can also be put on a long handled fork and charred over the flame. Skinned peppers are used for fried peppers: Slice, remove seeds, and saute in olive oil with a little garlic 4 to 5 minutes. Serve as a vegetable.

Chilis, jalapeno peppers, and serranos peppers are among the hot peppers used in Mexican cooking. With the popularity of Mexican cooking, more of these little hot peppers are finding their way into the market. For very hot food, do not remove the seeds when using them.

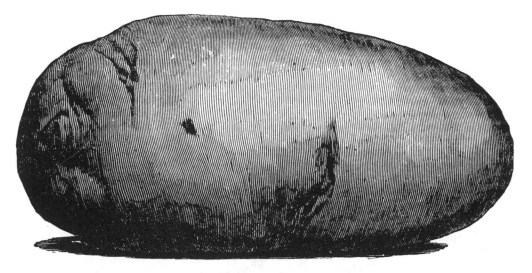

Potatoes

Potatoes are one of our most used vegetables. They are not fattening. It is the butter, sour cream, etc. that goes into them that adds the calories. They are nutritionally a good buy, too, having fair vitamins B, C, and G (riboflavin) and a good content of iron, phosphorus, and other minerals.

Store in a cool, dry, dark area.

Potatoes can be steamed, boiled, fried, or microwaved and are frozen in many forms as well as dehydrated. There are so many varieties it is not practical to list them all. The major varieties in this market area are those from Idaho (long russets, which make an excellent baking potato); round whites from Maine or other Eastern areas, good for boiled potatoes, salad, or frying; long whites from California, a good boiled potato; and round reds up from Florida, for boiling and salad.

To cook potato skins: Scrub and bake 6 russet potatoes (pierce with fork) at 400° F for about one hour. Cool and cut in half lengthwise. Scoop out potato and reserve for other use. Cut skins in 1-inch strips crosswise. Dip in flour, shake off excess. Deep fry in oil heated to 375° F for 2 minutes. Drain on paper towels. Sprinkle with seasoned salt to taste. Makes 60 potato strips.

Sweet Potatoes

Thick, chunky, medium sized sweets tapering toward the end are the best to choose. The skin of the dry potato is usually light yellowish tan; the moist potato, brownish red or whitish tan. Yams are more moist when cooked than other types. Sweet potatoes are a nutritionally excellent food. They can be boiled, baked, or fried and come canned with or without a sugar syrup. Sweet potatoes are also used in breads, pies, cookies, and cakes.

Pumpkin

The pumpkin is a member of the squash family. Cut up and remove seeds; steam until tender. Use pulp for pies, biscuits, breads, desserts. Pumpkin also comes canned.

Rutabagas and Turnips

Both are a strong flavored root vegetable and should be stored at 32° F. Both can be steamed or boiled and mashed or are used in stews. Cape Cod grows a special mild, white turnip. Regular turnips come in both yellow and white. To my taste, turnips and rutabagas should both be served with lots of freshly ground pepper and butter. They cook very well in the microwave and are also good sliced raw into salads.

Spinach

Fresh spinach is good both raw, as a salad green, and cooked. It also comes frozen or canned. It can be steamed, boiled, or microwaved. Wash the greens well to remove sand, cut out any heavy ribs, and cook 1 to 2 minutes in the water which clings to the leaves. Serve cooked spinach with butter and vinegar or chopped hard cooked eggs. Store fresh spinach in the refrigerator.

Squash

Squash is an overall name for a great variety of different squashes.

There are the winter or hard shell squashes such as acorn, butternut, banana, and Hubbard which steam and bake very well. They also can be cooked in the microwave, following the manufacturer's directions. You will also find spaghetti squash, whose flesh when cooked (steamed or boiled) comes loose in ribbons like spaghetti.

Summer squashes include zucchini, yellow crookneck and yellow straight neck, and patty pan or scallops.

Butternut, Hubbard, and banana squashes are sometimes made into pies or rolls after being steamed, scraped from the shell, and mashed.

Winter squash is enhanced with brown sugar or maple syrup, butter, salt, and pepper.

The summer squashes fit into many recipes, though they are good served plain with butter and seasoning. Some of the squashes are frozen and canned.

Tomatoes

Tomatoes, botanically, are a fruit; but for cooks they come into the vegetable classification. They are widely used both fresh and cooked. There are many varieties, but the biggest differences are found between the regular salad tomatoes, the Italian plum, and the cherry. Choose tomatoes that are ripe and have no blemish. If you cannot buy them as ripe as you wish, put in a brown paper sack with a fresh apple and close tightly. The apple releases a gas which helps ripen the tomatoes. Write the date on the sack with a pen, and remember to check each day or so. It should take about 3 days. (This method of ripening works well for peaches or pears, too.)

Sauteed cherry tomatoes with herbs are easy to prepare. For enough to serve 4, plan about 24 cherry tomatoes. Heat 2 or 3 tablespoons butter in a skillet. Add washed cherry tomatoes and saute until tomatoes' skins just begin to break. Season with salt, freshly ground pepper, chopped fresh parsley, and dill or basil.

Herbs

Fresh herbs are one of the most lovely additions to cooking. If you have a small space of land to spare, and have not grown herbs, try growing some. Thyme is a perennial so that once you get it started it will come up each spring. Oregano can sometimes be temperamental and some years does not reappear, but is hardy in many situations. Sage, chives, winter savory, tarragon, and mint all are very faithful and come up year after year. Basil is an annual but will grow and prosper in the kitchen so you will have it all year round. Some people have luck bringing in rosemary in the fall, but if it doesn't work for you it has to be purchased each spring. Dill must be planted each year and it does grow to large plants, if space is a problem.

Just the short list of herbs above will be enough to add flavor to your cooked dishes and salads. If you have fresh herbs and the recipe calls for dried, use 3 times as much chopped fresh herbs as dried.

Here are some food-herb combinations

BASIL: Tomatoes, eggplant, green beans, zucchini, cheese, and spaghetti dishes
WINTER SAVORY: Green or dried beans, poultry, meat salads, stuffing, scrambled eggs
TARRAGON: Green salads, mayonnaise, fish sauce, vinegar
OREGANO: Tomato dishes, cheese, eggs, vegetable and beef broths, fish
THYME: Fish, poultry, tomatoes, spaghetti dishes
DILL: Sour cream sauces, green beans, cabbage, cucumber, potato salad, fish
ROSEMARY: Chicken, eggs, cheese, lamb, veal, tomatoes, zucchini
PARSLEY: Can be added to most any cooked dish or salad
CHIVES: A relative of the onion family; chopped, goes into meat and vegetable salads and soups; nice as a garnish
SAGE: Pork, chicken, stuffings, seafood, cheese.

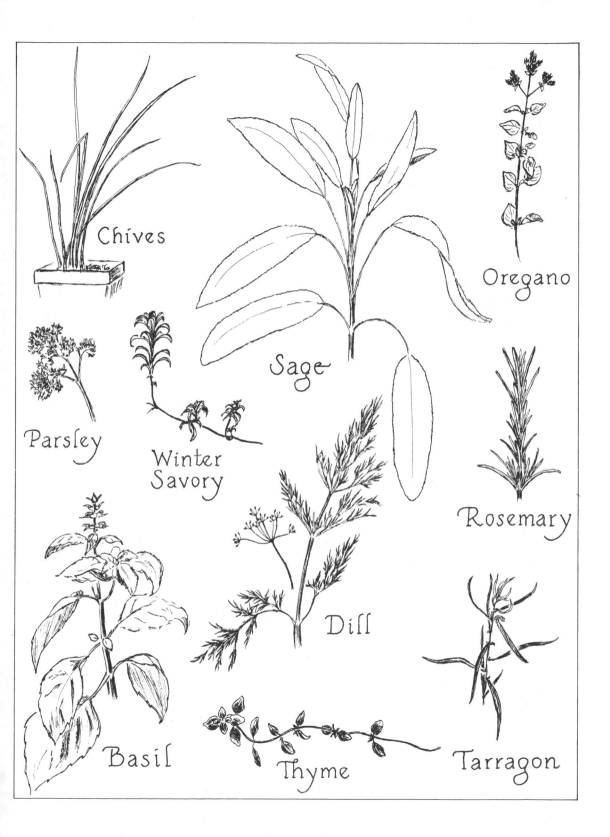

Chives

Oregano

Parsley

Sage

Winter Savory

Rosemary

Basil

Dill

Thyme

Tarragon

Coriander Mushrooms

1 pound fresh mushrooms
3 tablespoons lemon juice
2 teaspoons coriander seed
6 tablespoons olive oil
2 bay leaves
½ teaspoon salt
Freshly ground pepper to taste

The lovely juice from these mushrooms should be sopped up with crusty bread, so serve in individual vegetable dishes. Good with steak.

Wash mushrooms, if necessary. Cut off stem end; if large, cut mushrooms in quarters. Sprinkle with lemon juice. Crush coriander seeds with a mortar and pestle, or fold in wax paper and crush with a rolling pin.

Heat olive oil in a heavy skillet over low heat. Add coriander and allow to heat through. Add the mushrooms and bay leaves. Season with salt and pepper. Cook and stir one minute and then cover pan and let cook five minutes longer. Let mushrooms cool to serve. Makes 4 servings.

Cottage Cheese and Spinach Dumplings

1½ cups very well drained chopped cooked or canned spinach (a 1-pound, 13-ounce can, or 2 10-ounce packages frozen chopped spinach)
2 tablespoons butter, melted
1 cup dry cottage cheese
¼ teaspoon monosodium gluta-mate (optional)
½ cup grated sharp American cheese
¼ cup fine soft bread crumbs
1 egg, beaten
Flour
3 cups well-flavored beef bouillon
3 or 4 tablespoons butter, melted
Additional grated sharp cheese (optional)

Serve buttered noodles with the dumplings. For a vege-table, peas and carrots; for dessert, a fresh fruit cup and cookies.

Mix spinach with butter, cottage cheese, mono-sodium glutamate, grated American cheese, bread crumbs, and egg until well blended. Chill. Make into balls containing one tablespoon each. Roll in flour.

Heat bouillon to boiling. Drop dumplings into bouillon, and when they rise to the top remove from bouillon with a slotted spoon or fork. Keep hot. Serve with melted butter and extra grated sharp cheese, if desired. Makes 4 servings.

from B. A.
Confidential Chat Column

Baked Stuffed Potatoes

Potatoes prepared this way are boon to hostesses because they can be prepared in advance and heated at the last minute. My recipe is for four, but it can easily be multiplied.

Scrub potatoes well. Pierce in several places with a fork and rub all over with oil. Bake at 400° F for 50 to 60 minutes or until tender.

Cut about 1 inch off top of each baked potato lengthwise and scrape out insides of potatoes, leaving the shell intact. Mash potatoes and beat in sour cream or yogurt, butter, chives, and parsley, beating until fluffy. Season to taste with salt and pepper. Spoon back into potato shells. Sprinkle top with paprika. Reheat in a 400° F oven for 10 to 15 minutes. Makes 4 servings.

If potatoes are prepared in advance, refrigerate, and reheat at 400° F for 20 to 30 minutes.

4 large baking potatoes
Oil
3 to 4 tablespoons dairy sour cream or plain yogurt
4 tablespoons butter or margarine
2 tablespoons chopped chives
2 tablespoons chopped fresh parsley
Salt and freshly ground pepper to taste
Paprika

Parsley Chive New Potatoes

Delicious in the spring with roast chicken or fish or ground beef patties.

Scrub potatoes and put in a saucepan. Put about 1 inch water in pan and add salt. Bring to boil and steam, covered, for 20 minutes or until tender. Drain and shake over heat until potatoes are dry. Add remaining ingredients and carefully stir potatoes until all are covered. Makes 4 servings.

1½ pounds tiny new potatoes, unpeeled
Water
½ teaspoon salt
¼ cup butter or margarine
2 tablespoons chopped chives
2 tablespoons chopped fresh parsley
Freshly ground pepper to taste

Sherried Sweet Potato Casserole

3 tablespoons butter or
    margarine
½ cup 40% bran flakes
5 tablespoons brown sugar
½ teaspoon cinnamon
¼ teaspoon nutmeg
1½ cups cooked sweet potatoes,
    sliced ¼ inch thick
1 chopped peeled apple
1 tablespoon lemon juice
¼ cup dry sherry

Put a slice of ham in the oven to bake at the same time as this sweet potato casserole. Serve cranberry relish and peas and mushrooms.

Melt butter and add bran flakes. Mix sugar and spices. Put one half cereal in bottom of a buttered 1-quart casserole. Place half sweet potatoes and apples on top. Sprinkle with half sugar mixture. Add remaining potatoes, apples, and sugar. Pour over lemon juice and sherry and top with remaining cereal. Cover and bake at 350° F for 45 minutes. Uncover and let brown, about 10 minutes. Makes 4 servings.

Ratatouille

¼ cup olive oil
2 cloves garlic, minced
1 onion, sliced
1 green pepper, seeded and cut
    in strips
3 medium unpared zucchini
    (about 1 pound), cut
    crosswise into ¼-inch slices
1 medium eggplant (about 1
    pound), pared and cubed
2 tablespoons chopped fresh
    basil or 2 teaspoons dried
    basil
1 tablespoon chopped fresh
    oregano or 1 teaspoon dried
    oregano
1 teaspoon salt
Freshly ground pepper to taste
3 ripe tomatoes, peeled and cut
    in wedges

Ratatouille is a vegetable combination which can be served hot or cold. If served cold, assorted cold cuts and cheeses, and toasted French bread, would make a good combination.

Heat oil in an 11- or 12-inch skillet. Cook garlic, onion, green pepper, and zucchini until onion is tender, stirring frequently. Add eggplant, herbs, and seasonings. Cover and cook over medium heat, stirring a few times. Add tomatoes and cook, covered, 5 minutes longer or just until tomatoes are heated. Serve hot or chill well and serve cold. Makes 4 to 6 servings.

Hot Pepper Relish

Quickly made to serve with grilled or roast meats, or good with scrambled eggs or as a filling for an omelet.

Cut peppers in half and remove seeds and cores. Wash well and slice thinly. Heat butter in skillet and saute onion and garlic until soft. Add peppers, sprinkle with salt, and continue cooking until just tender, 4 to 5 minutes. Serve hot. Makes 4 servings.

2 red sweet peppers
2 green sweet peppers
2 tablespoons butter or
  margarine
1 medium onion, finely
  chopped
1 garlic clove, crushed
½ teaspoon salt

Piquante Squash

A new touch to one of our favorite vegetables.

Peel (if necessary) and cube squash. Steam or cook in a little water about 5 minutes.

In a skillet or saucepan large enough to hold squash, heat oil and saute garlic, onion, and parsley until tender but not browned. Add salt, vinegar, tomato sauce, and bouillon. Bring to a boil and simmer about 2 minutes. Add squash, cover, and cook 5 minutes or until squash is tender. Makes 4 servings.

1 or 2 yellow summer squash
  (about 1½ pounds)
Water
2 tablespoons oil
1 garlic clove, chopped
1 medium onion, chopped
1 tablespoon chopped fresh
  parsley
¼ teaspoon salt
1 tablespoon vinegar
¼ cup tomato sauce
1 tablespoon Bovril

Baked Yellow Squash

It is smart use of heat to cook vegetables in the oven when baking the main course. Here is one suggestion.

Slice enough yellow squash into a casserole to serve the desired number of people. Add butter or margarine, a generous amount of lemon juice, and a little salt and freshly ground pepper. Cover and bake at 350° F for about 35 minutes.

Yellow squash
Butter or margarine
Lemon juice
Salt and freshly ground pepper
  to taste

Variations

Add a few onion slices or chopped green pepper or finely sliced celery.

Honey Glazed Vegetables
(pictured between pages 198 and 199)

¼ cup honey
2 tablespoons butter
½ teaspoon salt
1 pound carrots, parsnips, or
   turnips

An ideal companion for a meat loaf and baked potato dinner.

Mix honey with butter and salt. Peel vegetable of your choice and slice or cube. Put vegetable in a buttered casserole and pour the honey mixture over. Bake at 350° F, covered, for 35 to 40 minutes, or until tender. Turn vegetables occasionally with a spoon. Makes 4 servings.

Harvard Beets

2 tablespoons sugar
2 teaspoons cornstarch
3 tablespoons vinegar
3 tablespoons beet juice
½ teaspoon salt
Freshly ground pepper to taste
2 tablespoons butter or
   margarine
2 cups diced cooked beets

The recipe labeled "Harvard Beets" is pretty much a standard. Either cooked fresh beets or canned beets can be used.

Mix sugar with cornstarch, vinegar, beet juice, salt, pepper, and butter in a 1-quart saucepan. Bring to a boil, then add and reheat beets. Serve hot. Makes 4 servings.

Variations
Orange Beets: Add ½ teaspoon fresh grated orange rind, and substitute ⅓ cup orange juice for vinegar and beet juice.
Lemon Beets: Substitute lemon juice for vinegar and add a dash each of cloves and cinnamon.
Ginger Marmalade Beets: Add a generous tablespoon of ginger marmalade to sauce.

Gingered Parsnips

1 pound parsnips, peeled
2 tablespoons butter or
   margarine
1½ teaspoons chopped candied
   ginger
Salt and freshly ground pepper
   to taste

Parsnips are an old time vegetable. Choose smaller size parsnips as they are less likely to be woody.

Steam parsnips over boiling water until tender, about 25 minutes. Put into a bowl and mash. Stir in butter and ginger and salt and pepper to taste. Serve hot. Makes 2 to 3 servings.

Braised Escarole with Pine Nuts

My first taste of braised escarole was in an Italian restaurant in New York City. It was something special then and still is.

Wash escarole well and cut up leaves so they will be easy to handle with a fork. Measure. There should be about 2 quarts. Heat olive oil over moderate heat in a large saucepan. Add nuts and garlic and saute until lightly browned. Add greens and salt and pepper and cook, covered, just until wilted, about 2 minutes. Mix nuts into cooked escarole to serve. Makes 4 to 6 servings.

1 medium bunch escarole
3 tablespoons olive oil
¼ cup pine nuts or slivered almonds
1 clove garlic, chopped (optional)
½ teaspoon salt
Freshly ground pepper to taste

Parsnip and Apple Casserole

A lovely flavor combination for a fall meal.

Arrange parsnips and applesauce in layers in a greased 1-quart casserole. Sprinkle with brown sugar, salt, nutmeg, lemon juice, and bits of butter. Top with buttered crumbs and sprinkle with paprika. Bake at 375° F for 25 to 30 minutes. Makes 4 to 6 servings.

from Grandma at 35
Confidential Chat Column

2 cups parsnips, cooked and mashed
1 cup applesauce
¼ cup firmly packed brown sugar
1 teaspoon salt
½ teaspoon nutmeg (optional)
1 tablespoon lemon juice
4 tablespoons butter
½ cup buttered bread crumbs
Paprika

Lemon Barbecued Chicken
(recipe on page 236)
and Barbecue Spare Ribs
(recipe on page 14)

Barbecues

Numbers refer to pages where recipes appear in this book.

Barbecuing Equipment and Techniques   232
Tips on Food for Barbecuing   233
Approximate Cooking Times   234
Barbecue Glaze   235
Basting Sauce for Fish and Shellfish   235
Steak Basting Sauce   235
Marinade for Fish   236
Lemon Barbecued Chicken   236
Herbed Marinade   236
Marinated Lamb Cubes   237
Vegetables for Marinated Lamb Cubes   237
Barbecued Turkey   237
Grilled Fish Steaks with Tomato Sauce   238
Oyster Roast   238
Potato Carrot Packages   239

Barbecues

One of the pleasures of summer is the barbecue. Here are a few general rules and some recipes.

Barbecuing Equipment and Techniques

The camaraderie and informal fun of cooking over the coals are hard to beat. But a good barbecue meal for the family or for a party requires some planning to make it successful.

● Be sure your grill is in good shape, whether it is a small hibachi or an elaborate gas fired barbecue.

● Collect the barbecue equipment in one place, such as in a plastic caddy easy to transport to the grill site.

● Equipment should consist of long handled spoon, fork, spatula, and tongs; basting brush (a paint brush purchased especially for this purpose is a good baster); padded mitts; and a water filled spray bottle to control flareups. Be sure to have sharp knives readily available.

● Spray grill rack with nonstick coating or oil it well.

● Before you start the fire, line the fire pit (except for a gas fired one) with aluminum foil, shiny side out. This helps in cleanups and the shiny foil throws out the heat. Some grills work better if an inch or two of sand or gravel is placed in the bottom of the grill and the fire is built on that.

● Twenty to 25 briquets are enough to cook several steaks, hamburgers, or chops, and 18 briquets for two pounds of fish, to serve two to four people. If using the rotisserie, build fire under the rotisserie and add more fuel as needed.

● Briquets should have a gray ash and a reddish glow underneath before cooking is started. With long handled tongs, arrange coals in an even layer.

● Start fire 30 to 40 minutes before cooking is due to begin, unless you are using briquets impregnated with fluid so they start rapidly; those coals will be ready in 15 to 20 minutes.

- To start a fire, four methods work well:
  1. Use electric starter according to manufacturer's directions.
  2. Arrange crushed paper and small pieces of kindling in center of grill fire box. Add a few briquets and light. When they begin to burn well, carefully add more briquets.
  3. Pour liquid starter over briquets. Allow a few minutes for the fluid to soak in and then light the fire.
  4. Build briquets in a pyramid or pile in a coffee can with holes punched around the bottom with a beer can opener.
- *Never* pour liquid starter on a fire that is already going, even if not enough to suit you.

Tips on Food for Barbecuing

- Score edges of steaks, chops, or ham slices to avoid their curling.
- Trim excess fat from meat so that it won't drip and cause flareups.
- Remember that cooking time for meat will vary with the cut, thickness, shape, temperature of meat when placed over coals, weather conditions, amount or arrangement of charcoal, position of meat on the grill, and degree of doneness desired. Test steak, chops, etc., by cutting into the center to see the extent of doneness.
- When kebabing meat, use long enough skewers so ends reach off the grill. Cook meat and vegetables on separate skewers, since they cook done in different times. Parboil vegetables like whole onions before barbecuing them.
- Plan ¼ to ½ pound boneless meat per person, ¾ to 1 pound meat with bone, depending on amount of bone.
- Toss a few herbs on the fire to give a new flavor. Sage for pork, rosemary for chicken or fish, oregano or basil for beef, tarragon for lamb, are possibilities.
- If the basting sauce has a lot of sugar in it, baste toward the end of cooking time so the food won't get too charred.
- Individual serving sized foil packets of partly cooked vegetables, seasoned with butter and herbs, can go on the grill with the meat or before, depending on timing. The foil packets generally take about 20 minutes to finish cooking; turn once. Be certain to seal them well.
- Fish is perfectly marvelous cooked over charcoal. To make the job easier, get a hinged fish grill. The fish is securely held and can be turned easily. The fish grill fits right over the cooking rack on the barbecue.

Approximate Cooking Times for Some Barbecue Items			
Beef steaks (time indicated depends on degree of doneness desired)	1 to 2 inches thick	4 to 5 inches from coals	20 to 30 minutes for 1 inch 30 to 45 minutes for 2 inch
Ribs, spareribs, loins, back ribs	serving size pieces	6 to 7 inches from low to moderate coals	1 to 1½ hours, turning frequently
Ham, fully cooked slice	¾ to 1 inch slice	5 to 6 inches from low to moderate coals	20 to 25 minutes turning frequently
Lamb chops, arm, loin, rib	1 to 1½ inches thick	5 to 6 inches from low to moderate coals	30 to 40 minutes depending on thickness
Whole fish	2 to 5 pounds dressed	4 to 5 inches from moderate coals	15 to 20 minutes per pound, or until meat flakes easily with a fork.
Fish fillets and steaks	¾ to 1 inch thick	4 to 5 inches from moderate coals	10 to 20 minutes depending on thickness
Chicken halves and pieces		5 to 6 inches from low to moderate coals	50 minutes to 1 hour
Ground beef		3 to 4 inches from hot coals	10 to 20 minutes depending on thickness of patties and degree of doneness desired

Barbecue Glaze

This combination of ingredients gives a nice flavor and look to the meats suggested below.

½ cup catsup
¼ cup Dijon mustard
½ teaspoon Tabasco sauce

Mix all ingredients well. Brush onto steaks, chicken, hamburgers, or hot dogs during latter part of cooking. Makes about ¾ cup.

Basting Sauce for Fish and Shellfish

Especially good for swordfish, flounder, salmon, and shrimp.

½ cup butter or margarine
4 tablespoons lemon juice
⅛ teaspoon Tabasco sauce

Melt butter and add lemon juice and Tabasco. Use as a baste sauce for grilled fish. Makes about ⅔ cup, enough for 2 pounds fish.

Steak Basting Sauce

A very tasty sauce to use only for basting. The ingredients can be doubled for a larger amount. However, this should be enough for one steak, with no leftover sauce to store.

2 tablespoons vinegar
1 tablespoon sugar
2 tablespoons water
2 teaspoons Dijon mustard
Freshly ground pepper to taste
½ teaspoon salt
Dash Tabasco sauce
½ lemon, thickly sliced
1 small onion, sliced
1 tablespoon Worcestershire sauce
¼ cup burgundy wine
2 tablespoons butter or margarine

Combine vinegar, sugar, and water with mustard, pepper, salt, Tabasco, lemon, and onion in a small skillet. Cover and simmer on low heat 15 minutes. Add Worcestershire sauce, wine, and butter and bring to a boil. Strain. Use as a basting sauce for steaks while grilling. Makes ¾ cup.

Marinade for Fish

2/3 cup oil
1/3 cup tarragon vinegar
1/2 teaspoon salt
1 teaspoon Worcestershire
   sauce
Freshly ground pepper to taste
2 pounds fish steaks, cut 1 inch
   thick

Codfish, haddock, or swordfish would be well flavored if soaked in this marinade.

Combine oil, vinegar, salt, Worcestershire sauce, and pepper in shallow dish. Add fish. Cover and refrigerate about 3 hours, turning occasionally.

To broil, place fish steaks on a greased hinged fish grill 4 to 5 inches from coals for about 10 minutes on each side. Makes 4 servings.

Lemon Barbecued Chicken
(pictured between pages 230 and 231)

1/4 cup melted butter or
   margarine
1/4 cup lemon juice
1/2 teaspoon garlic salt
1 teaspoon paprika
1 teaspoon Italian seasoning
4 chicken quarters

A change for a barbecue flavor, the lemon enhances the chicken. Wrap potatoes in foil and put in with charcoal when you start the chicken.

Combine butter and lemon juice with seasonings. Brush on chicken and let stand in refrigerator 1 hour.

Broil over charcoal 45 minutes to 1 hour, turning to cook both sides. Brush with butter-lemon mixture during cooking. Makes 4 servings.

Herbed Marinade

1 cup beef bouillon
1/2 cup red wine vinegar
1/2 cup oil
2 teaspoons liquid for browning
   gravy
1/2 teaspoon salt
1/2 teaspoon crushed dried
   oregano
1/2 teaspoon crushed dried
   thyme
Freshly ground pepper to taste
1/4 teaspoon garlic powder

Combine all ingredients and use to marinate lamb, beef, or chicken. Makes 2 cups.

Marinated Lamb Cubes

By cooking lamb and vegetables separately, it is possible to control time so that neither is overcooked.

Put lamb cubes in a bowl. Mix remaining ingredients and pour over lamb. Marinate in refrigerator for 6 hours or overnight, turning lamb in marinade occasionally, or put lamb and marinade in a plastic bag which can be tightly closed.

To cook, string lamb on 4 to 6 skewers and cook 4 to 5 inches from hot coals, turning occasionally, for 15 to 20 minutes. Serve while lamb is still pink. Makes 4 to 6 servings. Serve with vegetables for marinated lamb cubes.

2 pounds boneless lamb cut in 1½-inch cubes
½ cup lemon juice
½ cup olive oil
1 teaspoon dried rosemary leaves
1 teaspoon dried oregano
½ teaspoon salt
½ teaspoon freshly ground pepper
1 medium onion, sliced
1 large clove garlic, pressed

Vegetables for Marinated Lamb Cubes

Remove seeds from peppers and cut into 1½-inch squares.

Put vegetables loosely on 2 or 3 skewers and brush with melted butter. Cook over coals 10 to 15 minutes while lamb is cooking.

1 or 2 green peppers, depending on size
12 small whole onions, parboiled 5 minutes
12 mushroom caps
12 cherry tomatoes
3 tablespoons melted butter

Barbecued Turkey

Make a rice or macaroni salad, a bowl of crisp vegetables, and finger rolls to serve with the turkey.

Wash and dry turkey. Combine soy sauce with wine, oil, and onion powder. Place turkey in a leakproof plastic bag and add sauce. Close securely. Marinate in refrigerator 3 hours or overnight, turning occasionally. Remove turkey, saving sauce. Grill about 7 inches from heat for 1 hour, turning several times. Baste with reserved sauce the last 15 minutes. Carve to serve. Makes 4 to 6 servings.

2 turkey breasts (about 1½ pounds each)
⅓ cup soy sauce
¼ cup dry white wine
3 tablespoons oil
¼ teaspoon onion powder

Grilled Fish Steaks with Tomato Sauce

4 salmon or swordfish steaks,
    about 1 inch thick
2 tablespoons butter or
    margarine, softened
Salt and freshly ground pepper
    to taste
3 tablespoons oil
2 tablespoons butter or
    margarine
1 medium onion, finely chopped
1 clove garlic, finely chopped
1 teaspoon dried dill weed
½ teaspoon Tabasco sauce
2 tablespoons lemon juice
½ teaspoon salt
1 cup chopped fresh tomatoes

Baked potatoes wrapped in foil in the coals (put them in 20 or 30 minutes before cooking the fish), a tossed green salad, and sourdough bread sound good with the fish.

Rub salmon or swordfish steaks with 2 tablespoons softened butter and add salt and pepper to taste.

Heat oil and 2 tablespoons butter together and cook onions and garlic until soft. Add dill, Tabasco, lemon juice, salt, and tomatoes. Simmer, uncovered, about 10 to 15 minutes, stirring occasionally. Makes about 1⅓ cups.

Oil well a hinged fish grill, put in steaks, and cook about 5 inches above coals for 20 minutes, turning once. Serve with tomato sauce. Makes 4 servings.

Oyster Roast

Select good sized oysters and scrub well. Grill small lid up about 4 inches from coals until shells open. Serve with melted butter and lemon juice. Plan number of oysters depending on people present and whether this is a first course or the meal.

If it is the meal, have plenty of buttered French bread, a platter of tomato and cucumber slices with oil and vinegar and fresh herbs, and baskets of French fried potatoes.

Potato Carrot Packages

Potatoes cooked this way may be prepared well in advance to add to the grill at cooking time. I still get out my old 4-sided grater for this recipe. The grated potatoes seem lighter when this piece of equipment is used.

Scrub potatoes and carrots and cook in boiling water 15 minutes. Drain, cool, and chill.

Peel potatoes and carrots and grate on the coarsest grating side of a square grater. Cut up both green and white parts of onions. Lightly mix potatoes, carrots, onions, salt, and pepper.

Cut 4 squares of aluminum foil about 12×9 inches and oil on one side. Divide potato mixture between pieces of foil and dot top of each pile with 1 tablespoon butter. Close packages tightly by folding foil over at edges. Cook over hot coals about 20 to 25 minutes, turning once. To serve, cut top open and eat from foil. Makes 4 servings.

4 medium potatoes
3 carrots
3 green onions
¾ teaspoon salt
Freshly ground pepper to taste
Aluminum foil
Oil
4 tablespoons butter or
    margarine

Cakes and Cookies

Numbers refer to pages where recipes appear in this book.

Cakes   242
Baking Guidelines   242
Equipment   243
Chocolate Sour Cream Cake   244
Mystery Cocoa Cake   244
Banana Carrot Spice Cake   245
Harvey Wallbanger Cake   245
Heavenly White Fruitcake   246
Gingerbread   246
Nancy's Orange Rum Cake   247
Boston Cream Pie   248
Boston Cream Pie (Short Version)   249
Apple Raisin Pound Cake   249
Blueberry Cheese Cake   250
Fresh Blueberry Topping   250
Cookies/Bars   251
Cocoa Oatmeal No-Bake Cookies   252
Coffee Hermits   252
Pecan Bars   253
Orange Sugar Cookies   253
Molasses Whoopie Pies   254
Honey-Nut Cookies   254
Butterscotch Nut Cookies   255
Double Chocolate Nuggets   255
Fudge Nut Brownies   256
Chocolate Chippers   256
Oatmeal Raisin Saucers   257
Krispy Scotcheroos   257
Aunt Jennie's Monadnock Bars   258

Most people who like to cook also enjoy making sweets of all sorts. Part of this enjoyment might come from the praise of those who eat the sweets and the fact that on most occasions the results of the cooking stick around a little longer than in other areas of the art. This is a sampling, many from Chat correspondents.

Enjoy.

Cakes

With such a proliferation of mixes for cakes, cookies, bars, you name it, available to the homemaker, a chapter on cakes may seem redundant. But there are times when a special cake is on the program, even if it is a mix with additions.

Baking Guidelines

Even with mixes, there are baking rules to make better products. When using mixes, particularly in those recipes where additions are called for, purchase exactly what the recipe calls for. There are new formulas being manufactured constantly, so it is important to watch what you buy. In a recipe, cake mix without pudding could react completely differently to one with pudding in the mix. The recipe should specify the weight of a product. Then follow directions. It's fun to freelance a recipe when making stews and casseroles, but baked goods recipes should be followed religiously. Cake and cookie recipes are actually a scientific mixture of ingredients designed to give a proper flavor and texture.

Recently, when spending a weekend with a friend, I offered to make us some processor French bread, a recipe I had made dozens of times. But somehow I'd forgotten the differences that can exist in ovens—and there was nothing wrong with the bread except that it burned on the bottom. My face was red, but another lesson relearned. Get to know how your oven acts. Should the racks be set at center, or higher or lower? If the recipe calls for 350° F, does your oven produce 350° F heat? If there is a question in your mind, buy an inexpensive oven thermometer and check it out when you bake.

For any home cake, cookie, or bread baking, the oven should be preheated to the proper temperature before the food is put in.

Equipment

Good measuring cups are a must. It is generally recommended to have a cup for liquid measure (one with a space above the measure mark and a lip for pouring) and dry measuring cups which can be leveled off with a spatula. They come in sets of 1, ½, ⅓, and ¼ cup measures.

Other equipment to make baking easier (actually *all* cooking) includes a **timer.** My range has a fancy timing setup which I've never learned to use, but the hand timer is easy and dependable. It is used for timing the length of mixing, when that is specified, and for all other timed processes. When I need to leave the kitchen while food is cooking or baking, I just take the timer with me.

Pans should be used that fit the specifications of the recipe. New pans may have the size stamped on the bottom. If yours do not, measure from inside the rims to get the proper sizing, and down from the top on the inside. You could write the size on the outside of the bottom with a little fingernail polish if you wish.

If you are purchasing new pans, you might consider those with teflon lining. They are helpful in that food is released more easily from the pan, and they are easier to wash.

Cake racks are another helpful piece of equipment. They allow cooling around the product to avoid the food steaming itself when it is placed directly on the counter.

Equipment such as mixers should suit your own style of cooking. A **hand-held electric mixer** may be adequate for some homemakers who do not do a tremendous amount of baking. And **food processors** can take over some of the work that mixers used to do.

Years ago, when I was just starting out, I lived with a girl friend who had inherited some kitchen equipment from her bachelor brother who was being married. She had incorporated it with her own things so I had the opportunity to see both. He was a graduate of M.I.T. and knew the advantage of good equipment. He had translated that knowledge into his own purchases for cooking and they were far superior to what his sister had bought for herself. The difference the good stuff made in getting the job done was fantastic. That lesson has always stayed with me. Wait until you can get a good piece of equipment. In the long run you will save time and energy and money in your investment.

Alternate Pan Chart

Three 8×1½-inch round pans are equivalent to **two 9×9×2-inch square pans.**

Two 9×1½-inch round pans are equivalent to **two 8×8×2-inch square pans** or **one 13×9×2-inch oblong pan.**

One 9×5×3-inch loaf pan is equivalent to **one 9×9×2-inch square pan.**

Chocolate Sour Cream Cake

Cake

1 cup water
½ cup butter or margarine
2 squares (1 ounce each)
    unsweetened chocolate
2 cups ground oat flour*
1½ cups sugar
½ cup all-purpose flour
1 teaspoon baking soda
½ teaspoon salt
2 eggs
½ cup dairy sour cream

Topping

1 square (1 ounce) unsweetened
    chocolate
1 teaspoon butter or margarine
1 cup confectioners sugar
5 teaspoons (about) hot water
¼ cup chopped nuts

This is one of the best chocolate cakes I've ever made. It also has the advantage of the nutrition from the cereal flour.

For cake, combine 1 cup water, ½ cup butter, and 2 squares chocolate in a 3-quart saucepan. Bring to a boil. Remove from heat and stir in oat flour which has been mixed with sugar, all-purpose flour, soda, and salt. Mix until well blended. Add eggs and sour cream and mix well.

Pour into a greased 13×9-inch baking pan. Bake at 375° F for 30 to 35 minutes or until cake tester inserted in center comes out clean. Cool completely in pan on rack.

For topping, melt together 1 square chocolate and 1 teaspoon butter in a heavy small saucepan over low heat. Stir in sugar. Add water, 1 teaspoon at a time, until drizzling consistency is reached. Drizzle on cooled cake. Sprinkle with nuts. Makes 18 squares.

* To make 2 cups oat flour, grind 2½ cups uncooked quick or old fashioned oatmeal, 1¼ cups at a time, in the blender or food processor until very fine, about 60 seconds.

Mystery Cocoa Cake

⅔ cup margarine, softened
1½ cups sugar
3 eggs, beaten
1 teaspoon vanilla extract
2¼ cups all-purpose flour
½ cup unsweetened cocoa
1 teaspoon baking soda
1 teaspoon baking powder
¼ teaspoon salt
1 cup water
⅔ cup canned sauerkraut

The mystery ingredient gives the cake a coconut-like texture.

Cream margarine and sugar together in a large bowl. Beat in eggs and vanilla. Sift all dry ingredients together and add to bowl alternately with water.

Rinse and drain sauerkraut well. Chop, then stir into batter. Turn batter into a greased and floured 13×9-inch pan. Bake at 350° F for 30 minutes, until cake springs back when lightly pressed. Serves 16.

from Field of Corn
Confidential Chat Column

Banana Carrot Spice Cake

To all Chat bakers, Cakes and Cookies says the allspice in this recipe gives added flavor, which is true.

Sift together flour, baking powder, soda, salt, allspice set aside.

In mixer bowl, combine sugar, oil, vanilla. Beat at medium speed until well blended. Beat in eggs one at a time, beating well after each addition.

Blend in flour mixture alternately with mashed bananas at low speed. Stir in shredded carrots, mixing thoroughly.

Turn into well-greased 13×9-inch pan. Bake at 350° F about 35 minutes, or until it tests dones. Serves 20.

from Cakes and Cookies
Confidential Chat Column

2¼ cups sifted all-purpose flour
2½ teaspoons baking powder
1 teaspoon baking soda
⅛ teaspoon salt
¼ teaspoon allspice
1½ cups sugar
⅔ cup oil
1 teaspoon vanilla extract
4 large eggs
3 medium bananas, mashed
    (about 1 cup)
1 cup finely shredded carrots

Harvey Wallbanger Cake

The HW Cake was named after a drink of the same name. The original recipe calls for an 18½ ounce box of orange cake mix. When I couldn't find one, I bought lemon flavor cake mix and the result was excellent. Be warned, however: By the time all the ingredients are purchased it is an expensive cake, albeit good.

Combine cake mix and pudding mix in a large bowl. Stir to mix. Add eggs, ½ cup cooking oil, ½ cup liqueur, vodka, and ½ cup orange juice, and beat batter with hand-held electric mixer until smooth. Spoon batter into a greased and floured 10-inch bundt or tube pan. Bake at 350° F for 45 to 55 minutes or until a cake tester comes out clean. Let cool in pan on rack for 10 minutes and then carefully remove from pan to a cake plate.

While cake is still sightly warm, cover with following glaze.

Glaze: Mix confectioners sugar with Galliano, vodka, and orange juice. Spoon over cake.

Any uneaten portion of cake can be frozen.

1 box (18½ ounces) orange or
    lemon cake mix (not the kind
    with pudding in it)
1 box (3¾ ounces) instant
    vanilla pudding mix
4 eggs
½ cup oil
½ cup Galliano liqueur
2 tablespoons vodka
½ cup orange juice

Glaze

1 cup sifted confectioners sugar
2 tablespoons Galliano liqueur
1 tablespoon vodka
1 tablespoon orange juice

Heavenly White Fruit Cake

3 cups all-purpose flour, sifted
1½ teaspoons baking powder
½ teaspoon salt
1½ cups filberts
¾ cup blanched almonds
4 cups glace fruit, cut up
2 cups white raisins
1 cup butter or margarine,
   softened
2 cups sugar
5 eggs
½ cup sherry
Additional sherry

Mission Bells states that this cake truly stands up to its name "Heavenly."

Sift flour, baking powder, and salt together. Break pecans in pieces, leave filberts whole, cut almonds in thick slices. Mix nuts and glace fruits with raisins and several tablespoons of flour mixture.

Start oven at 300° F (or very slow). Grease two loaf pans, 9×5×3 inches. Line bottoms with wax paper and grease the paper.

Cream butter; add sugar gradually and cream until very smooth. Add eggs one at a time and beat well after each addition. Add flour mixture and sherry alternately, and last mix in the fruits and nuts. Put in pans, pressing batter down gently. Bake two hours or until cake tester inserted in center of cake comes out clean. Cool, remove from pan and peel off paper. Wrap in foil and store in an airtight container about a month before serving. Sprinkle several times a week with a little sherry. Keeps for months in refrigerator or freezer. Makes 2 loaves.

from Mission Bells
Confidential Chat Column

Gingerbread

1 cup sugar
1 cup molasses
2 tablespoons shortening
2 eggs, beaten
1 teaspoon cloves
1 teaspoon ginger
1 teaspoon cinnamon
3 cups all-purpose flour
2 teaspoons baking soda
Pinch of salt
1 cup boiling water

For Fine and Dandy, this is a dark, moist gingerbread and light in texture, says A Fireman's Wife.

Cream sugar, molasses, and shortening together; add beaten eggs and spices, then flour with soda and salt. Lastly add water. (If an electric mixer is used, combine all ingredients except boiling water. Beat it in by hand.) Pour batter into a greased and floured 9×13-inch pan. Bake at 350° F for 30 to 35 minutes or until tests done.

from A Fireman's Wife
Confidential Chat Column

Nancy's Orange Rum Cake

To my thinking, this is definitely a special occasion cake. It is work, but it is yummy good.

Cream butter in a large bowl until fluffy. Gradually add 1 cup sugar, beating until light. Stir in grated rinds. Add eggs, one at a time, beating well after each addition.

Mix flour, baking powder, soda, salt, and buttermilk powder. Add in installments alternately with 1 cup water, beginning and ending with flour mixture. Beat well after each addition. Fold in nuts. Spoon batter into a 9-inch tube pan which has been greased and floured. Bake at 350° F for 50 to 60 minutes or until cake tester inserted in center of cake comes out clean. Cool cake in pan on rack for 10 minutes. Carefully remove cake to a large cake plate.

While cake is baking, make rum sauce. Boil ½ cup sugar with ¼ cup water for 1 minute. Cool slightly and add juices and rum. Carefully spoon over warm cake on plate until all sauce is absorbed. Let cool. Before serving sprinkle with confectioners sugar. To store, cover cake loosely. Makes 1 9-inch cake.

* 1 cup fresh buttermilk may be substituted for the 4 tablespoons buttermilk powder and 1 cup water; in that case, add buttermilk alternately with dry ingredients as directed in recipe.

1 cup butter or margarine, softened
1 cup sugar
5 teaspoons grated fresh orange rind
1½ teaspoons grated fresh lemon rind
2 eggs
2½ cups all-purpose flour
2 teaspoons baking powder
1 tespoon baking soda
½ teaspoon salt
4 tablespoons buttermilk powder*
1 cup water
1 cup finely chopped pecans

Confectioners sugar

Rum Sauce

½ cup sugar
¼ cup water
¼ cup orange juice
3 tablespoons lemon juice
2 tablespoons rum

Boston Cream Pie

When is a pie not a pie? When it is a Boston cream pie—which is actually a cake with cream filling and chocolate frosting.

Cake

1 cup all-purpose flour
1 teaspoon baking powder
¼ teaspoon salt
3 eggs
⅔ cup sugar
1 teaspoon vanilla extract
1 tablespoon lemon juice
2 tablespoons cold water
3 tablespoons butter or
   margarine, melted

Filling

⅔ cup sugar
5 tablespoons flour
¼ teaspoon salt
2 cups milk
2 eggs, lightly beaten
1 teaspoon vanilla extract
2 tablespoons butter or
   margarine

Frosting

1 cup sifted confectioners sugar
1 tablespoon hot water
1 square (1 ounce) unsweetened
   chocolate, melted

Cake: Mix flour with baking powder and salt. Separate yolks and whites of eggs and beat whites until stiff, gradually beating in one-half of the sugar.

Beat egg yolks until thick and lemon colored with remaining sugar and the vanilla and lemon juice. Slowly add water. Fold in egg whites, dry ingredients, and butter, just to blend.

Line the bottom of a 9-inch round layer cake pan, 1½ inches deep, with wax paper. Spoon cake batter into pan and bake at 350° F for 25 minutes or until top springs back when touched lightly with tip of finger. Cool in pan on rack 10 minutes. Carefully remove from pan and cool cake on rack.

Filling: Combine sugar, flour, and salt in a saucepan. Gradually stir in milk. Cook and stir over low heat until mixture boils and is thickened. Mix a few spoonfuls into eggs and return eggs to cooked filling, stirring well. Hold over low heat, stirring, about 2 minutes; do not boil. Stir in vanilla and butter. Pour into a bowl. Cover with wax paper or plastic wrap and chill.

Frosting: Stir together sugar, hot water, and melted chocolate until blended. If necessary to make a spreadable texture, add a few more drops water.

To assemble Boston cream pie: Place cake layer on a decorative cake plate. With a sharp knife, cut crosswise into 2 layers. Spread filling on bottom layer and place other layer on top of filling. Spread top of cake with chocolate frosting. To serve, cut into wedge. Makes 6 to 8 servings.

If cake is not to be served within the hour, refrigerate until serving time.

Boston Cream Pie
(Short Version)

Buy an 8- or 9-inch sponge layer and cut cross-wise into 2 layers. Make one 4-serving package vanilla pudding according to package directions, using 1½ cups milk. Chill. Spread between layers and top with chocolate frosting (recipe at left).

8 or 9-inch round sponge layer
Vanilla pudding mix (4 serving package)
1½ cups milk
Chocolate frosting (page 248)

Apple Raisin Pound Cake

Start with a mix to make this flavorful cake. Good with ice cream for dessert, or serve sliced thin with tea.

Peel, core, and grate apples to measure 1 cup.

Mix cake mix with cinnamon in a bowl. Add milk, blend, and beat 1 minute on medium speed of mixer or 150 strokes by hand. Add vanilla, eggs, and apples and blend. Beat 1 minute on medium speed of mixer or 150 strokes by hand. Fold in raisins. Spoon into a greased and floured 9×5×3-inch loaf pan. Bake at 325° F for 1 hour and 15 minutes or until cake tester inserted in center of loaf comes out clean. Cool cake in pan on rack for 10 minutes. Carefully remove from pan and cool on rack.

When cool, glaze cake as follows: Mix 1 cup sifted confectioners sugar with 4 or 5 teaspoons hot water just so it will run from spoon. Dribble over top of cake.

4 medium size apples
1 package (17 ounces) pound cake mix
¾ teaspoon cinnamon
½ cup milk
½ teaspoon vanilla extract
2 eggs
½ cup raisins

Blueberry Cheese Cake
(pictured between pages 6 and 7)

The fact that this cheese cake is made with cottage cheese makes it less rich than some, but good nevertheless.

Mix graham cracker crumbs with ½ cup sugar and cinnamon. Reserve ½ cup and put remainder in the bottom of a well-buttered 9-inch spring form pan.

Beat eggs until fluffy. Mix in 1 cup sugar, lemon juice, salt, cream, cheese, flour, and lemon rind. Beat until smooth with an electric mixer. Fold in blueberries. Pour carefully into pan. Sprinkle with reserved crumbs. Bake at 350° F for 1 hour. Turn off heat and let cool in oven 1 hour. Chill and remove from pan. Makes one 9-inch cheese cake.

from Medico
Confidential Chat Column

Crust

2 cups graham cracker crumbs
½ cup sugar
1½ teaspoons cinnamon

Filling

4 eggs
1 cup sugar
1½ teaspoons lemon juice
⅛ teaspoon salt
1 cup light cream
3 cups cottage cheese
¼ cup all-purpose flour
2 teaspoons gated lemon rind
1 cup fresh or frozen blueberries

Variation
Top with Fresh Blueberry Topping

Fresh Blueberry Topping
(pictured between pages 6 and 7)

3 cups fresh blueberries
½ cup currant jelly

Rinse and remove stems from fresh blueberries. Pat dry. Melt currant jelly in a small saucepan over low heat. Let cool slightly. Brush melted jelly over top of chilled cheesecake. Arrange berries on top.

Cookies/Bars

Most of the rules that apply to making cakes also apply to cookies, but there are tips that make cookie baking easier.

It is a fuel saver to have several cookie sheets. My oven will hold two on one shelf so I have four. That way the oven never waits for me. If using more than one shelf in the oven do not place cookie sheets directly under those on the shelf above. This will block heat and result in uneven baking.

Most cookie recipes make quite a few cookies. If the quantity is more than can be used in a reasonable time, freeze part of the batter in a freezer container for future baking. Mark the container with the name of the cookies, baking temperature, and baking time. They will keep from 1 to 2 months at 0° F. Or if you wish, the cookies can be frozen after baking—I prefer freezing the batter, but it is a personal and not technical preference.

Use two iced tea spoons to drop the batter on the cookie sheet. If baked cookies are a soft type, store with wax paper or plastic wrap between layers.

Unless recipe specifies otherwise, remove cookies at once to a cooling rack with a broad spatula. The cookie sheet is hot and they keep on baking if not transferred.

Cocoa Oatmeal No-Bake Cookies

(pictured between pages 262 and 263)

2 cups sugar
5 tablespoons unsweetened
    cocoa
½ cup margarine
½ cup milk
1 teaspoon vanilla extract
3 cups uncooked quick oatmeal
    (not instant)
Hot water, if needed

Green Thumb Lady has had this recipe for more than 20 years and enjoyed making them when she was a child. You will too.

In heavy 3-quart saucepan, put sugar, cocoa, margarine, and milk. Cook, stirring constantly, over medium heat until mixture comes to a boil. Continue to boil for 6 minutes, stirring constantly. Remove from heat; stir in vanilla and oatmeal. Immediately drop by tablespoonfuls onto wax paper. Makes 36 cookies. If the mixture starts to get sugary before I finish, I add a few drops of hot water, then continue after stirring mixture back to proper consistency.

from Green Thumb Lady
Confidential Chat Column

Coffee Hermits

1 cup shortening
2 cups firmly packed brown
    sugar
2 eggs
½ cup cold coffee
3½ cups all-purpose flour
1 teaspoon baking soda
1 teaspoon salt
1 teaspoon nutmeg
1 teaspoon cinnamon
2 cups raisins
1¼ cups broken nuts (optional)

Always Sewing replaces molasses with cold coffee in her hermit recipe, one which her family and friends love, and it is good.

Mix shortening, sugar, and eggs thoroughly. Stir in coffee. Stir together the flour, baking soda, salt, nutmeg, and cinnamon; blend into shortening mixture. Mix in raisins and nuts. Chill dough at least one hour.

Drop rounded teaspoonfuls of dough about 2 inches apart on lightly greased baking sheets. Bake at 400° F for 8 to 10 minutes or until almost no imprint remains when a hermit is touched lightly in middle. Makes 6 dozen.

If you want them shaped like store hermits, place the dough on the cookie sheets in long strips, about 1 inch wide and ¾ inch high. Put only 2 strips on a cookie sheet at one time, as they spread out when cooking. After they come out of the oven, slice into size bars desired.

from Always Sewing
Confidential Chat Column

Pecan Bars

In my oven Muffy's Mom's pecan bars needed to bake a little longer than specified below. These are very rich, and if making them for a tea or even at Christmas I'd cut them into small squares.

⅓ cup margarine, softened
2 eggs
1 package (18½ ounces) yellow cake mix (not the kind with pudding in it)
1 can (14 ounces) sweetened condensed milk
1 teaspoon vanilla extract
½ cup butterscotch morsels
½ cup ground pecans

Combine margarine, 1 egg, and cake mix; beat on high speed of electric mixer until crumbly (or mix with a pastry blender). Press into bottom of greased 13×9-inch pan.

Beat remaining egg and combine with condensed milk and vanilla. Stir in butterscotch bits and pecans. Spread over first layer, out to the edge. Bake at 350° F for 30 to 35 minutes (or longer), until center leaves no dent when touched with finger. Makes 36 bars or 72 squares. Pack with wax paper or plastic between layers.

from Muffy's Mom
Confidential Chat Column

Orange Sugar Cookies

Amaryllis sends her recipe for flavorful sugar cookies.

½ cup margarine, melted
1½ cups sugar
¼ teaspoon salt
1 egg
½ cup orange juice
3 cups sifted all-purpose flour
½ teaspoon baking soda
Dash nutmeg
Colored sugars

Cream margarine, sugar, salt, and egg. Add orange juice, flour, baking soda, and nutmeg, then chill for an hour or so. Roll out to ¼ inch thick on a lightly floured surface. Cut cookies with a 2½-inch cookie cutter; bake at 350° F about 10 minutes. These can be sprinkled with sugar (or colored nonpareils) before baking. Makes 3 dozen.

from Amaryllis
Confidential Chat Column

Molasses Whoopie Pies

Whoopie pies are a New England tradition. Sometimes they are made with chocolate, but molasses is more traditional.

2 eggs
1 cup molasses
1 cup sugar
1 cup shortening
1 teaspoon vinegar
4½ cups all-purpose flour
2 teaspoons cinnamon
1 teaspoon ginger
½ teaspoon salt
2 teapoons baking soda
1 cup hot coffee (drinking
   temperature)
6 tablespoons marshmallow
   fluff
1 cup confectioners sugar
½ cup shortening
1 teaspoon vanilla extract

Beat together eggs, molasses, sugar, 1 cup shortening, and vinegar. Mix together flour, spices, and salt. Dissolve soda in coffee and blend well the sugar and flour mixtures and coffee. Drop by spoonfuls 2 inches apart onto ungreased cookie sheets. Bake at 350° F for about 15 minutes or until tops are firm to touch. Cool cookies on rack. Makes 6 dozen 2½-inch cookies.

Beat together marshmallow fluff, confectioners sugar, ½ cup shortening, and vanilla. Spread on bottom of one cookie and press bottom of another cookie to it. Makes 3 dozen double cookie "pies."

Honey-Nut Cookies

A good cookie for the lunch box or for an after school snack. Not too sweet.

⅓ cup butter or margarine,
   softened
½ cup honey
2 eggs
½ cup dairy sour cram
1 teaspoon vanilla extract
1¾ cups all-purpose flour
1 teaspoon baking powder
½ teaspoon baking soda
¼ teaspoon salt
½ cup chopped nuts
½ cup chopped dates
1 cup Rice Krispies cereal

In a bowl blend butter and honey with the electric mixer. Add eggs, sour cream, and vanilla and continue beating 3 to 4 minutes. Mix flour, baking powder, soda, and salt and blend into butter-honey mixture on low speed. When mixed remove beater and fold in nuts, dates, and cereal.

Drop by teaspoonfuls on lightly greased cookie sheets. Bake at 375° F for 10 to 12 minutes or until nicely browned. Makes about 4 dozen 3-inch cookies. Store in a covered container.

Butterscotch Nut Cookies

This is a quickly mixed cookie which is crisp and chewy. It is a good keeper and has a marvelous flavor.

Melt margarine and butterscotch morsels in top of double boiler. Stir in soda and boiling water and then add all remaining ingredients. Shape into 1-inch balls and place 2 inches apart on greased baking sheets. Bake at 350° F 10 to 15 minutes.

Remove cookies to rack and cool. Makes about 5 dozen. Store tightly covered in cookie jar.

¾ cup margarine
1 package (6 ounces) butterscotch morsels
1 teaspoon baking soda
2 tablespoons boiling water
¾ cup sugar
1 cup all-purpose flour
2 cups uncooked quick oatmeal
½ teaspoon salt
¼ cup chopped pecans

Double Chocolate Nuggets

The next time I make these cookies, I will add 1 teaspoon vanilla extract. The size indicated is great for kids of all ages, but for grownups at functions (such as a library tea) use less batter for each cookie to make them smaller.

Combine cake mix with eggs and oil and stir until blended. Fold in chocolate chips. Drop by teaspoonfuls on ungreased cookie sheets. Put a piece of pecan on each cookie. Bake at 350° F for 12 to 15 minutes. Let stand on baking sheet 1 minute before removing to rack to cool. Makes 48 3-inch cookies.

from Beaucoup D'Amour
Confidential Chat Column

1 package (18½ ounces) devil's food cake mix
2 eggs
½ cup oil
1 cup chocolate bits
24 pecans, cut in half

Fudge Nut Brownies

⅓ cup shortening
1 cup sugar
2 eggs, lightly beaten
2 squares (1 ounce each)
    unsweetened chocolate,
    melted
1 teaspoon vanilla extract
¼ teaspoon salt
½ cup all-purpose flour
½ cup broken or chopped
    walnuts

Painted Nails has used this brownie recipe for 40 years. It's her all-time favorite way to make brownies. We like it, too.

Cream together the shortening, sugar, and beaten eggs. Add melted chocolate, then add vanilla, salt, flour, and nuts. Blend by hand until fairly smooth—batter may be slightly lumpy.

Pour batter into a greased 8- or 9-inch square pan. Bake at 350° F for 25 to 30 minutes. The lesser time makes them more fudge-like. Makes 16 brownies.

from Painted Nails
Confidential Chat Column

Chocolate Chippers

1 cup butter or margarine,
    softened
¾ cup sugar
¾ cup firmly packed brown
    sugar
1 teaspoon vanilla extract
½ teaspoon water
2 eggs
2¼ cups all-purpose flour
1 teaspoon baking soda
1 teaspoon salt
1 package (12 ounces) chocolate
    morsels

A cookie that always has a friend. A close relative of the famed Toll House cookies.

Combine in bowl and beat until creamy the butter, sugars, vanilla, water, and eggs. Add flour, soda, and salt. Stir in chocolate morsels. Drop by well-rounded teaspoonfuls onto greased cookie sheets. Bake at 375° F for 10 to 12 minutes. Makes about 5 dozen.

from Evening Star
Confidential Chat Column

Oatmeal Raisin Saucers

These are delicious cookies, but be sure to leave a good 2 inches between as they spread to become quite large. Let them stand on cookie sheet about 40 to 50 seconds before removing. Whether you get 36 or (as I did) about 50 cookies depends on how big you make them. Store cookies with wax paper or plastic wrap between layers, so they will not stick together.

Mix shortening, sugar, eggs, and molasses together well. Add flour, soda, salt, and cinnamon and mix well. Finally, add oats, raisins, and nuts. Drop by teaspoonfuls onto greased cookie sheets. Bake at 400° F for 8 to 10 minutes. Makes 36 cookies.

1½ cups shortening or margarine
1¼ cups sugar
2 eggs
2 tablespoons molasses
1¾ cups all-purpose flour
1 teaspoon baking soda
¼ teaspoon salt
1 teaspoon cinnamon
2 cups uncooked oatmeal (not instant)
1 cup cut-up raisins
½ cup chopped walnuts

from Cakes and Cookies,
Confidential Chat Column

Krispy Scotcheroos

A cross between a cookie and a candy, Krispy Scotcheroos will be a pleaser.

Combine sugar and syrup in a 3-quart saucepan. Cook over moderate heat, stirring frequently, until mixture begins to bubble. Remove from heat. Stir in peanut butter; mix well. Add Rice Krispies and stir until well blended. Press mixture into buttered 13×9-inch pan. You have to work fast at this point because it hardens quickly.

Melt chocolate and butterscotch bits together over very low heat, or over hot but not boiling water, stirring until well blended. Remove from heat and spread evenly over cereal mixture. Cool until firm. Cut into 48 2×1-inch bars.

1 cup sugar
1 cup light corn syrup
1 cup peanut butter
6 cups Rice Krispies
1 package (6 ounces) chocolate morsels
1 package (6 ounces) butterscotch morsels

from Tickled Pink
Confidential Chat Column

Aunt Jennie's Monadnock Bars

1 cup chopped dates
½ cup boiling water
1 cup butter or margarine
½ cup sugar
½ cup firmly packed light
　brown sugar
2 eggs
1 teaspoon vanilla extract
2 cups all-purpose flour
¼ cup unsweetened cocoa
1 teaspoon baking soda
½ teaspoon salt
1 package (6 ounces) chocolate
　morsels
1 cup chopped nuts

Aunt Jennie's bars are good keepers and always popular.

Combine dates and boiling water and let stand until cooled. Cream butter until light. Add sugars and beat until light and fluffy. Beat in eggs and vanilla. Stir in cooled dates and water.

Mix flour with cocoa, soda, and salt and stir into creamed mixture. Fold in chocolate bits and nuts. Spread into a greased and floured 13×9-inch baking pan. Bake at 350° F for 35 minutes or until top is firm to touch of fingertip. Cool and cut into squares. Makes 3 dozen. Store covered.

Pies and Desserts

Numbers refer to pages where recipes appear in this book.

Pies   260
Equipment and Techniques   260
Pastry Mix   262
Pastry for One Pie   263
Crumb Crust   263
Meringue Pie Shell   264
Squash Pie   264
Pecan Pumpkin Pie   265
Marlborough Pie   265
Apple Pie   266
Cherry Crumb Pie   266
Strawberry Rhubarb Pie   267
Grasshopper Pie   267
Mincemeat Pie with Hard Sauce   268
Orange Chiffon Pie   268
Frozen Chocolate Sundae Pie   269
Indian Pudding   269
Grape-Nuts Pudding   270
Fall Cranberry Pudding   270
Brazilian Avocado Dessert   271
Oranges with Wine Sauce   271
Chilled Lemon Souffle   272
Rhubarb Medley Sauce   273
Frozen Strawberry Chantilly   273
Cranberry Fruit Ice   274
Poached Pears au Chocolat   274
Ginger Chill   275
Butterscotch Sauce   276
Chocolate Sauce   276
Blueberry Sauce   277
Strawberry Sauce   277
Cheese as Dessert   278

Suggestions for Fruit in Wine   278
Sherried Bananas   279
Nectarines in Red Wine   279

Fruit or cheese is always my favorite dessert, and the pieces of pie consumed by me during a year could probably be counted on one hand. Which is rather an anomaly since making pies is a facet of cooking I love.

Here are some recipes for a variety of desserts and pies—since meals never seem to be complete without some sweet.

Pies

With pastry mix, frozen pie shells, and packaged graham cracker crusts on the market, pie making can be as simple or as time consuming as you want it to be.

Equipment and Techniques

If you prepare your own pastry or use a commercial mix, there are several pieces of relatively inexpensive equipment I recommend. (1) A **pastry blender** enables you to mix the shortening and flour with ease. It can also be used to mix crumbs and butter for graham cracker or other cookie crusts, and to make the flour-sugar-butter base for some bar recipes and the like. (2) A **pastry canvas** to put over the board on which you roll the pastry, a **stocking** for the rolling pin, and a good **ball bearing rolling pin** are all invaluable. Sets of canvas and stocking can be purchased. I happened to have had some white canvas left over from another project and made my own, and purchased a pair of infant cotton lisle stockings (from which I cut the feet) for the rolling pin. The canvas and stocking should be washed after each use.

Pastry, after the liquid has been added, can be chilled for an hour or so before rolling out, but not much longer as it becomes too cold to roll well.

To roll pastry, flour pastry cloth and stocking. If making a 2-crust pie, divide pastry and shape each half into a flat round disc. Roll from center out with a light touch. As the pastry gets thinner and near the size of the pie plate, if the edges begin to split, pinch together in a crimped edge like the edge of a pie crust and reroll the edge. The **pastry circle** should be 1 inch larger than the pie plate all the way around. As you are rolling the pastry, add a small amount of flour to the canvas and stocking as needed, but not any more than necessary to keep the pastry from sticking.

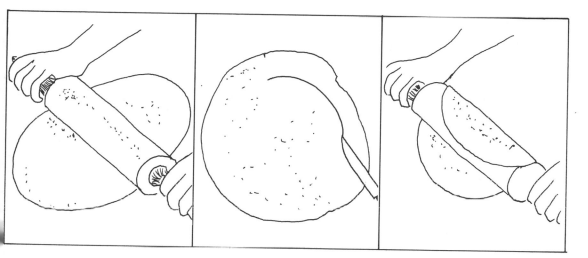

To transfer the pastry to the pie plate, put the rolling pin along one side and roll the pastry around the pin. Transfer over to the plate and unroll into the plate. Gently ease the pastry down into the pie plate. Do not stretch the pastry, as this is one of the reasons a single baked pie crust may shrink and buckle. **Trim the pastry** evenly around the pie plate. If it is not even all around, use some of the trimming for patching. Put a little cold water on the pastry in the plate. If this is a one-crust pie, turn the edges under to form a rim and crimp. Use a dinner fork and prick the pie shell all over, including around the sides. Bake at 425° F for 10 to 12 minutes for a baked single pie shell.

If you are making a two-crust pie, roll the pastry as you did for the bottom crust. Put the filling in the pie shell; with cold water wet around the edge of the bottom pastry; transfer the top crust onto the rolling pin as before and lay it over the filled pie. If necessary, trim crust evenly. Press the two crusts together. Bring bottom crust up around top and pinch together. Crimp to make a pretty edge. I do this by using my thumb and first finger on the inside; press pastry with two fingers around the inside fingers and continue around the pie until it is finished. Cut several slits in top to let steam out of pie as it bakes. Bake the pie as directed in the individual recipes.

Other pastry tricks include making a strip of aluminum foil long enough to fit around the top of a 9-inch pie plate plus several inches—it should be 4 inches in width, folded over to 2 inches. This strip can be used to cover the edge of the crust of the pie if it begins to get too brown before the rest of the pie is done. Gently ease it around the pie edge and fasten either by pinching the ends together or with a paper clip.

You will read directions for filling a single pie shell with beans or rice to keep it from shrinking and buckling while baking. This is done by cutting a circle of wax or brown paper to fit inside the pie shell, laying the paper in, and filling with beans (the cheapest variety you can buy) or raw rice. Leave the beans in about half the baking time and then carefully remove them by grasping the wax paper and lifting it out of the pie. The rice or beans should be stored separately from the regular stock and used only for pies. A new piece of paper should be cut each time, however, as it can become brittle from the heat and breaks easily.

Pastry Mix

8 cups (2 pounds) all-purpose
   flour
2 teaspoons salt
2 cups (1 pound) shortening

This is a very easy pastry mix to prepare, particularly if you buy the 2-pound package of flour and the 1-pound can of solid shortening. It will save money, however, if the flour is measured from a larger package and the shortening from a 5-pound can.

Put flour in a very large (4-quart) bowl. Mix in salt. Add half shortening and with a pastry blender or 2 knives cut into flour mixture until well blended. Add remaining shortening and cut into flour, lifting flour up from bottom so shortening is well mixed. This makes 8 cups of pastry mix. Store in a covered container. The mix does not need to be refrigerated.

To use for a 9-inch one-crust pie: Measure 1 cup and 2 tablespoons firmly packed pastry mix into a bowl. With a fork, lightly stir in 3 tablespoons ice water.

To use for a 9-inch two-crust pie: Measure 2¼ cups firmly packed pastry mix into a bowl. With a fork, lightly mix in ⅓ cup ice water.

This is a generous amount of pastry for a 9-inch pie. If there are scraps of pastry left over, you can cut them in cookie size, sprinkle with sugar and cinnamon, and bake 10 to 12 minutes in the 425° F oven with the pie.

If using an 8-inch pie plate, measure 1 cup pastry mix and add 2 tablespoons ice water for 1 crust or for a 2-crust 8-inch pie, 2 cups pastry mix and 4 tablespoons ice water.

Frozen Chocolate Sundae Pie (recipe on page 26?
with Chocolate Sauce (recipe on page 27?
and Cocoa Oatmeal No-Bake Cookies (recipe on page 25?